Transforming Cities and Minds through the Scholarship of Engagement

Economy, Equity, and Environment

Edited by **Lorlene Hoyt**

Transforming Cities and Minds through the Scholarship of Engagement

Transforming Cities and Minds through the Scholarship of Engagement

Economy, Equity, and Environment

Edited by Lorlene Hoyt

Vanderbilt University Press | Nashville

© 2013 by Vanderbilt University Press
Nashville, Tennessee 37235
All rights reserved
First printing 2013

This book is printed on acid-free paper.
Manufactured in the United States of America

Library of Congress Cataloging-in-Publication Data on file

LC control number 2012033268
LC classification HT175.T74 2012
Dewey class number 307.3'4160973—dc23

ISBN 978-0-8265-1904-7 (cloth)
ISBN 978-0-8265-1905-4 (paperback)
ISBN 978-0-8265-1906-1 (e-book)

For Mom & Dad,
Cynthia, Yeruksew, and Mitiku

Contents

Part III Engaging Environment

Acknowledgments

Both professionally and personally, this book represents the most rewarding experience of my academic career. This journey would not have been possible without the courage and wisdom of the students, staff, faculty, alumni, civic leaders, and residents with whom I have walked, stumbled and crawled, and climbed to new heights. It feels appropriate to begin by acknowledging the M.I.T. Community Innovators' Lab (CoLab), especially its fearless leader, Dayna Cunningham. When this book was nothing more than a nascent idea in my mind, she fervently nurtured it. I also express my heartfelt gratitude to the diverse and dynamic CoLab community—too many people to name here have had a hand in shaping the chapters in this book. A special thanks to Amy Stitely and Alexa Mills for their inclination to challenge conventional thought and practice and for joining me on this adventure without hesitation; Annis Whitlow Sengupta, Danielle Martin, Anya Brickman Raredon, Kevin Feeney, Robert Goodspeed, Stefanie Ritoper, and Aspasia Xypolia for lending a hand with the creation of the how-to guides, short films, and blog posts that made student theses readily available to a wider public; Anne Emig, Yeseul Kim, and Polina Bakhteiarov for conducting research and for talking through the ideas in my chapters with me; and the people living in and working together to improve the quality of life in cities, particularly Camden, New Jersey; Cleveland, Ohio; Lawrence, Lowell, and Boston, Massachusetts; Kansas City, Missouri; and Oakland, California. A very special shout-out to my dear friends and colleagues in Lawrence, Massachusetts, among them Kristen Harol, Jessica Andors, Maggie Super Church, Tamar Kotelchuck, Bill Traynor, Armand Hyatt, Chet Sidell, and Andre Leroux.

I also wish to thank my editors; the late Jeannette Hopkins, for teaching me to avoid academic jargon, listen to the evidence, and live in the world of ideas; Ray Huling, for providing thoughtful feedback on early drafts; Lily Song, for refashioning Nick and Eric's theses into chapters; Ben Winters, for joining me on the arduous and playful final mile, and Andrew Lopez, for jumping into the mix to craft an index to make this book useful for years to come. An infinite expression of thanks goes to Mom, who read each chapter with care and cheered me on in my darkest hours. You are amazing. Last, but not least, I thank Michael Ames at Vanderbilt University Press; every author needs a publisher who believes in her.

With deep admiration and affection, I acknowledge the six thesis writers who dared to reinvent their graduate experience without any guideposts to follow: Gayle (and Bug), Nick, Marianna, Leila, Ben, and Eric. As we ventured from the high, hard ground into the swampy lowlands and back again, you remained steadfast in your commitment to the project, each other, and me. Your humility, grit, and brilliance are an inspiration to those around you.

In closing, I sincerely thank all of my colleagues in M.I.T.'s Department of Urban Studies and Planning (from 2002 to 2011) for the gift of "embodied knowledge." I experienced a transformative education; what I have come to know is who I am. A special thanks to Phillip Clay, Anne Whiston Spirn, J. Phillip Thompson, Ceasar McDowell, Eric Klopfer, Annette Kim, Tunney Lee, John de Monchaux, Bish Sanyal, Bob Fogelson, Larry Susskind, Karen Polenske, and Judith Tendler, for being extraordinary mentors, colleagues, and friends. I thank too my colleagues at the University of Pennsylvania (from 1995 to 2001), including Gary Hack, Eugenie Birch, Seymour Mandelbaum, Peter Brown, Nisha Botchwey, Stephanie Boddie, and Amy Hillier. My deepest gratitude to all of the women who blazed new trails in urban planning education, especially Marcia Marker Feld.

I am profoundly grateful for the ongoing support I receive from the people at the Kettering Foundation, the New England Resource Center for Higher Education at the University of Massachusetts–Boston and the Talloires Network at Tufts University who skillfully and relentlessly advance the burgeoning civic engagement movement in higher education.

Foreword

Dayna Cunningham, Executive Director,
M.I.T. Community Innovators' Lab

My first serious conversation with Lorlene Hoyt was my interview for the job of executive director of what was then called the Center for Reflective Community Practice (CRCP). CRCP was the predecessor to the M.I.T. Community Innovators' Lab (CoLab), where she and I have partnered for the last five years. Until then, the interviews had been very friendly, focused mainly on my fundraising experience and work in civic engagement. I had met Lorlene several times socially and knew her better than any of the other interviewers; I figured she would be even friendlier. She was nice enough to start but quickly dropped her engaging smile and began grilling me about my intentions for the future CoLab. How did I intend to meld the very disparate interests of students, community practitioners, and faculty into something coherent and useful? What were my ideas about knowledge cocreation across these groups? How did I plan to sustain involvement in communities despite the ever-changing mix of students? How would I accommodate and leverage the students' coursework and degree requirements? Lorlene was not, it turns out, being mean. She was being strategic: these were the dilemmas for which she was, at that very moment, developing highly creative responses. She wanted a partner in crime.

Lorlene had spent the prior seven years working in Lawrence, Massachusetts, one of a group of disinvested, abandoned, formerly industrial cities that she had come to call "forgotten cities." She now understood that the fundamental problems of these cities were as much political and social as economic and technological. After almost three generations with no coherent urban policy guiding the development of American cities, Lorlene could see that a central challenge in the United States, manifested first and most poignantly in forgotten cities, was the lack of political will and imagination to see cities as the future of the nation. Instead, politically dominant and, for a time, racially homogenous suburban voters had consistently voted to defund urban development, undermining the engines of their own prosperity. I am not myself a planner, but as a former voting rights lawyer I understood something of this dilemma of divided constituencies.

Given this ongoing collective irrationality at the heart of current urban challenges, Lorlene sought to explore the role of the planner and the task of planning education. For her, a vexing dilemma of planning pedagogy is its reluctance to attend to the identity of the planner; imparting planning knowledge and skills without creating space for students to explore their own purpose in becoming a planner is insufficient. She consistently pressed students to explore important questions: Who are you in relation to the discipline? What do you care about? How will you apply your talents to advance the discipline? How will you come to see and challenge your own assumptions and the field's blind spots—your own, and the field's, failures of imagination?

Lorlene also understood that these queries fundamentally are not just academic: only in practice, immersed with actual communities grappling with real problems of budget shortfalls, political failure, warring factions, racism, weak leadership, ineffective governance, unsuccessful coalitions, and unintended consequences—topics impossible to fully explore in the classroom—can the student begin to grasp them. Only within the context of practice can students begin framing their critique of the discipline, probing their own identity and role within it, and cultivating a prodigious imagination about cities. And here, Lorlene perceived a second vexing challenge of planning education: forgoing engagement in the neighborhoods that are crucibles and laboratories for urban innovation meant that planning students were missing a critical source of knowledge for improving cities. How, then, to develop a pedagogy that actively incorporated practice? How to accommodate the rigors of a traditional academic curriculum—in-class time, exams, master's theses or doctoral dissertations, and the like—with the requirements of a practice-based approach? She set out to refashion the traditional mechanisms into robust "instruments-for-action" to support critical professional development. Her research in the city of Lawrence, Massachusetts, evolved into a multiyear practicum with opportunities each semester for students to deepen their involvement and explore their roles with neighborhood-based organizations and issues in that city.

The Lawrence practicum each year produced highly usable reports and recommendations for local organizations, student papers exploring structural issues in the city, master's theses developing new knowledge about and recommendations for forgotten cities more generally, and highly engaged students learning who they were as planners and what they might contribute to the field. This experience in Lawrence informed the development of CoLab in multiple ways; Lorlene was integrally involved in its creation at every stage. She sat on the faculty committee that assisted CoLab staff in deciding everything from its vision and mission to its name. Using Lawrence as the example, she helped us all agree that CoLab would commit itself to merging theory and practice, to creating opportunities for students to immerse themselves in real-world problems where they could figure out what it meant to them to be a planner. We thought we might help them explore the seemingly irreconcilable conflict between the need of social science to reliably predict outcomes and the realities of life, particularly for people living in socially marginalized communities that consistently refuse to be scripted.

L orlene was the first faculty member to firmly locate her teaching inside CoLab, asserting the seamless unity between research, practice, and pedagogy in her work. Perhaps the most important invention of Lorlene's rogue pedagogy was the collaborative thesis. The collaborative thesis engaged a dedicated group of students in a yearlong critical inquiry loosely organized around what we called at the time planning's "sweet spot"—the intersection of economy, equity, and environment that may drive development in communities in the emerging future. The collaborative process not only enabled students to reflect on their own relationship to the field of planning, it also allowed them to engage in a comparative exercise, looking at this set of themes across diverse cases in cities across the country. Lorlene, however, was not satisfied with the thesis effort alone. For her, it was insufficient for her students to learn something important about social change processes; she also required them to give something specific and concrete back to the communities on which their research was based. Each student was required, with help from CoLab staffers Amy Stitely and Alexa Mills, to turn their thesis into a practical step-by-step how-to guide and a popular media piece such as a short film, blog post, or op-ed. In this way, Lorlene sought to increase the possibility of students' work having an effect in the real world, and, in so doing, she created a potential alternative metric for determining the value of their scholarly conclusions—impact, rather than replicability, of results.

The Lawrence practicum and the collaborative thesis became joint Lorlene-CoLab projects that did more than offer encounters between theory and practice. They enabled students to immerse themselves in neighborhood social-justice efforts with guidance from Lorlene and CoLab staff, then reflect and write about their experience individually and collectively. Inside CoLab, the weekly collaborative thesis meetings became a rich hive of intellectual creativity in which students simultaneously wrestled with their research inquiries and with their actions and obligations as planners working on social change in actual places. Above all, they sought to understand the relationship between the two.

Ultimately, the theses became the chapters of this book, a documentation of the process, methods, and results of the students' engaged research. Lorlene surrounds the chapters with her insights about the collaborative thesis process in an accessible narrative that follows the students' experience and probes its impact on them as aspiring planners. Moreover, she provides a candid personal view of her approach as a teacher and scholar and its impact on her work at M.I.T. All of this makes the book necessary reading for anyone brave enough to explore the uncharted and challenging ground of community-engaged research from within the academy and for anyone hoping to partner with an institution capable of supporting such research efforts.

For me this was the ideal marriage of our two worlds. As a civil rights lawyer, I had become interested in working with communities after experiencing the limits of litigation strategies that focused on the lawyers' expertise and knowledge without directly engaging community residents. Such strategies were doomed to failure because it was the day-to-day work of building social justice into the habits, practices, institutions, and culture of the community, not only the legal advocacy, that ultimately made a difference for the people who lived there. This work often did not begin until after the lawyers left. Similarly, Lorlene understood that physical planning, development finance, and the like, though critically necessary elements of a functional community, were inadequate when applied without resident leadership and ownership of the processes. We both understood that this requirement of engagement for success implied a teaching model that prepared students to be involved collaborators, not merely detached researchers or professional experts.

As the head of CoLab, I had been successful, with the staff team, at creating opportunities for students to do meaningful work with community organizations. Our staff were all M.I.T. Department of Urban

Studies and Planning alumni who understood firsthand the rigors of the program and had creative ideas about how to wedge practical engagements into the students' workload each semester. But we were under some scrutiny, as this alone did not justify our presence within, and support from, an academic institution. There were ongoing debates within our department, as in the broader field, about the appropriate connections between the practical and theory-making work of the planning discipline. Among the questions on the table was, and remains, the perennial issue of whether replicability is the only metric for determining the success of research results.

Introduction

Lorlene Hoyt

It's obvious that the problems of urban life are enormously
complex; there are no simple solutions. I'm almost embarrassed
to mention it as a problem because it is so enormously complex,
but we live in cities. They determine the future of this country.
And I find it ironic that universities which focused with such
energy on rural America a century ago have never focused with
equal urgency on our cities. —Ernest L. Boyer (1996, 19)

Converging Crises

Cities

In September 2008, the country was in economic free fall. Hundreds of
banks, large and small, were failing, corporations were filing for bank-
ruptcy, and the stock market plunged. Thousands of Americans lost
their jobs and their pensions. Families lost their homes to foreclosure.
But for cities from Camden, New Jersey, to Kansas City, Missouri, to
Oakland, California, this Great Recession was only the latest chapter
in a decades-long crisis. Such cities and their people, who worked in
mills and factories to supply clothing, food, and luxuries to the world,
have long been intimately familiar with the devastating consequences
of urban decline. They watched their cities decay as mills and factories
closed down or took their jobs to the South, where unions were few or
nonexistent, and wages lower. They watched neighbors move away, housing deteriorate, downtown centers empty, crime increase, and debris fill
alleyways. As the American economy soared in the 1990s, these small
cities and portions of large cities were left behind and, in effect, forgotten (Hoyt and Leroux 2007).

The idea of uniting city planning education and practice for the purpose of transforming cities and minds—reciprocal knowledge—is not
my own (Hoyt 2010). It evolved in collaboration and over the course of

1

a decade as I co-led MIT@Lawrence, a sustained city-campus partnership between M.I.T. and the city of Lawrence, Massachusetts. A former textile-mill city located thirty miles from Cambridge on the banks of the Merrimack River, Lawrence was designed in 1845 as an efficient industrial machine. Like other forgotten cities, Lawrence has struggled with a legacy of deindustrialization and globalization—unemployment, racial and ethnic conflicts, environmental contamination, and a faltering civic infrastructure. But devoted civic leaders in Lawrence, like their counterparts in other small cities, have learned to cope with, and in many ways thrive in, a rapidly changing world.

Today Lawrence boasts a growing population of Caribbean and Central American immigrants and is the most heavily Latino city in New England. The ethnic conflicts between Latinos and Anglos in the 1980s and 1990s have been replaced by dynamic partnerships among rooted institutions. Tied to, dependent on, and embedded in neighborhoods, universities and colleges, hospitals, churches, community development corporations, and community foundations are helping to bring cities like Lawrence back to hope and to productive life. Together, civic leaders and residents are learning the norms and advancing the values of democracy by replacing long-standing habits of distrust with new ideas and relationships. Collective action among these and other rooted institutions is resulting in large-scale iconic projects like Union Crossing and the Spicket River Greenway, which exhibit new ways of linking and thinking about issues of economy, equity, and environment.

The knowledge necessary for transforming cities is, in large part, born and developed in neighborhoods, not universities; it is cultivated by civic leaders and residents, day by day, through seemingly insignificant interactions that culminate in tangible outcomes. The guiding principles of democratic engagement are created, tested, and recalibrated locally in response to ever-changing conditions. As more Americans come face-to-face with the same crises and struggles people in cities are beginning to overcome, the need becomes increasingly urgent to synthesize and disseminate local knowledge to society at large. City-campus partnerships expose faculty, staff, and students to relevant and pressing issues while giving them an opportunity to witness and acquire the skills needed to solve them. Cities can benefit from the new ideas and added skills that people inside the university bring to the challenges at hand as well as their motivation to publish and share what they have learned far and wide (Reardon 2000).

Universities and Colleges

> It seems to me that for the first time in nearly half a century, institutions of higher learning are not collectively caught up in some urgent national endeavor. Still, our outstanding universities and colleges remain, in my opinion, among the greatest sources of hope for intellectual and civic progress in this country. I'm convinced that for this hope to be fulfilled, the academy must become a more vigorous partner in the search for answers to our most pressing social, civic, economic, and moral problems. —Ernest L. Boyer (1996, 11)

As the Great Recession took hold, I was facing my own career crisis: the fight for tenure. This crisis was not a surprise to me; the clock was ticking and the odds were slim. Only one in three tenure-track faculty at M.I.T. win tenure, a promotion that guarantees job security and academic freedom for life. For an engaged scholar like me, the odds were even slimmer. Though invented by M.I.T.'s own Kurt Lewin in the 1940s, action research is as lost a tradition at M.I.T. as at most other research universities. Instead, technical rationality reigns supreme (Schön 1995). Professors are expected to conduct research and dispense knowledge to students. A one-way flow of highly specialized knowledge is privileged. Professors are rewarded for their individual contributions to narrowly focused bodies of knowledge in the form of peer-reviewed journal articles, which are accessible only to a small cadre of academic experts (Benson, Harkavy, and Hartley 2005). Faculty promotion policies are well established, rarely challenged or revamped, and designed to reinforce intellectual autonomy. I was aware of and understood the institutional culture and prevailing epistemology, but chose to resist it.

An institutional culture dominated by technical rationality creates systemic tensions for engaged scholars on the tenure-track as well as for students, tenured faculty, and administrators. For example, early-career faculty, especially women in applied fields such as health sciences, education, and city planning, are more likely to collaborate with local communities in ways that integrate research, teaching, and service (Vogelgesang, Denson, and Jayakumar 2010). As it stands, doctoral students of all stripes are socialized to conform to the dominant paradigm, which emphasizes competitive individualism and discourages research for public purposes. If doctoral students are not exposed to engaged scholarship, it is unlikely they will have the desire or the ability to do so later in their academic career (O'Meara 2011). Those doctoral students who do become engaged scholars on the tenure-track are faced with the dilemma of choosing career or calling (Hoyt 2010), which presents a difficult choice: do they conform to traditional academic standards prioritizing research over teaching and advising to achieve tenure, or do they explore an epistemology of reciprocal knowledge to solve pressing economic and social problems and risk the reward of tenure? Many reluctantly choose to postpone their calling and, as they seek, admit, and train doctoral students to assist with their research, enhance the already dominant culture. Others are unable to make a suitable home of the academy and make a calculated exit. In both cases, the academy and society at large loses. A greater diversity of faculty augments intellectual diversity. Over time, intellectual diversity among faculty may result an institutional culture that values specialized knowledge while making room for other ways of knowing.

Such a shift has profound implications for increasing campus diversity as well as access to higher education. Administrators, faculty, and staff charged with leading change initiatives are keenly aware of the mismatch between the rhetoric on diversity embedded in their mission statements and the reality of their institutional policies and culture. Fortunately, some universities and colleges are vigorously examining the relationship between civic engagement and faculty assessment, on the one hand, and diversity, on the other. Land-grant universities, which have historically had a mandate to collaborate with their communities, are boldly leading the way, and momentum is building among some private universities. In 2007, Syracuse University announced a commitment to Scholarship in Action, a robust framework for public scholarship, broadly defining what constitutes scholarly work while maintaining high standards for early-career faculty. Here, a coherent body of work that ameliorates a social, political, or economic problem is on par with a substantial contribution to theory. What matters is impact.

During my first week at M.I.T, I made a commitment to connecting the people at M.I.T. with the people in Lawrence for the purpose of generating relevant knowledge through interaction with the actual world. Experts on both sides developed knowledge through a "multiply-connected system" in which ideas and people flow from the community to the university and back again. I was driven by what I had learned as a graduate student at the University of Pennsylvania, a rooted institution in West Philadelphia: universities have a responsibility to respond to pressing problems, for society's sake and for their own.

And now, in 2008, to make an intense situation more acute, the U.S. Department of Housing and Urban Development's funding award for the MIT@Lawrence partnership was due to expire by the end of the academic year; I was running low on both money and time. As luck would have it, a longtime community organizer and collaborator left Lawrence and enrolled in the M.I.T. Department of Urban Studies and Planning's graduate program. She helped me by recruiting an exceptional group of fellow students to join the MIT@Lawrence partnership, and we set the goal of producing a final round of top-notch scholarship with the people of Lawrence.

But a crisis loomed on the horizon for this group of students, too: the dreaded task of producing a thesis. The process of thesis research and writing, for so many graduate students before them, was an isolating and daunting experience. In the beginning, students struggle with focusing a topic of general interest into a manageable research project. They need and search for guidance, but faculty are rarely rewarded for advising and often focused on their own research. Nonetheless, students pitch their nascent ideas only to discover that faculty are selective with respect to the topics they will agree to explore as well as the number of students they will advise. Once a student finds an advisor, they may get some pointers on books and articles to read; the advisor may provide some feedback on the student's overall research design, but many students are left to fend for themselves. They rely on peers to cope with the obstacles and setbacks all research projects bring. With little to no institutional incentive to support the thesis research or writing process, and with demanding research projects of their own, many advisors postpone interaction with students until the student produces a few draft chapters. As the thesis deadline approaches, students who have been the intellectual and social lifeblood of the university disappear into dark corners of the library or stop coming to campus altogether.

When the students reappear, they look haggard and voice their disappointment. They are not confident about the work they have produced, and they are desperate for detailed feedback from their advisors. The thesis defense, sometimes the only opportunity students have to discuss their work at length with their advisor and other committee members, traditionally takes place behind closed doors. Students present their work in an hour or so, and committee members enumerate, in general terms, the types of improvements that need to be made to the manuscript for the student to graduate on schedule. Faculty who are either on nine-month contracts, away, or intensely involved in their own research are reluctant to advise students during summer months. In the end, the quality of student theses within an academic department varies tremendously; both rigorous and inadequate theses are concealed from public view. More often than not, the culmination of student ideas and efforts, the thesis itself, is doomed to molder on library shelves. Increasingly, student theses are available online for academics who have access to the university's library. On occasion, a student thesis is cited in an academic journal article. My students at M.I.T. had the smarts and tenacity to muddle through the thesis, a requirement for graduation, but the process was antiquated. My new cohort of engaged students, too, would have to endure the medieval ritual (Chang 2004).

As I surveyed the economic landscape, the landscape of my own life, and that of my students, I felt a powerful realization that in these difficult times, dramatic action was called for. I had a long-standing feeling that the thesis-writing process needed modernizing; it seemed to me, given the imminent tenure decision and given the heterogeneous group of bright, ambitious scholars I found around me, that here, now, was my "do or die" moment. I decided to risk the reward of tenure to push the boundaries of reciprocal knowledge. This book is the result of that cathartic moment and the two years of innovative, collaborative work that followed.

Once I had lured them into taking part, these students approached an old problem—how to write a thesis that won't end up ignored and forgotten—through what we came to call the scholarship of engagement. Instead of working in isolation, we met regularly and we worked together. Each student in the group selected an American city and identified civic leaders with whom they would engage. We deliberately searched for cities that were grappling with the challenge of understanding and securing stimulus funding and selected cities in different parts of the country. Our aim was to improve the thesis as an opportunity for learning by making it a collective intellectual endeavor. Each student became an expert in issues of economy, equity, and environment in the city where she or he worked. And by frequently exchanging ideas, strategies, and stories, each student in the group gained an understanding of his or her own work in relation to the work happening in other cities. Throughout the process, we identified common themes across the individual projects and created common and publicly accessible products.

In addition to producing a thesis, each student in the group agreed to disseminate his or her work in alternative formats including "how-to" guides, short films, blog posts, and public presentations inside and outside the university. The how-to guides are about twenty-five pages in length, written for a local audience, and rich with colorful charts and photographs; they are available free of charge on the Internet. The short films include interviews with residents and distill student research into practical recommendations; they, too, are available online. The collaborative thesis group organized and held a weeklong series of public presentations on campus in April. Each session had twenty to forty students, staff, faculty, family, and friends in attendance. Six first-year graduate students volunteered to write and post a blog on M.I.T.'s CoLab Radio that captured the key points of the presentation for people outside the university to see. In my view, our approach to the collaborative thesis is best characterized as a student-centered model of collaborative learning that aims to reestablish "a communal authority over the cult of the expert" (Rendón 2009). Strikingly, the work they produced argues that the *old* challenges facing America's cities also need to be approached in a *new* way: by engaging people from all walks of life in the task of galvanizing rooted institutions to function as nimble and responsive agents of change in the world.

Transforming Minds

The Scholarship of Engagement

The scholarship of engagement is an emerging field of theory and practice. For academics, it is an integrated view of scholarly activity where research, teaching, service, and professional practice overlap and are mutually reinforcing. Engaged scholars, such as the chapter authors, strive to become "participants in the larger public culture of democracy." Instead of seeing ourselves as experts who produce knowledge for laypersons, we aim to generate and discover knowledge by way of collaboration. Expert knowledge that is rational and analytic is not at odds with local knowledge that is relational and contextual; we seek to blend both ways of knowing. We value inclusiveness, participation, and reciprocity in problem solving, and we believe that everyone can contribute to education and community building (Saltmarsh and Hartley 2011). The concluding chapter unpacks the collaborative thesis project through the lens of the scholarship of engagement. It points to our success in reaching the goals described above, highlights where we fell short, and offers recommendations for those who might dare to replicate the experiment within their own college or university. Because we learned along the way that creating and sustaining meaningful human relationships is fundamental to the enterprise of knowledge production, I introduce you now to my students such that you are left with an impression of both their wholeness and uniqueness.

Marianna Leavy-Sperounis: The first student I drafted into what we would later call "the collaborative thesis project" was Marianna Leavy-Sperounis, whom I had known for several years. She was one of a handful of colleagues at Lawrence CommunityWorks, a community development corporation led by four M.I.T. alumnae who moved to Lawrence after they graduated in 1999. Marianna was a community organizer with a deep commitment to social justice she attributed, in part, to her father's mother, Stella Sperounis, who immigrated to Lowell, Massachusetts, from Greece in 1935. An illiterate factor worker and single mother of three boys, Stella's frequent moves and loneliness made an indelible impression on Marianna as a young girl. As an undergraduate student, Marianna focused on women's studies and politics at Oberlin College in Ohio. "Outraged and distressed" by the unfolding war in Iraq during her senior year, she channeled her energy into organizing and led a student walkout and rally on the day the war began (Leavy-Sperounis 2008). Her matriculation at M.I.T. signaled to me an opportunity to improve the scholarship we had been coproducing through the MIT@Lawrence partnership and to make more meaningful connections with the next cohort of students entering our department.

It was Marianna's personal ties with both cities and her experience creating a more flexible, friendly, and productive public sphere in Lawrence that she brought to bear on her investigation of Lawrence and Lowell, Massachusetts. Though widely understood as "urban twins," Marianna felt, and shows in her chapter, that Lawrence and Lowell are fundamentally different. Her frustration about Lawrence's apparent inability to secure funding from the Obama administration's 2009 Recovery Act was magnified by Lowell's success in doing so. Marianna talked with residents and civic leaders in each city as well as state officials and elected representatives to figure out why, when, and how the two cities diverged. In the end, Marianna makes the case for applying the network organizing strategies she developed and deployed on the ground in Lawrence at the state level. Cities like Lawrence and Lowell, she argues, don't have to compete for funding in a zero-sum game where one city wins and the other loses: they can collaborate and leverage each other's resources.

Gayle Christiansen: The second student to join the MIT@Lawrence partnership was Gayle Christiansen, who applied to M.I.T. because she was "burnt out from being in the trenches." Originally from Cedarburg, a small town near Milwaukee, Wisconsin, Gayle majored in sociology at Kenyon College in Gambier, Ohio. As a senior, she checked the box labeled "region most in need" on her Teach for America application and ended up in a public school in Camden, New Jersey. Somehow, teaching seventh- and eighth-grade science to more than one hundred teenagers consumed only a portion of her energy. Gayle channeled the rest of it into leading the science fair committee, coaching volleyball, choreographing the tap dance team, and mentoring students at Mount Zion Church (Christiansen 2008a, 2008b, 2010). I didn't know Gayle before she applied to M.I.T., but she had studied the department's offerings and expressed the desire to get involved with the MIT@Lawrence partnership. We met at the annual open house for newly admitted students, where I realized that Gayle was the best candidate to lead Lawrence@ MIT, a program created in 2007 to combat the high school dropout crisis in Lawrence. Inserting dozens of eighth graders from the Lawrence Family Development Charter School into chemistry and physics classes at M.I.T. every month was a tall order, but Gayle could handle it.

It was Gayle's dedication to Camden and its people, and her frustration with the *New York Times'* depiction of Camden as "America's most dangerous city" that led her to a thesis that would uncover and highlight the city's strengths. Knowing she thrived while working with mainstreet business owners in New Orleans, I guided her to an investigation of the potential role of small businesses in transforming Camden. The title of Gayle's chapter, "Makin' a Way Where There Is No Way," points at once to Gayle's modus operandi and to the perseverance of Camden's entrepreneurs. By knocking on doors, making phone calls, sending e-mail messages, and shopping in their stores, she found sixteen struggling yet resilient entrepreneurs and convinced them to share their stories with her. Gayle was as relentless in her quest to meet them as they are in creating jobs, providing services, filling vacant buildings, and giving hope to Camden's next generation. Gayle's chapter adopts an experiential mode of inquiry, eschewing academic jargon and bringing voices from Camden to a wide audience, thus providing a model for Camden and articulating the need for the city to change the way it views and interacts with its small businesses.

Nick Iuviene: Another student, Nick Iuviene, was raised in Columbia County in rural New York and lived for a short time on East Eighty-Ninth Street between Second and Third Avenue on the island of Manhattan. Before beginning at M.I.T., Nick worked as a draftsman at the Architectural Bureau in Chatham, New York, and as a community organizer for the Northwest Bronx Community and Clergy Coalition. Determined to figure out how to transform a neighborhood "without displacing low-income residents," Nick focused his attention on the Kingsbridge Armory redevelopment project—an effort to create a massive mixed-used complex, complete with shops, schools, a movie theater, and recreational and community space (Iuviene 2008). Quiet, unyielding, and politically savvy, Nick spent years rallying union representatives, residents, small-business owners, and youth groups who pressured developers to hire locally and pay living wages. He left before a decision was made and ultimately the project did not materialize.

The uphill climb took its toll on Nick, who often felt "ineffective and lacking creativity." When Nick met Marianna on M.I.T.'s campus, he was "amazed" by the position she held as deputy to the regional field director for the Obama Campaign in Denver, Colorado, and "wanted to know more." Marianna introduced me to Nick, and I hired him to work with her on the MIT@Lawrence Story Project, a documentary about the partnership's seven-year history, as told by participants on both sides—city and campus.

Throughout his time at M.I.T., Nick shared and probed his experience in the Bronx. He was determined to find a solution to the problem of gentrification; he refused to believe it was an inevitable outcome. He used his thesis to search for and study economic development models that benefited rather than exploited communities and workers. Nick discovered the idea of worker cooperatives, a strategy that prioritizes community needs above individual benefits; nobody gets rich quick and everybody has a job for life. He carefully examined living examples throughout Europe and America. During visits to Cleveland, Ohio, he talked with leaders of the Evergreen Cooperative Initiative who had imported and implemented a model from Spain. Nick believes in the power of big ideas, and his thesis presents the fundamental components of a strategy for cooperative economic development, a framework he is now applying in the Bronx.

Eric Mackres: Eric Mackres, like Gayle, was "a product of the Rust Belt" who wanted to stay "grounded" while studying at M.I.T. An environmentalist, Eric grew up in and around Michigan's cities, among them Detroit, Jackson, and Lansing. After earning his undergraduate degree in political science and environmental studies at Albion College, he ran door-to-door campaigns across Michigan for the Human Rights Campaign, the Sierra Club, and the Public Interest Research Group. He also worked in San Francisco, where he advocated for the development of affordable housing. Aware of this strong background in environmental policy, community organizing, and policy advocacy, I chose Eric to launch and run the Green Jobs Project in Lawrence. Eric found Lawrence to be "a beautiful city" and quickly engaged an array of civic leaders who were eagerly looking for a new way of doing business in the failing economy (Mackres 2008a, 2008b, 2010).

Eric's interest in social movements, especially those that leverage environmental issues to "catalyze a social and economic renaissance," led him to study Community Labor United, a regional base-building organization across the Charles River in Boston. Because of his prior professional experience, he was able to recognize and illustrate how Community Labor United adopted sophisticated techniques of collaboration that helped overcome conflicts that arise in their advocacy campaigns. Eric advances the discipline of collaborative planning by explaining how organizations and social movements can best employ such techniques to strengthen themselves in their causes and in negotiations with their opponents. The type of work necessary for building effective partnerships between community, labor, and utility companies is as complex, thoughtful, and nuanced as his chapter.

Leila Bozorg: Leila joined MIT@Lawrence reluctantly, but felt "lucky" to be part of the partnership after her first visit to "the immigrant city." She "loved watching Marianna introduce her old colleagues" as she led a tour of Nuestra Casa (Our House), a community center designed and built by Lawrence CommunityWorks. After studying international relations and government at Wesleyan University, Leila worked in Ahmedabad,

India, where one of her projects focused on community mapping in informal settlements (Bozorg 2008b, 2010). She was a perfect fit for the iHouse Project, a new initiative aimed at training undergraduate M.I.T. students living in the "international house" dormitory to map manholes, fire hydrants, and catch basins in the Arlington and Whitman Street neighborhoods in Lawrence.

Leila, the "daughter of secular revolutionaries turn[ed] academicians," had traveled extensively and learned as a child "what it means to dedicate one's self to a cause, take big risks, and make big sacrifices" (Bozorg 2008a). Driven in part by this conviction, Leila scoured the country looking for a civic leader with a bold strategy for making the most of the Recovery Act. This brought her to Kansas City, Missouri, where she talked with people to learn about the newly enacted Green Impact Zone, created by Congressman Emanuel Cleaver. A prominent figure in Kansas City politics for nearly forty years, Cleaver conceived of the zone to concentrate federal funds in an area of the city plagued by severe racial and economic divisions. Leila's chapter illuminates the significance of history in creating discriminatory systems and practices, which result in "unjust geographies." It also reinforces the dire need for leaders to recognize and seize emerging opportunities in real time.

Benjamin Brandin: The sixth chapter contributor, Benjamin Brandin, did not participate in MIT@Lawrence during his first year as a graduate student. Ben and Nick were close friends who met serendipitously at an open house at the University of California, Los Angeles, for newly admitted graduate students, where Nick gave Ben "a hard pitch about going to M.I.T." (Iuviene 2010b). Ben, a socially conscious bartender from San Francisco, had taken a somewhat circuitous road to M.I.T. After high school, he attended California Polytechnic State University in San Luis Obispo. He later transferred to City College of San Francisco where he embraced his "Creole and Spanish heritage" by "exploring Latin American and Jazz history." Ben finally enrolled at the University of California, Berkeley, where he studied urban public policy and graduated with honors (Brandin 2008, 2010).

Ben's connections to San Francisco and a nagging feeling that his prior professional experience was "inadequate" relative to his peers led him to Oakland, California, a city that has long struggled to create opportunities for its least advantaged. Oakland has misused the federal funding it received in the past and Ben sets out to help chart a different course for the city that is receiving the second-largest amount of Recovery Act funds in the United States. He relies on best practices, looking to Seattle, Washington, and Portland, Oregon, cities that are thriving because of citywide retrofits to create green jobs. Oakland, Ben argues, can learn from them. His analysis is detailed and disciplined, offering novel solutions to long-standing problems. While his recommendations are tailored to help Oakland with its own transformation, the lessons are transferable and may be applied to other cities.

Transforming Cities

Engaging Issues of Economy, Equity, and Environment

Transforming Cities and Minds showcases scholarly student engagement in several cities across the country. Each chapter emphasizes the three issues that the next generation of city planners must understand and solve: economy, equity, and environment. The authors proceed from the premise that problems of economy, equity, and environment are interdependent and must be treated as such. To illuminate how old problems can be viewed from a new perspective, I organized our book thematically. Though each author examines all three issues, chapters are grouped in pairs for the purpose of highlighting a particular issue: the reader's journey begins with "Engaging Economy," moves to "Engaging Equity," and concludes with "Engaging Environment."

Engaging Economy

In Part 1, "Engaging Economy," Gayle and Nick focus on new strategies for transforming two former industrial powerhouses: Camden, New Jersey, and Cleveland, Ohio. Gayle and Nick find both cities striving to reinvent themselves in a new millennium by leveraging the resources of rooted institutions to strengthen the local economy. Camden's waterfront strategy—with its new aquarium, minor-league baseball stadium, and decommissioned battleship—is insufficient because it fails to reach and improve the lives of city residents. Gayle turns her attention instead to the city's smaller, yet deep-rooted institutions—its bodegas, hair salons, flower shops, restaurants, and day care centers. These small businesses, she argues, are the city's true change agents because they provide important goods and services to residents, enhance civic life by reclaiming neighborhood streets, and give back frequently to the community they love. Gayle reveals the struggles small-business owners endure on their own and offers a set of strategies for improving their relationship with the city, the agencies charged with assisting them, and one another.

Nick focuses on emerging partnerships among Cleveland's large and rooted institutions, including the Cleveland Foundation, University Hospitals, Case Western Reserve University, and the Cleveland Clinic. He tells a story of how the leaders of these institutions studied and imported a cooperative economic development model from Mondragon, a small city located in the Basque region of Spain. Instead of contracting services to firms in outlying cities and regions, Cleveland's Evergreen Cooperative Initiative is uniting the city's largest employers and leveraging their procurement dollars to stabilize the faltering local economy. In the same way that small businesses in Camden capture and reinvest local dollars while providing goods and services to city residents, Cleveland's civic leaders created new firms, including the Evergreen Laundry Cooperative and Ohio Solar, to employ local residents and give them an ownership stake in the company. Both Gayle and Nick contribute to a new way of thinking about the economy of cities, advocating growth from within and direct participation and control over local markets. They make the case that such economies are better able to cope with sudden economic crises and, over time, will grow and begin exporting goods and services to other markets. At the same time, they warn that strong and diversified local economies require support systems.

In Camden, dozens of agencies were established to support small businesses. But while small businesses need their support, financial and otherwise, these agencies and businesses cannot seem to find each other. Small-business owners in Camden rarely receive bank loans, and many perceive city hall to be nothing more than a bureaucratic "merry-go-round." For a cooperative economic development model to thrive, Nick argues that coordinated and ongoing support from such rooted institutions such as banks, universities, philanthropic foundations, and government entities is needed. Cooperative firms and small for-profit businesses are critical economic engines for ensuring a culture of collective ownership, prosperity, and well-being. Gayle and Nick follow different paths in the chapters that follow, but arrive at broadly similar conclusions: strategies for solving the economic problems of a given city must come from *all the people* that live and work there. Here, as throughout this work, democratic and collaborative processes are found to be essential. In Camden, Gayle finds that small-business owners must be given greater access to information and that the city must be given greater incentive to listen to the small-business community. Detailing the early efforts of the Evergreen Cooperative, Nick discovers that a cooperative effort cannot exist independent of the city's rooted institutions; to the contrary, it succeeds by leveraging the resources of those larger institutions. In "Engaging Economy," Gayle and Nick teach us to begin the job of transforming cities by engaging rooted institutions, large and small. Economic success requires new connections—listening and cooperation between what may seem, at first blush, conflicting parties and institutions.

Engaging Equity

The next part of *Transforming Cities and Minds* brings our attention to questions of equity. To appreciate the difficulties Kansas City, Missouri, and Lawrence, Massachusetts, face in the present, Leila and Marianna turn to the past. Both authors uncover a history replete with overt and protracted patterns of racial discrimination and corporate exploitation. People of color living in these cities were not only left behind, they were, in a variety of ways, systematically oppressed. Leila's chapter lays out a courageous attempt to transform Kansas City by way of the Green Impact Zone, an idea brought to life by Congressman Emanuel Cleaver, a former city councillor and Kansas City's first black mayor. Rather than spread federal dollars from the Recovery Act "thin," Cleaver aims to right the wrongs of the past by concentrating investment in a 150-block area. The neighborhoods in question, according to Leila, represent an "unjust geography" resulting from chronic disinvestment in the form of race-restrictive covenants, school segregation, and displacement. Leila finds that though the Zone was designed with good intentions, and while more than a $100 million have been poured into it to retrofit housing and improve transportation efficiency, there is room for improvement. Administered by the Mid-America Regional Council, the Zone leadership team has engaged rooted institutions with strong track records such as the University of Missouri, Ivanhoe Neighborhood Council, and Brush Creek Community Partners in data collection and decision-making processes. At the same time, many neighborhoods have been excluded and points of entry for engagement remain unavailable to them. If not remedied in short order, the Zone could evolve into yet another policy imposed on people of color and modest means rather than one that is governed by them.

Marianna examines the way the city of Lawrence was designed and built, how those decisions influenced the concentration of capital with the city's limits, the kind of leadership that emerged, and, ultimately, the quality of life its people experience today. Her analysis of Lawrence's history is understood relative to its "urban twin," the neighboring city of Lowell, Massachusetts, located fifteen miles southwest of Lawrence on the Merrimack River. Unlike both Lowell and Kansas City, Lawrence has not received a windfall of dollars from the Recovery Act. Lawrence aims to create green jobs, but the city was designed to be self-sustaining; its founders were intent on maximizing profit and the "lack of economic diversity in Lawrence, relative to Lowell, persists today." Lawrence struggles to generate revenue from its tax base, while Lowell's organized elite have successfully secured state funding for its national historic park and the Lowell campus of the University of Massachusetts. Today, Lawrence is largely without the political leadership necessary to get the attention it needs. Marianna argues that Massachusetts needs to rethink its current policy for transforming small cities; in assuming all small cities are the same, it disadvantages cities like Lawrence and favors cities like Lowell. Like Leila, Marianna recognizes the importance of a regional perspective on city transformation. She creatively applies to the Merrimack Valley region the principles of network organizing that she developed and used to strengthen civic life in Lawrence, offering a new way of thinking about the allocation of state resources. She argues that transforming cities requires an up-close understanding of their histories, needs, and aspirations. In "Engaging Equity," both Leila and Marianna find that past history is a large determining factor in present inequality, and both search for new ways to end and reverse the discriminatory policies and practices in cities. Developing a nuanced understanding of history—its relevance to and its continual influence on the present—offers readers a new perspective on cities and, therefore, an opportunity to transform their minds.

Engaging Environment

In "Engaging Environment," Ben and Eric highlight the new kinds of partnerships, both in terms of participants and goals, needed to make the building stock in cities more energy efficient. Energy-efficient cities, as noted by Ben, alleviate the nation's dependence on foreign and domestic oil, decrease greenhouse gas emissions, and improve air quality. Ben examines unlikely partnerships among community-based organizations and labor unions in Seattle, Washington, and Portland, Oregon, to inform leaders in Oakland, California—whose city council members recently committed to reduce greenhouse gas emissions by more than a third in less than a decade. Financing, he finds, is key to a citywide retrofitting strategy, and fortunately all three cities have established revolving loan funds, creating an unregulated and recycled pool of capital for small businesses. Both Seattle and Portland have signed legally binding community workforce agreements with dozens of partners to define contracting, training, and employment policies outlining specific requirements. Such agreements functionally regulate the market and allow for community-controlled economic development. Mayors and development agencies in all three cities play an active role in retrofitting strategies, but Ben emphasizes that Oakland would benefit by engaging its rooted institutions.

Eric takes us to back to the East Coast to discover that Massachusetts, too, is trying to figure out how to meet the aggressive energy-efficiency standards it recently adopted by way of the Green Communities Act. Eric brings us into the world of social movements, suggesting they might be viewed as new strategies for building partnerships between community, labor, and utility companies. His chapter focuses largely on Community Labor United, an alliance of social-movement organizations that has run three successful campaigns. The most recent, complex, and ambitious among them—Green Justice—is an example of how successful community-labor-utility partnerships bridge historical differences, build trust, and cultivate a shared identity. In the case of Green Justice, an inside-outside game was necessary to reach a common goal; once strong linkages between community and labor were established, members both confronted and negotiated with utilities to bring them into the fold. As a result, Green Justice has a tangible win: they were assigned with implementing a set of energy-efficiency retrofit pilots for buildings in communities throughout the state. But, even pilots in neighborhoods where strong local partnerships are in place (such as Boston's Chinatown with NSTAR, the Chinese Progressive Association, and the International Union of Painters) were delayed because revolving loan funds and other financing mechanisms were not available.

Both Ben and Eric make the point that engaging the environment is not opposed to addressing issues of economy or equity, but dependent upon it. They illustrate that it is not only desirable, but necessary, to seek out connections between economy, equity, and environment. Ben details the struggle to design a citywide retrofitting strategy in Oakland, California, and offers an instructive example—a project that brings with it a lot of jobs, a lot of resources, and a lot of community and government involvement. It is an opportunity to give a sense of purpose and vitality to a region. Eric focuses on environment through Community Labor United's battle for better energy policy, but his work also illuminates the importance of including issues of economy and equity: the organizations involved are attempting to create jobs and raise the standard of living for the city's working class.

Our Scholarly Engagement

M.I.T.'s Community Innovators' Lab

Creating a book from six graduate student theses was not, it perhaps goes without saying, an easy or straightforward process. There were twists and turns, conflicts and near implosions—all of which I will detail more in the concluding chapter, when I reflect on the scholarship of engagement. Among the crucial partners in this project was M.I.T.'s Community Innovators' Lab (CoLab), a center connecting faculty, staff, and students inside the university with seasoned civic leaders outside the university to cocreate innovative solutions to complex urban challenges. CoLab supported sustained engagement with the people of Lawrence and introduced students to the "sweet spot," the idea that effective city planning practice involves three distinct but interrelated issues: economy, equity, and environment. CoLab also provided the institutional infrastructure and intellectual culture the collaborative thesis project required. This book would not exist without CoLab.

Developing Habits of Collaboration

We survived the twists and turns associated with the collaborative thesis project because we had already developed habits of collaboration. During our first year together, some students made enormous strides in Lawrence, while others floundered. Through it all we met weekly to compare notes, share advice, and vent concerns to one another. Mirroring the principles of network organizing developed by civic leaders in Lawrence, we adopted a horizontal management structure, which meant rotating responsibilities among group members. By the end of their first year in graduate school, chapter contributors knew how to work with one another; they had taken classes, started new student groups, gone on road trips, helped each other through personal tragedies, and developed productive habits of collaboration and a feeling of solidarity.

Overcoming Obstacles to Engagement

At the start of the summer of 2009, the collaborators went their separate ways, all but Leila planning to work side by side with civic leaders to secure stimulus funds from the Recovery Act. When they returned to campus in the fall, I actively recruited them, one by one, to join me in my experiment to transform their theses into a collaborative project. Slowly, and for very different reasons, each student agreed to venture with me into the unknown. As soon as it seemed we were all poised to move forward, the experiment began falling apart: one student was diagnosed with two serious illnesses, another learned his mother was living with cancer, and the department chair warned me that investing in this collaborative initiative would prevent me from getting tenure.

In need of support, I turned to two friends, both MIT@Lawrence alumni, now staff in M.I.T.'s Community Innovators Lab. Together, we created and circulated an agreement that looked a lot like a syllabus and began meeting regularly. One student's thesis advisor gave an ultimatum: stick with me as your advisor and leave the group or join the group and find another advisor. During the long holiday break, spanning from mid-December 2009 through January 2010, students dug through library archives, read journal and newspaper articles, and talked with civic leaders and residents in cities. In early February, a student expressed concern about how we were using our time together, suggesting we "help each other dig deep into the issues we are exploring." In response, we added a series of "miniretreats" to our schedule, creating the opportunity to listen to each other's ideas, ask challenging questions, and identify similarities across the cities under investigation. We organized and held "New Strategies for an Old Crisis," a three-day event in mid-April, which included a roundtable discussion, a public defense for each student, and a happy hour to celebrate the completion of an important milestone. But when the event arrived, only two of the six writers were prepared to defend their work. Though some of us felt defeated, we stuck together, each student showcasing his or her work publicly to an audience of faculty, staff, and students as well as community partners, friends, and family.

"We Wondered If It Would Work"

In the end, Ben summed up the collaborative thesis project best: "There were points along the way where we wondered if it would work. It was experimental. It went rather smoothly" (Bozorg et al. 2010). Students agreed that a collaborative approach to a graduate thesis was beneficial, especially for learning from one another. By working together, they heard different perspectives on other cities and their own work was consistently challenged. Our regular meetings ensured students received ongoing feedback. This helped them to gain confidence in their ideas and feel less isolated. The CoLab provided a respectful space for our discussions as well as staff who helped students hone their arguments, sharpen their writing, and disseminate their research in alternative formats like how-to guides, short films, and blog posts. CoLab staff also recruited a doctoral student at M.I.T., Lily Song, who worked closely with two thesis writers—Nick and Eric—to transform their theses into chapters for this book.

The Power of Human Relationships

At times, it was messy and unpredictable, and we fell short. Some students felt they relied too heavily on the group, failing to take advantage of the guidance other faculty could have provided. I was overwhelmed, especially near the end, and failed to give each student timely feedback. In the end, the students in the group were satisfied with the process and their work; perhaps most importantly, each has since found a job in which to put to work the ideas and relationships developed through their thesis research.

What began as converging moments of crisis evolved into a small community of engaged scholars devoted to reinventing city planning education and practice. To my surprise, we did not become a group of friends, though there were friendships among people in the group. But, we dared to try something new, identified a set of common goals, treated one another with respect, and saw the project through to its conclusion.

By simultaneously studying and practicing the idea of engagement, we created this book and a lifelong bond.

Reciprocal Knowledge

> Knowledge does not move from the locus of research to the place of application, from scholar to practitioner, teacher to student, expert to client. It is everywhere fed back, constantly enhanced. We need to think of knowledge in an ecological fashion, recognizing the complex, multifaceted and multiply-connected system by means of which discovery, aggregation, synthesis, dissemination, and application are interconnected and interacting in a wide variety of ways.—Ernest Lynton (1994, 88–89)

The idea of modernizing the thesis began to emerge as a consequence of our engagement with the people of Lawrence. Over time, we imagined curricular artifacts such as courses, fellowships, research assistantships, and theses as instruments for—rather than barriers to—action. The word "thesis" is Greek for "intellectual proposition" and originally materialized as a theological exercise in translation. By the thirteenth century, Oxford University had instituted the practice of teaching scholars to dispute in public, a formal event and celebrated occasion at the university. Over the course of a few centuries, the disputation evolved into an exercise in answering, by way of writing, a proposed question. The thesis became standard practice in the seventeenth century as the cost of writing paper became more affordable and universities, beginning with the University of Berlin, codified the thesis requirement into their statutes (Chang 2004). By way of imitation, the idea spread to universities and colleges across the globe.

The thesis, too, can be reworked into a powerful instrument-for-action; it demands a substantial amount of student time and energy, the work spanning at least a semester, often two or more. Students engaged in Lawrence started using their theses as means for working closely with engaged faculty and civic leaders to identify, define, and address pressing problems for which resources were limited. Some theses made their way, tattered and torn, to city council meetings where their findings were referenced and recommendations were debated; they became instruments-for-action that enriched students' learning, informed and impacted decisions in Lawrence, and strengthened relationships among civic leaders and residents.

In 2008, I started to explore new possibilities for the thesis and searched for additional instruments-for-action. Other scholarly publications, such as peer-reviewed journal articles and books, it occurred to me, too, could serve a larger purpose. The idea of an edited volume, created by a team of faculty, staff, and students in collaboration with civic leaders in cities, struck me as a good way to further explore the kind of epistemology we had been developing through our partnership with the people of Lawrence. And, rather than looking for resources to fund such a project, I considered the vast resources already at my disposal. Why not bring a group of thesis writers together, focus their attention on a set of issues, and ask them to produce research relevant to the larger society? In short, what is now known as the collaborative thesis project was known, in my mind, as the edited-volume project. I did not have a plan for making it happen. I was surrounded by talented people, we brought our resources to bear, and we improvised.

The kind of work that went into this book is the kind of work necessary to transform America's cities. For decades, unlikely partnerships and big ideas have thwarted decentralization—the unrelenting migration of firms, retail establishments, and customers from downtown to outlying suburban communities. Pittsburgh, Boston, and Baltimore are widely known in both the academic and popular press as cities that turned the corner by engaging business leaders and local government in coalitions of common cause. Downtrodden downtowns have been transformed by way of partnerships that introduced public spaces and activities designed to attract large crowds, namely festival marketplaces, waterfront attractions, sports arenas, and convention centers (Sagalyn 1990). According to urban regime theory, these flagship projects are the material result of a shift in local politics whereby economic development is understood as the social production of governance (Logan and Molotch 1987; Cox and Mair 1988). To function effectively, urban governments need not exert power "over" the citizenry; they only need to facilitate the power to act. The question then for city planning educators and practitioners is this: who has the capacity to act?

The answer is *everybody*. But where does a city like Camden, Cleveland, or Lawrence—where corporate and government leadership is lacking or nonexistent—begin? Simply put, they begin by identifying and connecting their rooted institutions because such institutions will never relocate and they are motivated to invest in the communities where they are located.[1] Moreover, rooted institutions are rich with seasoned civic leaders, employees who live in nearby neighborhoods, political and financial clout, and the space and equipment necessary for public meetings, dialogue, and deliberation. By creating an informal yet stable type of "civic cooperation" among leaders working "to produce a capacity to govern and bring about publicly significant results," rooted institutions can provide jobs and workforce training, incubate the development of new businesses, and invest their purchasing power in local businesses (Stone 1989, 5–7). In these ways, they create a reinvigorated civic sphere that attracts new residents, knowledge-industry workers, and tourists. The ability of alliances among civic leaders representing private interests as well as community development corporations, community foundations, and public colleges and universities to transform cities is well-documented (5–7).

Forging productive relationships among rooted institutions for the purpose of improving the quality of life in cities is easier said than done. Each rooted institution has its own unique history, culture, and purpose. Many are inward-looking. University and college campuses are often physically designed to be separate from the community, turning their back to the public streets or sitting on a plinth (Blaik, 2007). They are idiosyncratic, dedicated to an academic calendar that separates academic and public life by artificially segmenting the year into semesters and long holiday breaks that disrupt continuous engagement with the world beyond the gates. The real challenge is in transforming rooted institutions from the inside. For example, how can we mold universities and colleges, which are preoccupied with knowledge production and control by and for a few, into democratically engaged institutions committed to generating relevant knowledge with and for the larger public? Calling into question the relevance of curricular artifacts like the thesis and modernizing them is one way forward.

Conclusion

Innovative city planning education is a prerequisite for innovative city planning practice. The job of the city planning educator is to meet students where they are, create respectful spaces for dialogue, engage with them in ways that reveal their individual strengths and weaknesses, uncover their aspirations, embrace their uniqueness as well as their wholeness, and support the discovery of bold ideas. Similarly, every city has its own unique history, challenges, and potential futures. The city planning practitioner needs to invite citizens from all walks of life to participate in public discourse and decision making in a way that gets them excited about creating a vision for and taking action in their own neighborhoods.

Transforming Cities and Minds provides a daring set of solutions and routes of exploration for solving the multiple, interlocking problems that face the American city today. Just as we decided it would not work to pursue the thesis in the old ways, we feel—and argue, in the essays that follow—that it would be wrong to pursue the transformation of cities in the old ways. While it is undeniably a crisis of massive proportions, the Great Recession is also an opportunity. The collapse of the nation's real-estate and private investment markets, along with the downfall of global investment markets, has intensified economic, social, and environmental challenges that are long-standing: disappearing manufacturing jobs, failing public education, rising income inequality, and dependence on foreign oil. More communities across the country, not only its cities, are becoming vulnerable and beginning to suffer. Ironically, this new reality gives us new insights and the courage to approach old problems in new ways.

Transforming Cities and Minds is intended to inspire action. Our work makes the case that universities and colleges still in ivory towers should respond to the urgent societal needs of people living beyond the campus boundaries, generating new and relevant knowledge with and for the use of communities and receiving knowledge in return in an "ecological system of knowledge" (Lynton 1994, 89).

Central to the enterprise is the power of human relationships, a vital resource the United States cannot afford to squander. We must emerge from our isolation, engage with one another, learn from each other, and share our discoveries far and wide. We must recruit and invest in the next generation in ways that narrow the growing divide between the rich and the poor; we must also press onward with optimism and a full appreciation for the natural world upon which we all depend.

The practice of city planning appeals to people who are amazed by and want to learn more about cities—why and how they thrive and fail. *Transforming Cities and Minds* is primarily for high school students who are thinking about college, college students in search of their calling, and everybody who has an impulse to take part in making their street, neighborhood, town, or city a better place to live and work. We welcome you to join us.

Notes

1. Though most academics and practitioners refer to them as anchor institutions, we refer to them as rooted institutions—vital and fixed resources in the civic landscape of cities that depend on the people in the community where they are located as much as the people in the community depend on them.

References

Benson, L., I. Harkavy, and M. Hartley. 2005. "Integrating a Commitment to the Public Good into the Institutional Fabric." In *Higher Education for the Public Good: Emerging Voices from a National Movement,* edited by A. J. Kezar, T. Chambers, and J. Burkhardt, 185–216. San Francisco: Jossey-Bass.

Blaik, O. 2007. "Campuses in Cities: Places between Engagement and Retreat." *Chronicle of Higher Education,* February 23, 25–26.

Boyer. E. L. 1996. "The Scholarship of Engagement." *Journal of Public Service and Outreach* 1 (1): 11–20.

Bozorg, L. 2008a. Personal statement. Massachusetts Institute of Technology.

———. 2008b. Essay from application to MIT@Lawrence. September 24.

———. 2010. Resume. March 29.

Bozorg, L., B. Brandin, G. Christiansen, L. Hoyt, N. Iuviene, M. Leavy-Sperounis, E. Mackres, and A. Stitely. 2010. Group meeting. May 17.

Brandin, B. 2008. Personal statement. Massachusetts Institute of Technology.

———. 2010. Resume. August 6.

Chang, K. 2004. "From Oral Disputation to Written Text: The Transformation of the Dissertation in Early Modern Europe." *History of Universities* 19 (2): 129–87.

Christiansen, G. 2008a. Personal Statement. Massachusetts Institute of Technology.

———. 2008b. Essay from application to MIT@Lawrence. September 21.

———. 2010. Resume. March 1.

Cox, K. R., and A. Mair. 1998. "Locality and Community in the Politics of Local Economic Development." *Annals of the Association of American Geographers* 78: 307–25.

Hoyt, L. 2010. "A City-Campus Engagement Theory From, and For, Practice." *Michigan Journal of Community Service Learning* 17 (1): 75–88.

Hoyt, L., and A. Leroux. 2007. *Voices from Forgotten Cities: Innovative Revitalization Coalitions in America's Older Small Cities.* Report sponsored by PolicyLink, Oakland, CA; Citizens' Housing and Planning Association, Boston, MA; and M.I.T. School of Architecture and Planning, Cambridge, MA.

Iuviene, N. 2008. Personal statement. Massachusetts Institute of Technology.

————. 2010a. Resume. June 13.

————. 2010b. Phone interview. July 14.

Leavy-Sperounis, M. 2008. Personal statement. Massachusetts Institute of Technology.

Logan, J., and H. Molotch. 1987. *Urban Fortunes: The Political Economy of Place.* Berkeley: University of California Press.

Lynton, E. 1994. "Knowledge and Scholarship." *Metropolitan Universities: An International Forum* 5 (1): 9–17.

Mackres, E. 2008a. Personal statement. Massachusetts Institute of Technology.

————. 2008b. Essay from application to MIT@Lawrence. September 28.

————. 2010. Resume. March 1.

O'Meara, K. A. 2011. "Faculty Civic Engagement: New Training, Assumptions, and Markets Needed for the Engaged American Scholar." In *"To Serve a Larger Purpose": Engagement for Democracy and the Transformation of Higher Education,* edited by J. Saltmarsh and M. Hartley, 177–98. Philadelphia: Temple University Press.

Reardon, K. 2000. "An Experiential Approach to Creating an Effective Community-University Partnership: The East St. Louis Action Research Project." *Cityscape* 5 (1): 59–74.

Rendón, L. 2009. *Sentipensante Pedagogy: Educating for Wholeness, Social Justice and Liberation.* Sterling, VA: Stylus.

Sagalyn, L. 1990. "Explaining the Improbable: Local Redevelopment in the Wake of Federal Cutbacks." *Journal of the American Planning Association* 56 (4): 429–42.

Saltmarsh, J. 2010. Personal correspondence. January 10.

Saltmarsh, J., and M. Hartley. 2011. "To Serve a Larger Purpose." In *"To Serve a Larger Purpose": Engagement for Democracy and the Transformation of Higher Education,* edited by J. Saltmarsh and M. Hartley, 1–26. Philadelphia: Temple University Press.

Schön, D. A. 1995. "Knowing-in-Action: The New Scholarship Requires a New Epistemology." *Change* 27 (6): 26–34.

Stone, C. 1989. *Regime Politics: Governing Atlanta, 1946–1988.* Lawrence: University Press of Kansas.

Vogelgesang, L., N. Denson, and U. Jayakumar. 2010. "What Determines Faculty-Engaged Scholarship?," *Review of Higher Education* 33: 437–72.

PART I

Engaging Economy

1

Strengthening Small Businesses

Strategies for Makin' a Way Where There Is No Way in Camden, New Jersey

Gayle Christiansen

"We Invest in Our Own"

Dominican and Puerto Rican music pours out the doors of the Caribbean Mega Center, a small electronics store in Camden, New Jersey—a city known for its entrenched poverty, crime, and failing schools. The storefront lights and awning portray a brightly painted beach. José Marrera, the store's owner, describes his place as

> a little Best Buy. Everything you can get in there we've got: radios, computers, cell phones, video games. We deal with DJ equipment, car equipment, DVDs, music, video systems, everything at once. People come here because it is cheaper and it saves you time. We've been here for eighteen years. Eighteen years serving the community.

But why is he in Camden? Why not a more affluent city with a better reputation, where doing business might be easier? José insists,

> We're from Camden . . . raised in Camden. We still live here. That is why the store is here. We love our city. It's not bad here. People think Camden is the worst city anywhere. People have to come here and see for themselves that we aren't bad people. We are good people. We work hard. I think we are friendly with everybody and when you are friendly, people like you. When everyone is nice to each other, you don't have a problem. Camden is not what people think. There is a great opportunity here.

Though business is slower for the Caribbean Mega Center thanks to the recession, José has a track record of success and remains hopeful for the future. He does, however, question the city's economic development strategy. He explains,

> They build stuff around the nice parts. They invest in the good, not the bad. If they never invest in the bad, it will stay bad. We invest in our own. We're about to open another store that was abandoned. We bought it, and now we are fixing it to make the street look better. It will be a fruit and vegetable shop, like a little market, Jumbo's Fruit and Vegetables. It is going to be another business coming to the area. (Marrera 2010)

José's entrepreneurial knowledge and his understanding of this East Camden neighborhood raise several questions. Are there other small-business owners with the same determination who care as much as José about the city? And, if so, why does José feel like the city supports only the "nice parts" of town, instead of helping people like him? Would investing in small businesses improve the economy and civic life of the city?

In this chapter, I present a narrative of Camden's dominance and decline, how it tried to turn itself around and why it failed. I argue for a storefront in addition to a waterfront strategy by showing how Camden's small businesses have survived despite the obstacles they encounter. Lastly, I present a set of strategies for unleashing the power of small businesses in Camden and other American cities.

Camden's Dominance and Decline

Camden, New Jersey, was once home to many entrepreneurs and innovators. Jersey tomatoes helped the Campbell Soup Company grow to international fame. New York Shipbuilding Corporation built some of the largest World War I battleships in Camden. RCA, Radio Corporation of America, led the world in the manufacture of "talking machines," and its technology later allowed people to hear the first words uttered from the moon. Both the iconic poet Walt Whitman and the first drive-in movie theater called Camden home. The city's vibrant, ethnically centered, commercial corridors of Broadway, Kaighn, and Haddon Avenues boasted "movie theaters, real estate operations, doctors, dentists, and lawyers mixed with a host of commercial and retail services" (Gillette 2005, 22). Local family businesses thrived during World War I and the Great Depression as they met the needs of their neighbors (Gillette 2005).

Then came industrial decline, white flight, the building of the Cherry Hill mall, the 1971 riots, and various attempts at urban renewal—all of which left Camden, like small postindustrial cities across the country, in a state of decline. In 1973, Mayor Angelo Errichetti explained, "The years of neglect, slumlord exploitation, tenant abuse, government bungling, indecision and short-sighted policy had transformed the city's housing, business and industrial stock into a ravaged, rat-infested cancer on a sick, old industrial city" (Gillette 2005, 89). Today, Camden is one of America's poorest cities. It is also largely uneducated (in 2009, 54.9 percent of high school seniors graduated) and shrinking (the city had 124,555 people in 1950 and has 79,904 today) (CamConnect 2010).

In places like Camden, the challenges of urban decline threaten to overwhelm numerous positive assets. These cities have developed infrastructure, access to a waterway, a walkable downtown, and historic architecture. They enjoy cultural institutions such as universities alongside a wide diversity of immigrant populations, niche markets, and entrepreneurship (Hoyt and Leroux 2007; Fox and Axel-Lute 2008). When it comes to the task of revitalizing cities like Camden, the crucial question is how to leverage assets to overcome the challenges facing these cities and the people who live and work in them. However, selecting which assets should be targeted, and developing an investment strategy around them, is more difficult than it sounds.

Camden's Waterfront Strategy

In 1981, newly elected New Jersey governor Tom Kean and Camden mayor Randy Primas focused redevelopment efforts on what was felt to be the city's greatest asset: the waterfront. Primas considered Baltimore's Inner Harbor redevelopment a successful model that Camden could replicate. "I don't believe you're going to find private-sector investment in the neighborhoods. ... The only way to change that is by creating a viable downtown and having it grow from there" (Gillette 2005, 129). By the start of the twenty-first century, Camden's waterfront contained an expanded aquarium, children's garden, minor-league baseball stadium, decommissioned battleship, concert venue, and RCA factory converted into loft apartments. But this investment was not enough to turn the city around: over the two decades that followed, decline steepened to the point where Camden required state-level intervention.

In 2002, New Jersey enacted the Municipal Rehabilitation and Economic Recovery Act (also known as the Receivership Act), placing Camden under state receivership and affecting the direction of redevelopment. The Receivership Act aimed to stabilize the local economy, stimulate investment, and reform municipal government (Kromer 2009). Following the trail laid by previous development decisions—and, inevitably, political interests—$175 million of reinvestment money went largely to grow waterfront tourism and the city's educational and medical facilities (Katz 2009; Kromer 2009). Receivership Act funding passed over community development corporations and nonprofit projects because Receivership Act administrators saw such organizations as too small to create tangible city improvement. John Kromer, former director of city planning and the Camden Redevelopment Agency, a quasi-government department created under the Receivership Act, reflects on the legislation's approach:

> In years prior to the Receivership Act, major commitments of state funding had been made to finance development on the waterfront, with relatively little comparable state investment in neighborhoods, and a continuation of this pattern was reflected in the Receivership Act's financing approach: the aquarium received a $25 million allocation of its own, while the city's neighborhoods had to vie for a share of the $78 million available in the two generically designated "neighborhood" funds (some of which would pay for demolition that would not be followed by new development). (2009, 214)

Over the years, some Camden residents and researchers have questioned the way this revitalization strategy focused solely on expanding waterfront tourism and the rooted educational and medical institutions downtown. In 1981, they wondered if Mayor Primas's waterfront focus would create a handful of highly paid professional jobs and many unskilled, low-paying positions to be held disproportionately by minorities (Gillette 2005, 136). In protest of the aquarium expansion, one resident told the *Philadelphia Inquirer*, "We got two and three families living in one house and beautiful fish living in tanks by themselves" (Gillette 2005, 137). A 2005 resident survey conducted by Camden Churches Organized for People and the Concerned Black Clergy of Camden found only 26 percent of Camden residents felt the three-year-old Receivership Act revitalization was going in the right direction (Ott 2005). Investment in the waterfront and in rooted institutions has had no effect on education, unemployment, poverty, or violence levels. According to Matt Katz (2009), a reporter for the *Philadelphia Inquirer:* "Camden residents are just as poor today and just as likely to be murdered. They are just as unemployed and lacking in the skills to succeed at work. Their children's reading and math skills are just as abysmal. And the city is twice as reliant on state taxpayers as before."

The failure of Camden's waterfront- and rooted institution-based approach to economic development makes plain that the city needs a new approach. An economically comprehensive revitalization strategy, in which all residents contribute to the city's prosperity, is crucial to creating sustainable, long-term vitality (McGahey and Vey 2008). Acknowledging and leveraging the city's overlooked assets needs to be part of an economic strategy that spurs equitable investment while supporting and serving those who call Camden home.

Investing in Entrepreneurs

In Camden and other cities that have been left behind, small businesses are hidden assets. Valuable as they are, they go unrecognized. Small businesses—defined by the Small Business Administration (SBA) as those firms employing fewer than five hundred people—account for 44 percent of the total U.S. private payroll and employ over half of all private-sector employees. Between 1993 and the third quarter of 2008, they accounted for 14.4 million new jobs, or 64 percent of all the jobs created in that period. In 2004, the number of jobs created by small businesses approximately equaled the number of jobs lost by large firms during that period (U.S. Small Business Administration 2010a).

Small businesses, meanwhile, provide everyday goods and services that residents would otherwise have to leave the neighborhood to get (Boston 2006; Gittell and Thompson 1999; Bendick and Egan 1993). They fill vacant spaces in neighborhoods, reducing blight and bringing vitality and stability (Bendick and Egan 1993). Small businesses contribute to the tax base of the city, increasing the pool of money available to improve citywide services and infrastructure (Gittell and Thompson

1999). Finally, business owners are often important political and social leaders and often serve as spokespeople for community interests (Gittell and Thompson 1999).

In Camden, the time is ripe for the development of small businesses. New leadership, in the form of New Jersey governor Chris Christie and Camden mayor Dana Redd, has made room for strengthening the city's small-business presence. Governor Christie recognized that "efforts to upgrade the downtown waterfront will be undermined as long as Camden's neighborhoods remain unsafe and unschooled" (Hirsch and Walsh 2009). Investing in entrepreneurs is one way to revitalize neighborhoods. At the city level, Mayor Redd expressed her belief that "the strength of our City lies within our children, our families, small businesses, our neighborhoods" (Redd 2010). And "what does not work is top-down planning. It has to be grassroots-driven, in terms of redevelopment and how we revitalize and stabilize our neighborhoods" (Hirsch 2010). In 2011, Camden small-business owners and supporters have a rare opportunity to have their voices heard.

Finally, investing in Camden's small businesses makes sense from a city design perspective. Many small businesses are located in or near commercial corridors, which connect neighborhoods and surrounding suburbs to downtown. Unlike Baltimore's downtown, which redeveloped as an "economic island" from its neighborhoods, Camden's downtown can profit from its linkages with small businesses on connecting commercial corridors (Levine 1987). The size of buildings on many commercial corridors fits the square-footage requirements of small-business owners, and zoning often permits business use. Indeed, there is already evidence of small-business success on Camden's Federal Street. Businesses there, like Marrera's Carribean Mega Center, "have boosted a grassroots redevelopment effort as the city struggles to attract major employers" (Conaboy 2010).

These small businesses provide residents with jobs and may draw outside shoppers with Federal Street's unique concentration of Latino stores. Federal Street is slowly proving that a corridor of small businesses can revitalize an area and spur additional development (Lamboy 2009a). Following the Federal Street example, small businesses on and around other commercial corridors can improve Camden's economy, provide jobs, attract outside shoppers while meeting residents' needs, and beautify the city.

Imagining a Storefront Strategy

What would Camden be like today if a portion of the state-funded Receivership Act had gone to support small businesses? A quick, back-of-the-envelope calculation shows the potential impact if Receivership Act administrators had allocated $10 million, or approximately 6 percent of the total $175 million—less than one-half the funding that went into expanding Camden's one aquarium—to small businesses. If each new business received $160,000 of support, perhaps $80,000 to obtain a commercial property, $35,000 in a business loan, $2,500 in entrepreneurship training, and the remaining $42,500 for building improvements, the $10 million could have opened sixty-two new businesses. To be conservative, if each business led to four new resident-held jobs (at the time of my investigation, Camden's small businesses each actually employed six people on average), the funding would have created 248 new jobs. Dividing these sixty-two businesses among Camden's nine commercial corridors results in approximately seven new businesses per corridor. Filling vacant storefronts to create at least one new whole city block on each corridor sends positive signals to other potential business owners that there is opportunity in Camden. The city government benefits from the tax revenue generated by sixty-two new enterprises, while neighborhoods benefit from sixty-two new leaders and role models working to improve their community.

Imagining a storefront strategy helps to illuminate the potential of small businesses when included in a larger, well-funded plan for economic development. But the reality is that federal and state governments are not likely to bail out the nation's postindustrial cities. The United States does not have enough money to pursue this strategy, even if it wanted to. So, in the absence of such resources, what has Camden already achieved? Where local government and institutions have failed, Camden's residents, especially its small-business owners, have succeeded. Though Camden's small businesses would benefit from proper investment, they have managed to thrive without it. An economic downturn, coming after years of disinvestment, requires us to think creatively about how to revitalize American cities. Camden's small businesses are a wellspring of just this kind of creativity and resiliency. But how have they been successful?

From, For, and Of the City: The Power of Small Businesses

My sample of successful small businesses consists of sixteen diverse enterprises. Three are in the field of construction, three are restaurants, four are involved in other services including a day care and a barbershop, and six are retail. The sixteen businesses are also geographically diverse. Three are on the Federal Street commercial corridor, four on or near River Road in East Camden, two on Haddon Avenue, two on Mt. Ephraim Avenue, three on Broadway, and two in the central business district. These business owners—twelve men and four women—come from all over the globe. They identify as African American, white, Dominican, Puerto Rican, Korean, and Indian. They have had varied life experiences. One graduated from an Ivy League university another worked as an executive in a Fortune 100 firm, and another spent time in prison. Finally, these businesses have been operating for different periods of time. The two businesses that have been open more than fifty years saw the city at its height and have survived its subsequent sustained decline. Four have been open a decade or two, six are between five and ten years old, and five opened their doors fewer than five years ago.

There were, despite their many differences, certain similarities among the small-business owners I surveyed. For instance, at least seven of the sixteen (44 percent) held a bachelor's degree, suggesting that business owners are better educated than the average Camden citizen—only 5.4 percent of the city's residents over the age of twenty-five have a bachelor's degree (U.S. Census Bureau 2000). Additionally, three salient patterns surfaced from my interviews: small-business owners care about Camden, they have and promote a positive image of the city, and they are tough and resilient.

Giving Back to the City

All sixteen owners have a business plan focused on profit and long-term growth, but thirteen of them also use their businesses as a means for giving back to the city. Their commitment takes many forms, from mentoring youth to complex civic activism to simple neighborhood beautification. Connie Jackson, who owns a construction management firm, says she located her business in Camden because she is "from here, grew up here, went to school here. I wouldn't have had my business anywhere else. I wanted to be able to give back to the city" (2010). In addition to her construction business, she served on the Camden City School Board from 1996 to 1999, started the Friends of Creative Arts, which raises money for student activities at the Creative Arts High School, is currently president of the New Jersey Chapter of the National Association of Minority Contractors, and mentors potential entrepreneurs (Jackson 2010). After more than two decades in the ophthalmology business, Esther Williams, who opened City Eyes, the city's only optical retail store, hosts meetings with other entrepreneurs to "come up with ideas of how we can better become successful, how we can partner to let each other know about other businesses that are here" (2010).

In early spring, Robert Lucas plants flowers along the sidewalk in front of and next door to Donkey's Place, the regionally renowned cheese steak restaurant opened by his parents over fifty years ago (2010). For Byron Gans, who owns the sneaker and sports-nostalgia store The Shoe Kings with his brother Darien, giving back means creating a welcoming ambiance and treating his customers with respect. He explained to me, "I say, why can't we have a nice store? Why should it be cold? And why should I serve you something through Plexiglas? I say we're not doing that to the people that's around here. People respect that" (Gans and Gans 2010).

For six of the business owners I interviewed, caring about Camden meant serving as a role model for youth. For example, Corrine Powers hires local youth to work at her soul food restaurant, Corrine's Place. She explains, "It's not just a job of serving food. They learn life skills, in terms of how to talk, how to walk, how to look . . . so it is like a training program also" (2010). She adds, "If I don't do anything else, I've made a difference. Children that leave up out of here and do fantastic. They reflect back on what I took them through and appreciate it." At Total Perfection, a unisex barbershop and salon, owner Barry Wilkins and his staff empower youth by showing them how to behave respectfully. The barbers in his shop teach children to shake hands when greeting customers, to speak courteously, and to exude confidence (Wilkins 2010). The professional tone he sets for his staff transfers to the customers they serve. Others expect to influence the next generation and have a clear vision of how they might give back. Kelly Chang, who owns Friends Café next to Rutgers University in Camden, wants "to get involved with the high schools and teach them about culinary arts. I'll give them a job here and teach them how to run a small business. Make it kind of a credited class—not just running a business, but paying the bills, showing them what a bill looks like and doing QuickBooks" (2010). Small-business owners aren't donating to philanthropic organizations, but they contribute to the community as role models, setting an example of success in a challenging environment (Wilson 1996).

"It's a Different Taste"

Eleven of the businesses owners I interviewed discussed the challenge of sharing their view of an opportunity-rich, peaceful Camden with outsiders who believe it to be an impoverished and violent wasteland. As the Gans brothers put it,

> Being from here we get categorized. Once you hear Camden, soon as you mention it to the corporations, immediately we're on the defensive. Don't walk down Mt. Ephraim Ave., don't say "Hi," because of the rap. But when you open the orange up, peel the orange, see the real fruit, then it's a different taste. (2010)

Thirteen of the sixteen business owners reject Camden's unsafe and violent reputation. Neither José Marrera nor Ralph Ishack, who owns the city's only school uniform retailer, have been robbed in all their eleven and eighteen respective years of operation. Over this time, Ralph actually observed an increase in safety. He notes, "There is more law enforcement and less drugs and hookers" in South Camden (2010). José Marrera wants people's perception of Camden to align with the reality. He told me, "Camden has changed a lot for the better. The people from outside, I'd like to invite them to come to Camden. They think of this as a scary area. This is not" (2010).

Only three of the sixteen business owners spoke about negative experiences in their neighborhood, including Barry Wilkins at Total Perfection, who decided that taking his business to the next level would require curbing "street" behavior and language. He instituted rules of conduct in his store and reinforced them through his own example and by admonishing those who failed to comply with them. As a native with an understanding of the local culture, Barry knew how to teach people to behave professionally. Today Total Perfection is a popular shop, known as a neighborhood favorite for quality hairstyles, especially for such special occasions as weddings and high school proms (Wilkins 2010).

Camden's small-business owners see opportunity where outsiders see obstacles. Ten of the sixteen business owners I interviewed grew up in Camden and, when asked why they chose Camden as a place for business, gave responses like José Marrera's: a long relationship with the city equips these business owners with local knowledge, and this knowledge allows them to see Camden as a place rich in business opportunities. While they have not performed traditional market analyses, they access similar information about supply and customer base from their experience in, and personal understanding of, the city (Waxman 2000). Tyrone Pitts, an entrepreneur raised in Camden and educated at the University of Pennsylvania, explains, "It is amazing that a lot of people don't recognize the opportunities that are available in the city of Camden. They kind of look at it as a place where business doesn't occur, and to be truthful there is a tremendous amount of business waiting to happen, but people just have to uncover the opportunity" (2010). Corrine Powers does not acknowledge the drawbacks to the city where she was born and raised. She exclaims, "I was born down at Cooper Hospital. I was educated from grammar to college right there in Camden. I graduated from Rutgers. I'm often asked, 'Why Camden?' and I say, 'Why not?' You know, why not?" (2010). One opportunity the small-business owners see is the consumer potential of the city's residents. Tyrone Pitts knows that just because people are poor does not mean they have no money to spend:

> What they don't understand is, and it's kind of worked to my benefit, is that most of the people here, although their incomes are low, they dispose of everything they have. So they utilize all their money, and it becomes disposable income, which makes for a very fertile business development endeavor. People live day-to-day, week-to-week, month-to-month, and a lot of what they receive or all that they receive can be put back into the local economy. (2010)

This is especially important to businesses selling convenience goods, that is, items people need on a daily basis. When people purchase these things close to home, instead of spending their money outside the city, small-business owners capture local money and keep it within the local economy. Before José Marrera opened the Caribbean Mega Center he wondered, "Why do people from Camden have to go out of Camden? I looked at Best Buy and thought, 'Maybe we can do the same thing in Camden.' My store is not as big as Best Buy, but here you can get everything they have" (2010). He views city residents as music lovers and video game players, not as people too poor to afford a television or cell phone. His store profits by meeting a community need.

Other small-business owners similarly cater to customers underserved by other options. Luis Japa, owner of Luis Records and Electronics, which started more than fifteen years ago selling pagers and Spanish-language music, explains, "In this city many people don't have a bank account so then they come here to pay their bills" (2010). He serves the community by operating a bill-payment and money-transfer center in his store. Tyrone Pitts entered the construction and tutoring businesses to meet Camden's two most important needs: housing and education. "What I try to do is meet the needs of the community I grew up in. We got evicted when I was like in eighth grade. I know what it is like to be homeless, and so I think housing is important. It gives people stability and a point of reference. A lot of people get into trouble because they don't have that point of reference" (2010). Rhonda Mendez and her partner operate the only flower store in Camden. "We have a lot of funeral work, a lot of weddings, sweet sixteens, sweet fifteens. There was a need for a floral shop in this area" (2010).[1]

Small-business owners in Camden see local residents not only as customers, but as potential employees. Construction contractor Marcellus Hill has capitalized on recent funding from the American Recovery and Reinvestment Act (also known as the Recovery Act) to hire workers from the neighborhood.

> The stimulus money is for bringing everybody up. . . . We have a lot of people out here who want to work; they just don't get a fair share and opportunity. I pick different people out in different distressed areas I work. I'm actually going to pull them in and let them work in the company for a minute and then push them through the union to get more training and benefits for their family. (2010)

He adds that the construction and weatherization fields have plenty of room to employ people on welfare or in halfway houses (Hill 2010).[2] While some businesses won't hire ex-convicts, Corrine Powers believes, "Sometimes there are a lot of unhorrible people that have been incarcerated" (2010). She knows the people of the city and does not shy away from hiring locally.

Surviving Tough Times

The Great Recession impacted small businesses across the country; for Camden's residents, the recent downturn only added to long-standing industrial decline and poverty. Ten of the sixteen business owners reported weathering the economic recession as their most pressing concern.

Manuel José owns Loida Daycare with his mother Eunice, a retired Camden schoolteacher. Rising unemployment during the recession means "within the last three months we've lost maybe fifteen customers, because parents are losing jobs. The economy is still not as good as it was. Parents, especially this fall, lost more jobs than I've seen" (José 2010). Out-of-work parents stay home with their children because they do not have the money to pay for daycare. At Friends Café, Kelly Chang suffered a similar decrease in customers because eating at home is less costly than eating out (2010). "I don't think that people are holding money and not spending. I think that it is they don't have money to spend. If you have high unemployment, people are going to buy the basics—food, shirts," explains Luis Japa (2010). Adam Woods owns the screen-printing shop Camden Printworks and is proud of employing local people at a living wage. Though he prepared for the recession, he finds enduring it more difficult than he anticipated:

> We were ready for it. We had some savings built up; we were keeping a minimal inventory. We were doing really short orders, all the stuff you are supposed to do to be a scrappy survivor. We did all those things and we did them right and so we were able to weather the storm for a long time. I would say by October 2009, we first started to see things pick up out of the slump, but they aren't picking up at a fast enough clip. So consequently we have people that are laid off. When we emerge from hibernation it is probably going to look a little different than it did before we went into it. (Woods 2010)

Miguel Benito, who immigrated to Camden from Mexico in 1995 and opened Universal Foto Estudio with help from his brothers, now advises potential business owners to wait until after the recession to open. "Before 2008 it was busy, but now there is hardly anything. We still make money, but not as much as before. We make only enough to feed ourselves" (2010).

For the small-business owners I interviewed, coping with the economic downturn requires a variety of tactics. Like Adam Woods, Connie Jackson had to let go of some employees. Downsizing is a measure that is often more difficult for small-business owners than for others. Connie explains, "With a small business, when things get slow you may have to lay off, and you're down to one or two people. The burden is heavier on you because you automatically wear three, four, five hats and you now put on a couple more hats" (Jackson 2010). Instead of laying off employees, Luis Japa has put store improvements on hold. "Small businesses are facing difficult times. Lately, it is like you make some money and you have already promised that money. You can't save it to do changes in the store or to invest in merchandise or inventory or changes to the environment or presentation or showcasing the store" (Japa 2010).

In contrast, contractor Marcellus Hill saw an opportunity for strategic expansion: the simultaneous collapse of the housing industry and increased federal support for weatherization led him to expand his portfolio. Marcellus describes his experience, "The market had changed to make the construction go down. I started trying to get other jobs, but the economy was so bad. It wasn't just me, everybody's going through it. So I just redirected my energy into weatherization because I got a whiff that was going on" (2010). José Marrera, too, finds creative ways to cope with the recession. He didn't rethink the nature of his business; he began renting some of his building space to smaller vendors instead. He explains, "The economy is bad. If I'm going to pay the mortgage for the building, being by myself I can't afford it. Now I have five stores in my one location. I rent out to people. And then these people help me to pay the mortgage and pay the bills" (2010).

These different survival tactics point to the tenacity and resiliency of Camden's small-business owners, a determination that many attribute to their Camden roots. According to Tyrone Pitts, "It is my makeup, coming from a place like Camden where things get tough a lot of times. You learn to endure and work through problems. Normal people would just quit" (2010). Connie Jackson agrees. She explains how growing up poor in Camden and fighting to make it turned her into the entrepreneur she is today: "My parents didn't have money. We basically didn't know what we were going to eat from day-to-day. My mother was on welfare because she got sick and couldn't work anymore. I was working at the age of thirteen and have worked all my life" (2010). Camden's small-business owners are resilient, which serves them well as they navigate an uncertain economic landscape. They find imaginative ways to overcome obstacles, persevere during tough times, and stay open for business.

Obstacles for Small Businesses: Isolation, Dollars, and Bureaucracy

Conversations with Camden small-business owners show they care about their city, believe in its positive image, and have the wherewithal to persist through an economic recession coming on top of years of disinvestment. These characteristics are even more remarkable when considered in the context of the obstacles they face, notably their disconnection from economic development entities meant to assist them, from financial resources, and from the city government.

Institutions as Strangers

My research identified twenty-three city, regional, and state institutions that are theoretically available to support small businesses through real-estate acquisition, financing, entrepreneurship training, business development, or networking. But when asked who supports them, business owners point to just three—the Latin American Economic Development Association, the Camden Empowerment Zone Corporation, and the Cooperative Business Assistance Corporation—and eleven of the sixteen businesses received no support from any formal organization. Notably, fifteen of the sixteen business owners have never received a bank loan.

The inescapable conclusion is not that Camden suffers from a lack of support institutions, but that business owners are unaware of the resources available to them. Adam Woods laments, "I guess I'm surprised by how little there is out there for small businesses. All my life I was told there was a lot of stuff for small businesses" (2010). According to Tyrone Pitts:

> A lot of people have great ideas about starting businesses but they don't have any support. There's not a whole lot of support here to help individuals trying to start them. I know I did most of my stuff by trial and error. A lot of the services for start-up businesses aren't readily available

or people don't know where they are or the access to information is sometimes a hindrance to those who want to start a business. (2010)

The Shoe Kings agree. "People are not informed. They don't know about a lot of different programs. A lot of people don't go through with things because they don't have the right information on how to do it. They might have great ideas, but they'll never take flight because they have no one around them to be the avenues to make it happen" (Gans and Gans 2010). These comments suggest that if business owners knew of services, they would use them.

Rutgers-Camden, a university with a business incubator, Small-Business Development Center (SBDC), and Office of Civic Engagement committed to making the campus a supportive member of the Camden community, is an example of the disconnection between resources and small businesses. The business incubator strives to bring high-tech, bio-tech, and life-science businesses to Camden and the region (Zammit 2009), but Camden's thriving small businesses are not in these sectors.

In January 2010, Rutgers-Camden held a civic engagement sympo-sium that included a session dedicated to successful entrepreneurship activities. It highlighted the work of students in developing business plans and briefly mentioned the idea of locating student businesses in the community. Little was said about students working with current Camden small businesses in a form of mutual learning (Pritchett 2010). At the end of the symposium, Chancellor Pritchett announced that to increase economic activity in the city, the university will

> host a series of small-business marketplaces inviting local business owners to come and present their goods and services to the Rutgers-Camden community. This initiative will work closely with students, faculty, staff, and the Camden Urban Enterprise Zone and other interested stakeholders to ensure local businesses understand the needs of the campus community as well as helping the campus community understand the depth and quality of the products and services offered by these businesses. (2010)

On the surface this sounds like a program bridging the business re-source chasm, but upon closer inspection it raises several concerns. First, none of the successful entrepreneurs interviewed mentioned a relationship with the Urban Enterprise Zone, making it an unlikely agency to represent business voices or ideas. Second, it would be better for the businesses if the Rutgers-Camden community came to them: people on campus would learn where the stores are so they can frequent them again, and businesses would benefit from increased foot traffic. Crucially, visiting the businesses on the commercial corridors would challenge students to reconsider their negative perceptions of the city; forcing businesses to come to campus only reinforces the idea that the outside neighborhood is unsafe. Overall, this proposal appears to have little benefit for the small-business owners.

Lacking deep-rooted support from local institutions, small businesses turn instead to family and friends; nine of the businesses in my survey rely on such informal assistance, and for five it is their only source of support. Miguel Benito learned how to start and run his business from his brothers, who had previously opened two businesses in the region (2010). Kelly Chang relied on the support of a former employee and friend, "He knows this town well. He still lives in Camden. He helped me with this building and decorating it. He's really handy and knows electric" (2010). The entrepreneurs benefit from the assistance of loved ones, even though the resources they can provide are less substantial than those of economic development organizations.[3]

"I Borrowed Money from Friends and Family"

Many potential small-business owners have the will and vision needed to start a business but lack the financial resources and/or technical knowledge required (Bates 1997). The well-documented difficulty of minority business owners in obtaining start-up and working capital is borne out in Camden. Even though thirteen of my sixteen interviewees set aside financial resources before opening, some owners were still surprised by the amount of up-front business costs. Kelly Chang admits he underestimated the amount of money needed to open a business. "I didn't know it was going to cost me $100,000! The building was in shambles and all the licensing and the furniture and the inspections, it just added up. Maybe I fell into a money pit" (2010). Esther Williams spent a year investigating what it would take to open an optical retail business in Camden but remains frustrated: "The biggest challenge is money. You never really have enough. I haven't had a paycheck in a year, but I've heard I can go up to three years without a paycheck" (2010). Being fully aware of the challenges associated with starting a business does not make the experience any easier. Business owners looked to banks to provide additional debt financing but found that getting a bank loan was nearly impossible. Adam Woods explains:

> If you want to start a small business, and you are not a person of privilege, you can't. You can't afford to start one. If you're not a person of privilege, you are not going to be creditworthy either, so the bank's not going to give you any money. The banks said no because I was like a twenty-four-year-old kid that didn't own a house. I owned a used car that was worth an eighth of what I needed to borrow. So when the government says they're going to shore up SBA lending, that's still discretionary for banks. (2010)

Ray Lamboy says Camden loan recipients "basically need to have A1 credit, resources, et cetera, and you have to be prepared to sign over your firstborn as well" (Lamboy 2009b). Manuel José of Loida Daycare, the only business owner to successfully borrow from a bank, accessed the loan in part through a childhood friend who manages Camden's Susquehanna Bank branch. Manuel recalls, "He'd been talking to us for a while and helped us do a consolidation loan and also gave us money to help us start this place" (2010). Manuel's experience highlights the importance of personal connections in securing commercial money.

Many of the business owners turn to family and friends for financial support because they are disconnected from mainstream financial institutions. Marcellus Hill says, "I have never gotten a loan from a bank. I borrowed money from friends and family members. I remember one time I borrowed money from my sister to pay for my insurance" (2010). Rhonda Mendez credits her husband for his help. "Thank god my husband was there to support me. For weeks I didn't receive a paycheck, I had him to fall back on" (2010). Manuel José received financing from a local economic development financing entity and two banks, but still fell short. He explains, "The biggest challenge is funding. Honestly, in the end, we were about $30,000 short and she [his mother] ended up taking out of her retirement to start this. So we have a big debt to her. We're paying her back little by little" (2010). José Marrera summarizes the lack of lending. "We need a chance. You go to the bank, you go to the city to get loans. We need more loans from the banks that help small businesses" (2010). In Camden, as in many places, the lack of financial capital for small businesses disproportionately impacts women and minority businesses but also affects the ability of all small businesses to launch, maintain, and grow their enterprises.

The Merry-Go-Round

The obstacles facing Camden's small-business owners extend beyond finances. Six of my interviewees complained about the complexity of city procedures relating to starting a business. The licensing and permitting process is discouragingly long and complicated. "There is a lot of red tape. People I guess don't know how to deal with the red tape," shares Marcellus Hill (2010). Kelly Chang at Friends Café describes his experience in city hall:

> Originally I thought I was targeted because I am Asian. . . . Nobody was helping me. Oh, go to this floor, oh, go to this floor, where do I ask about sanitation? Nobody wanted to give me answers. They were just like go everywhere, fill this out, pay here. Pay, pay, pay, that is all it is. Register for this, register for that, show me your bills. . . . It was so strenuous. Half of them are not there and you don't know where you are going. You don't know what you are doing. Nobody wants to help you. . . . If you have an issue with permitting, they'll answer your question about permits, but they may not follow up with you to let you know after this you need to do this. There's never a follow up as to next steps. . . . You're in the wrong office and you're sitting there for an hour. They finally say, oh, can I help you? You go up there, and they say you're in the wrong room. (2010)

Attempting to map the permitting and licensing process for small-business owners, I found incorrect phone number information listed on the city's website; when I called one number, I got a full mailbox. Another phone number, listed on a business license application, rang to a personal cell number. City employees working the front desk expressed frustration when I asked questions. When I called the Building Bureau with a question about architectural drawings, they put on me hold for twelve minutes. City directors and employees were unable to provide answers about average costs or time frames unless a specific zoning or planning law existed. Surely all these bureaucratic obstacles force would-be entrepreneurs to ask why they should jump through all the hoops in Camden when it is easier to open a business elsewhere.

These confusing processes mean that institutions devote a lot of their time to "hand-holding." The Urban Enterprise Zone explained:

> If they come to us, what we do, we really try to direct them to who they need to speak with. Joe Thomas, the community outreach individual, walks businesses through the process. Joe will take the time to walk them through this whole process. It is a lot of hand-holding. Everybody does it. Particularly they [small-business owners] feel like city hall is the worst place to deal with. (Basara 2009)

At the Latin American Economic Development Association, "Our position is to actually take them by the hand, take them to city hall, take them to meet with a realtor, or meet with this to get them into business" (Lamboy 2009b). Or at the Cooperative Business Assistance Corporation, "We'll send them over to Dubois and Sheehan [a law office], which is over on Cooper Street here and they'll shepherd them" (Diemer 2009). Instead of spending time assisting small-business owners in areas of their expertise, such as financing, entrepreneurial training, or business development, economic development organizations waste time leading entrepreneurs through the bureaucratic maze.

City department directors are familiar with complaints about permitting and licensing. Iraida Afanador, director of the Building Bureau and The Bureau of Licenses and Inpection, explains, "We are doing more with less. Sometimes things get tied up due to lack of staffing" (2010). Presently, the city lacks enough inspectors, which means getting a business license or construction permit may take longer. Afanador insists it is not always fair or right to always blame the city (2010). Ed Williams, director of development and planning, points to an additional challenge. On average, commercial properties turn over every eighteen to twenty-five months, which means that permits for the same properties are constantly cycling through the system (Ed Williams 2010). There are a limited number of employees available to review permits, which happens in addition to other zoning and planning obligations.

Strategies for Strengthening Small Businesses

> What is needed is to set entrepreneurs loose to identify
> the opportunities and to connect socially and economically
> unconnected parties who could derive mutual benefits from
> an association. . . . Overcoming the problems of inadequate
> information and social disconnection could foster the
> entrepreneurial spirit and business development in the inner
> city. —Ross Gittell and J. Phillip Thompson (1999, 489)

The small businesses I studied in Camden defy the odds, succeeding despite a profound disconnection from economic development entities, lending institutions, and city government. But it should not be this hard. Fostering and promoting the economic vitality and power of small businesses requires building stronger connections between and among city government, economic development organizations, established civic institutions, and the small businesses themselves.

Streamlining City Hall

To begin with, leaders in city government need to overhaul the process for opening and working with small businesses; existing permitting and licensing steps are unclear, drawn out, and confusing. If city hall offered a clearer process, more people who wanted to start a small business would be able to do so more efficiently. An increase in business activity means fewer vacant buildings, improved neighborhoods, new jobs, and additional city tax revenue—all top concerns for city officials.

Achieving a more efficient and effective system is not impossible.[4] A necessary first step would be to outline and share the current process with business owners, organizations working with small businesses, and city-hall departments. Posting the process on the city's website would be a good start. Once the current process is clearly established and made accountable, department heads, economic development organizations, and business owners could audit it with the purpose of retaining valuable aspects while removing what is unnecessary. In the longer term, the city could create a one-stop shop for businesses large and small. A Department of Business Growth and Development would coordinate all functions related to businesses for the city, recruit businesses, provide process-oriented business assistance, and be a business liaison with other business development entities (Lamboy and Davis 2010).

Introducing Entrepreneurs to Institutions

Economic development organizations need to find better channels to offer their services to small-business owners. This will require, first, improving access to information by compiling city, state, and national support into one location and, second, increasing understanding between the two groups through relationship building.

Gathering business-support information can start with economic development organizations meeting for a roundtable discussion to better acquaint one another with the services they offer and then making this information widely available, in English and Spanish, to each of the economic development organizations to distribute to potential businesses. Much like the process for streamlining the city permitting and licensing process, later discussions can look for synergies and inefficient redundancies, with the ultimate goal that each organization is providing the best services within its own niche—for instance, perhaps only one organization will offer entrepreneurship workshops, and other organizations can direct their resources elsewhere.

The economic development organizations could also consider creating a referral system by hiring an outside organization or creating a new function of an existing organization to be the initial first stop for all potential businesses. From here, this new office could refer people to different organizations. In the future, with enough funding and demand, the city might take over and turn the office into a one-stop business department similar to efforts led by the Mission Economic Development Agency's Plaza Adelante in San Francisco.

Beyond making their information more clear and available, economic development organizations need to better adapt their support to the communities they are trying to reach. Elizabeth Rodriguez, former community outreach coordinator at the Camden Empowerment Zone Corporation, explains how she reached out to small businesses:

> I was supposed to go to the stores all dressed up, but I would go home and change first. Nobody's going to talk to you looking like that.
> They'll think you're from the IRS. So I wore my big hoop earrings and talked to the businesses before really introducing myself. I'm from the

neighborhood. I know what to say. And then after a while I would explain who I was and why I was there. (2009)

Working effectively with small-business owners also means holding training sessions and workshops after the workday, sitting with business owners while they fill out paperwork instead of just dropping it off, and coming back to a business multiple times if the owner is not in the first time.

Building Solidarity among Small-Business Owners

Even more important than a revamped set of city processes is a stronger set of relationships between small businesses, or a business network. This does not have to be a formal business association, as small-business owners rarely have the time or financial resources to join a bureaucratic organization. But a network can serve as a forum for discussing topics of mutual interest, allow the creation of shared services agreements, and provide a collective identity to more strongly advocate their interests with city government, with bank lenders, or in larger redevelopment projects.

Investing in the Entrepreneurs of Tomorrow

For small businesses to have a truly transformative impact there must be a way to transfer the necessary business skills and values from current entrepreneurs to youth, the entrepreneurs of tomorrow (Fairlie and Robb 2008). Young people bring meaning to their studies by working with a small-business owner. Entrepreneurship training teaches students about goal setting and decision making, helps build their self-confidence, and encourages them to take school more seriously, given the need to apply classroom learning in math and economics to their business venture (Rasheed and Rasheed 2003). The youth also gain a positive role model absent in many urban neighborhoods (Wilson 1996). They can turn to the adult business owner for career and personal advice and emotional support (Bendick and Egan 1993). Even if the young person does not start his or her own business, entrepreneurship teaches critical thinking, imbues responsibility, and demonstrates how to contribute to the economy (Suggs 1995). Similarly, business owners benefit by working with young people, acquiring an extra set of hands, often at a low cost. For business owners planning for retirement, working with a younger person interested in entrepreneurship can increase the chances of business longevity.

A stronger relationship between youth and small-business employers is not out of reach. In Germany, some students use school time to participate in apprenticeship programs and then transition smoothly into a career, often with the apprenticing employer, after graduation (Rosenbaum 2001). To an extent this already happens with MetEast, Camden's Big Picture high school, which sends students into the community two days a week to work in a field of professional interest. In the future, school district administrators can incorporate this internship model into all high schools. As more students work with business owners, teachers will learn what applicable skills and knowledge need to be taught in the classroom, and business owners will have a better way to find, train, and evaluate potential new employees (Rosenbaum 2001).

Leveraging Rooted Institutions

Another way to strengthen and encourage small business in Camden is by building relationships between those businesses and the city's waterfront and long-standing institutions, leveraging the investments already made in these rooted institutions. At Rutgers-Camden, for example, the Office of Civic Engagement could encourage courses in which students work directly with small-business owners. Students will learn firsthand what it takes to successfully run a business in a challenging environment, while business owners will benefit from students who have the time and knowledge to investigate financing tools or develop marketing campaigns.[5]

Other rooted institutions should consider how their industries can spur small-business development. In Camden, City Eyes and Uniform City are two businesses that have benefited from the expansion of Camden's hospitals by providing, respectively, an optical retail option next to the doctor's office and uniforms for hospital personnel. As the rooted institutions continue to expand, more opportunities will open for small businesses offering complementary goods and services. For example, a new Rowan Cooper University Medical School will draw additional residential students looking for coffee shops, bookstores, restaurants, and entertainment options. The Cleveland Foundation, which helped established the Evergreen Cooperatives in Cleveland, Ohio, offers a current example of how to start new businesses using the cooperative model to meet the needs of a cluster of educational and medical facilities: Local people work at a laundry cooperative cleaning hospital linens, a solar panel cooperative installs solar panels on large building roofs, and a hydroponics greenhouse will produce food served in hospital and university cafeterias (Iuviene 2010). Small businesses benefit from a large and steady demand provided by the rooted institutions, and the institutions benefit by gaining tailored services close to home.

Conclusion

This chapter has enumerated specific steps that can be taken by Camden's small-business owners and city officials alike, and it endeavored in doing so not only to lay out a path forward for this particular "forgotten city" but to suggest a route that others might follow. Behind all the small, specific measures (e.g., reorientation of government small-business programming and better alignment of businesses and business-service organizations) there must lie a citywide commitment to small business and to the neighborhoods lying outside the radius of the visitor-friendly rooted institutions.

In countless conversations—with small-business owners, with employees at city hall, with the heads of social-service organizations—I found a city where such rooted institutions had long ago been given a place of privilege over small business, and the results of that foundational decision were plain: a sense of separateness between, on the one hand, a lavishly funded, much-promoted "city for tourists," and, on the other hand, the "real city," where small-business owners and their families struggle to thrive in neglected neighborhoods. If Camden is to experience a lasting recovery for all its citizens, it must consider both sides of this equation, not as a competition between small businesses and rooted institutions, but as parts composing a whole, a system in which attention to the needs of one can feed into the others. Camden's example shows a path forward, where the needs of both sectors can be recognized and integrated; it requires a city government willing to devote money, time, and the other resources of government to parties on both sides of the equation.

Notes

1. Michael Porter, a Harvard Business School professor and leading authority on competitive strategy, writes that the inner city has a great amount of unmet demand and local dollars for businesses to capture (1995). By meeting the needs of people in these neighborhoods, small businesses prosper by exploiting untapped consumer buying power (Giloth 2007). When people are able to purchase goods in their neighborhood, they stop bleeding dollars to outside towns and businesses, thus building wealth in urban neighborhoods and restoring local markets (Giloth 2007). Local circulation of money helps to staunch the gap in economic progress suffered by low-income neighborhoods (Suggs 1995).

2. See also Chapter 5, by Brandin and Levitt, for more on the Weatherization Assistance Program.

3. The phenomenon of a well-connected local community thriving apart from the city's decision makers and resource holders is described by William Julius Wilson, an American sociologist and Harvard Kennedy School professor. Wilson (1996) finds strong local neighborhood relationships without connections to the broader, mainstream society. Family and friends support small business ventures while the more institutionalized and "other" economic development organizations cannot reach these businesses.

4. Even though city government is often thought of as a large, bureaucratic machine resistant to change, overhauling and improving city departments is possible. In *The Wealth of Cities* (1998), John Norquist, former mayor of Milwaukee, Wisconsin, explains how he cut government spending while improving city services. City departments are now organized according to their intended outcomes with individual roles defined by the desired results.

5. The Social Entrepreneurs of New Orleans (now named Propeller) opened after Hurricane Katrina and concentrates on social entrepreneurs, or those who enter business in part to create positive change in their communities, across multiple sectors. Social Entrepreneurs offers a mentoring program that matches new business owners with experienced social entrepreneurs to coach them and provide advice in management, long-term financing, and business and media planning. They also maintain and grow a network of partners to assist businesses by offering pro-bono professional services, conducting market analyses, and framing different business opportunities. (Social Entrepreneurs of New Orleans 2010).

References

Afanador, Iraida. 2010. Personal interview. February 1.

Basara, Vince. 2009. Personal interview. December 16.

Bates, Timothy Mason. 1997. *Race, Self-Employment, and Upward Mobility: An Illusive American Dream.* Washington, DC: Woodrow Wilson Center Press.

Bendick, Marc, Jr., and Mary Lou Egan. 1993. "Linking Business Development and Community Development in Inner Cities." *Journal of Planning Literature* 8 (1): 3–19.

Benito, Miguel. 2010. Personal interview. January 21.

Boston, Thomas D. 2006. "The Role of Black-Owned Businesses in Black Community Development." In *Jobs and Economic Development in Minority Communities,* edited by Paul M Ong and Anastasia Loukaitou-Sideris. Philadelphia, PA: Temple University Press.

CamConnect. 2010. "CamConnect." *www.camconnect.org.*

Chang, Kelly. 2010. Personal interview. January 20.

Conaboy, Chelsea. 2010. "Hispanic Shoppers Revitalize Camden's Federal Street." *Philadelphia Inquirer,* January 27.

Diemer, Mike. 2009. Personal interview. December 17.

Fairlie, Robert, and Alicia Robb. 2008. *Race and Entrepreneurial Success: Black-, Asian-, and White-Owned Businesses in the United States.* Cambridge, MA: MIT Press.

Fox, Radhika, and Miriam Axel-Lute. 2008. *To Be Strong Again: Renewing the Promise in Smaller Industrial Cities.* Oakland: PolicyLink.

Gans, Byron, and Darien Gans. 2010. Personal interview. January 13.

Giloth, Robert. 2007. "Investing in Equity: Targeted Economic Development for Neighborhoods and Cities." In *Economic Development in American Cities: The Pursuit of an Equity Agenda,* edited by Michael I. J. Bennett and Robert P. Giloth. Albany: State University of New York Press.

Gillette, Howard, Jr. 2005. *Camden after the Fall: Decline and Renewal in a Post-Industrial City.* Philadelphia: University of Pennsylvania Press.

Gittell, Ross, and J. Phillip Thompson. 1999. "Inner-City Business Development and Entrepreneurship: New Frontiers for Policy and Research." In *Urban Problems and Community Development,* edited by Ronald F Ferguson and William T Dickens, 473–520. Washington, DC: Brookings Institution Press.

Hill, Marcellus. 2010. Personal interview. January 18.

Hirsch, Deborah. 2010. "Redd Looks to Produce Real Change in Camden." *South Jersey Courier-Post,* January 5.

Hirsch, Deborah, and Jim Walsh. 2009. "Camden's in Christie's Hands." *South Jersey Courier-Post,* November 8.

Hoyt, Lorlene, and Andre Leroux. 2007. *Voices from Forgotten Cities: Innovative Revitalization Coalitions in America's Older Small Cities.* Report sponsored by PolicyLink, Oakland, CA; Citizens' Housing and Planning Association, Boston, MA; and M.I.T. School of Architecture and Planning, Cambridge, MA.

Ishack, Ralph. 2010. Personal interview. January 15.

Iuviene, Nick. 2010. "Building a Platform for Economic Democracy: A Cooperative Development Strategy for the Bronx." Master's thesis, Massachusetts Institute of Technology.

Jackson, Connie. 2010. Personal interview. January 27.

Japa, Luis. 2010. Personal interview. January 26.

José, Manuel. 2010. Personal interv.ew. January 14.

Katz, Matt. 2009. "Camden Rebirth: A Promise Still Unfulfilled." *Philadelphia Inquirer,* November 8.

Kromer, John. 2009. *Fixing Broken Cities: The Implementation of Urban Development Strategies.* New York: Routledge.

Lamboy, Raymond. 2009a. Personal interview. July 14.

———. 2009b. Personal interview. December 15.

Lamboy, Raymond, and Kathleen Davis. 2010. "Economic Development and Entrepreneurship Committee Report Recommendations for Mayor-Elect Dana Redd." April 1. Camden, NJ.

Levine, Marc V. 1987. "Downtown Redevelopment as an Urban Growth Strategy: A Critical Appraisal of the Baltimore Renaissance." *Journal of Urban Affairs* 9 (2): 103–23.

Light, Ivan. 1995. *Race, Ethnicity, and Entrepreneurship in Urban America.* New York: Aldine de Gruyter.

Lucas, Robert. 2010. Personal interview. January 19.

Marrera, José. 2010. Personal interview. February 4.

Blackwell, Angela Glover and Radhika Fox. 2008. "Promoting Inclusive Economic Renewal in Older Industrial Cities." In *Retooling for Growth: Building a 21st Century Economy in America's Older Industrial Areas,* edited by Richard McGahey and Jennifer S Vey. 351–71. Washington, DC: Brookings Institution Press.

Mission Economic Development Agency. 2010. "Our Vision—Plaza Adelante Capital Campaign," *plazaadelante.org/main/en/about/plaza-adelante-vision.*

Mendez, Rhonda. 2010. Personal interview. January 29.

Norquist, John O. 1998. *The Wealth of Cities: Revitalizing the Centers of American Life.* Reading, MA: Addison-Wesley.

Ott, Dwight. 2005. "Revitalization Efforts Get Failing Grade, Survey Says." *Philadelphia Inquirer,* July 19.

Pitts, Tyrone. 2010. Personal interview. February 9.

Porter, Michael. 1995. "The Competitive Advantage of the Inner City." *Harvard Business Review,* May-June.

Powers, Corrine. 2010. Personal interview. January 28.

Pritchett, Wendell. 2010. "Rutgers Civic Engagement Symposium: Entrepreneurship." Speech, January 29.

Rasheed, Howard, and Barbara Rasheed. 2003. "Developing Entrepreneurial Characteristics in Minority Youth: The Effects of Education and Enterprise Experience." In *Ethnic Entrepreneurship: Structure and Process,* edited by Curt Stiles and Craig Galbraith, 261–77. London: JAI.

Redd, Dana. 2010. "Mayor Redd's Transition Reports." April 1. *www.ci.camden. nj.us/departments/transition_reports.html.*

Rodriguez, Elizabeth. 2009. Personal interview. July 16.

Rosenbaum, James E. 2001. *Beyond College for All: Career Paths for the Forgotten Half.* New York: Russell Sage Foundation.

Social Entrepreneurs of New Orleans. 2010. "SENO—Social Entrepreneurs of New Orleans." *www.seno-nola.org/index.php.* The organization's name has since been changed to Propeller.

Suggs, Robert. 1995. "Bringing Small Business Development to Urban Neighborhood." *Harvard Civil Rights–Civil Liberties Law Review* 30: 487–506.

U.S. Census Bureau. 2000. "Camden (city) QuickFacts from the US Census Bureau." *quickfacts.census.gov/qfd/states/34/3410000.html.* Accessed March 2010.

U.S. Small Business Administration. 2010a. "Frequently Asked Questions." *web. sba.gov/faqs/faqindex.cfm?areaID=24.*

Wilkins, Barry. 2010. Personal interview. February 5.

Waxman, Andy. 2000. "Why Improve Neighborhoods? Shifting the Goals of Inner City Neighborhood Commercial Revitalization." *Projections: MIT Student Journal of Planning* 1: 31–57.

Williams, Ed. 2010. Personal interview. January 28.

Williams, Esther. 2010. Personal interview. January 21.

Wilson, William J. 1996. *When Work Disappears: The World of the New Urban Poor.* 1st ed. New York: Knopf.

Woods, Adam. 2010. Personal interview. January 28.

Zammit, Suzanne. 2009. Personal interview. July 7.

2

Leveraging Rooted Institutions

A Strategy for Cooperative Economic Development in Cleveland, Ohio

Nick Iuviene and Lily Song

Introduction

Cities like Camden, New Jersey, and Cleveland, Ohio, have their own unique histories and unique sets of problems. But among the undeniable commonalities is a persistent mindset that sees two distinct groups—small players versus large players, small businesses versus rooted institutions—dangerously overlooking the reality of one whole economic ecology, in which the health of one sector contributes to the health of all. In seeking to escape from this trap, the Evergreen Cooperative participants in Cleveland imported the Mondragon model, reimagining the relationship between small and large. In this model, rather than casting themselves as economic Davids, hurling rocks at the rooted-institution Goliaths, small players pooled their resources and sought out symbiotic relationships with the city's big players. By examining both Cleveland's experience and the Spanish effort that inspired it, we aim to elucidate both the challenges to such an approach and the considerable benefits: providing jobs to the jobless, providing needed support to key rooted institutions, and providing a means to keep precious dollars within the local economy.

Economic Democracy

The last two decades have seen the rise across American cities of social movements, such as Justice for Janitors and living-wage campaigns, which have reconceptualized economic justice as an issue that goes deeper than the workplace, down to the bedrock of the urban economy. Accordingly, social movements have forged broader political coalitions encompassing labor unions, community and faith-based organizations, and elected officials (in contrast to the competitive interest-group dynamics that prevailed in the 1970s and 1980s). Beyond decent pay and work benefits, what drives many of these movements is their members' commitment to a particular place, coupled with a desire for democratic control over their collective economic prosperity. Cleveland's leaders aim to build on existing social networks and civic capacity, while also drawing on local assets to foster economic development and recast citizens as worker/owners.

The idea of economic democracy—that is, shared ownership of the local economy by all who participate in it—is a socioeconomic arrangement in which rooted institutions are controlled by those engaged in the local economy. With a wide ownership structure, such an approach removes the profit-maximizing motive from its position of primacy among economic decision makers. By realigning interests, economic democracy begins to reconcile conflicts between owners and laborers, meanwhile grounding wealth in local communities. Cooperative businesses—whether worker, producer, consumer, or housing cooperatives— are one type of firm that fits within the model of economic democracy.

Worker cooperatives are typically for-profit businesses, owned and democratically controlled by the employees of the firm, the "worker/ owners." Although the form of organization varies dramatically between firms, most worker cooperatives adhere to the set of principles set out by the International Cooperative Alliance: open, voluntary membership; democratic governance; limited return on equity; member-owned surplus; education of members and public in cooperative principles; cooperation between cooperatives; and concern for community.

The story of worker cooperative development is one of many efforts but few successes. Inspired by the negative consequences of industrialization and increased urbanization, workers have made efforts worldwide to build local, regional, national, and global worker cooperative sectors. In the United States, few initiatives have reached a significant scale in terms of firms created, people employed, or revenue generated. Some exceptions include the O&O Supermarkets in Philadelphia and the plywood cooperatives in the Northwest. And even these were unable to maintain their success over the long term.[1]

Internationally, however, there have been exceptional successes, notably the Mondragon Cooperative Complex in Spain, which has provided inspiration as well as strategic and organizational direction to other worker cooperatives. Some argue that Mondragon's success can be explained by its cultural, historical, geographic, and political circumstances—and that the success, therefore, is not replicable. Others make the broader claim that cooperatives cannot survive in America's competitive marketplace. We found, to the contrary, that the Mondragon model contains a set of strategic considerations that may be transferable to other contexts, including the American city. These considerations include an appropriately defined geographic area (*geography*), establishment of a cooperative network (*networks*), and growth from within (*endogeny*).

The Evergreen Cooperative Initiative in Cleveland, Ohio, has successfully imported and applied these three considerations of the Mondragon model to a postindustrial American city. While Evergreen is still in its preliminary stages, it is a working experiment in importing ideas from Mondragon while modifying aspects of the model to accommodate local conditions. In what follows, we examine the Mondragon Cooperative Complex and the Evergreen Cooperative Initiative to answer the question: how might other American cities initiate a cooperative local economic development model of their own?

Becoming Greater University Circle

Cleveland's precarious economic circumstances overall would be familiar to residents of America's other so-called forgotten cities, but there is one section of the city, about thirty minutes east of downtown, that is booming. The small area, known as University Circle, hosts an impressive concentration of rooted institutions, including Case Western Reserve University, the Cleveland Clinic, University Hospitals, and the Veterans Administration Hospital. These are not only among the city's preeminent institutions, but also among the largest employers. In recent years, they have collectively invested billions of dollars in the construction of new facilities as striking in their architectural aesthetic as they are in contrast to the built environment of the surrounding neighborhoods. Surrounding University Circle are some of Cleveland's poorest neighborhoods, including East Cleveland, Wade Park / Heritage Lane, Eastern Hugh / Upper Chester, Eastern Fairfax, Buckey/Shaker, and Little Italy. These neighborhoods have a median household income of $18,500 and a poverty rate of 30 percent (the analogous nation-wide figures are $52,174 and 13.2 percent). These neighborhoods suffer from rampant water shutoffs, tax foreclosures, and unsound building conditions.

In 2004, the Cleveland Foundation, the largest community foundation in the country, undertook an ambitious effort, which came to be called the Greater University Circle Initiative. The initial goal of the project was to engage the leadership of University Circle's rooted institutions and identify projects that could be collaboratively undertaken with them. The foundation describes the project this way:

> We were looking around the city and saw [rooted] institutions that were growing physically but also creating jobs. We saw an opportunity to leverage the institutions in a way that hadn't been done before. There were three new leaders at the institutions that the town had never seen before in terms of their willingness to collaborate. Before they wouldn't sit in the same room. It was a totally new day. The most valuable thing the Cleveland Foundation did was to say let's just sit around the same table and find crosscutting issues that we care about and can collaborate around. There was a conscious decision among the institutions to meet every quarter, and this became one of the most important pieces. (Pierce Lee and Kuri 2010)

Prior to this time, the institutions of University Circle had rarely coordinated their investment or development. In fact, the term "Greater University Circle" came into existence as a placeholder when the foundation and its new institutional partners needed a way to refer to their target geographic area. Previously, this area, characterized by a stark dichotomy between institutional assets and acute neighborhood poverty, had not been conceived of as a whole. However, as the foundation observed, the "institutional leaders [soon identified] with this orientation," and "[it was] powerful to have this new orientation in this town" (Pierce Lee 2010). Initially, however, the experience of the term's binding force remained limited to a small circle of institutional leaders.

Upon its formation, the group immediately focused on identifying and accomplishing a set of achievable objectives. The members agreed on four physical redevelopment projects, with three to be focused on transportation and one on mixed uses. After completing the four initial proposals, the foundation and its partner institutions contemplated their next step, eventually agreeing to expand their efforts beyond physical development and to directly engage the neighborhoods surrounding University Circle. Through the Program for the People, they aimed at social improvements in education, employer-assisted housing, community safety, community building, and economic inclusion. While the group was intent on meeting its goals, the content of its future work was not necessarily clear, particularly with respect to certain issues. As Cleveland Foundation program director India Pierce Lee recounted, at the time, no one was sure what "economic inclusion" would entail.

"A Focus on Institutions"

Shortly after, in September 2006, Pierce Lee attended a conference in North Carolina on community wealth-building strategies and met Ted Howard, the executive director of the Democracy Collaborative, a nonprofit based at the University of Maryland that focuses on wealth building and the role of rooted institutions in local economies. One area that Howard analyzed closely was the amount of money spent by rooted institutions on daily goods and services, which rarely benefit local businesses and residents. At the conference, Pierce Lee heard Howard explain how communities could partner with rooted institutions to leverage procurement dollars to stabilize the local economy. Howard describes the next step:

> In December 2006, the collaborative organized a community wealth-building roundtable in Cleveland, Ohio. The fortunate thing in the timing of that gathering was that the [Cleveland] foundation had already begun organizing a strategy around the [rooted] institutions of the city. The big [institutions such as the Cleveland Clinic, University Hospitals, the VA Hospital, and Case Western Reserve University] were serendipitously in the midst of major construction projects that would cost upwards of $2.5 billion and last over a couple of years. The foundation thought, if there's this much growth and money flowing through these institutions, how do we ensure some of it benefits the surrounding low-income neighborhoods? The truth was, most of the construction dollars weren't going to reach the surrounding neighborhood. But what about the ongoing spending these institutions do on

a day in, day out basis, even after the billions in construction go away? Every year Cleveland's biggest anchors spend $3 billion for goods and services in the normal course of doing business. Now that's the place to focus if you're interested in leveraging their business activity to benefit the community. What we lead with is a focus on institutions and their business side. Not that community education or health care delivery or diabetes classes for the community aren't important, but how can they conduct their business in a way that puts dollars into the community, and leads to jobs and wealth building? Given their enormous supply chains, what could they source locally in order to benefit the residents of Cleveland? (Howard 2010a)

After Howard's presentation and a series of conversations over dinner, Pierce Lee began to envision the economic inclusion consideration of their Program for the People.

The concept underlying the Evergreen Initiative grew out of a budding relationship between the Cleveland Foundation, represented by India Pierce Lee and Lillian Kuri, and Ted Howard's Democracy Collaborative. The two organizations together developed a proposal for redirecting a portion of the nearly $3 billion in procurement dollars spent annually by rooted institutions into the surrounding neighborhoods. Their proposal called for building employee-owned businesses designed to target the procurement needs of the rooted institutions, simultaneously redirecting procurement resources into the local economy and building wealth and productive assets that would be owned by local residents and rooted in their communities.

Putting this idea into action involved building consensus with the rooted institutions, demonstrating that the project was in their interest and had a reasonable chance of success. Many institutions viewed the Cleveland Foundation as a fair arbiter without an alternative agenda and a sophisticated and competent partner; they agreed to the foundation's proposal, therefore, despite professed skepticism. The Cleveland Foundation had the political, financial, and human capital to be a convener and facilitator, and the Democracy Collaborative provided the intellectual capacity to legitimize the employee ownership and rooted institution approach as well as the use of public funds. Once the foundation got the rooted institutions around the same table, the Democracy Collaborative convinced them that the proposal was in their interest, was plausible, and could provide a means for working with the neighboring communities in a mutually supportive and beneficial manner.

In addition to the core leadership team, which is responsible for daily management of the Evergreen Initiative as well as short- and medium-range planning, Evergreen also has a secondary leadership group composed of senior management from the rooted institutions and the city of Cleveland. The city, especially the economic development department, has been an important partner, providing access to the lion's share of start-up capital for the cooperatives. This secondary group meets with members of the leadership team on a regular basis to coordinate programs, assess challenges, and perform long-term planning. As reiterated by a number of interviewees, the active involvement of the senior members of the rooted institutions and the city has been critical to the success of the Evergreen effort to date. There is also a tertiary group, made up of the community development corporation housing network and a number of civic and nonprofit organizations, that is less active but still involved in the planning process. In essence, Evergreen is building a cooperative network, encompassing a broad array of local organizations, cooperatively owned firms, and support organizations with a range of capacities (e.g., organizing, technical, financial, program management) to nurture the development of worker cooperatives in and around Greater University Circle.

Learning from Mondragon

Encouraged by the Ohio Employee Ownership Center at Kent State University, members of the Evergreen project have made several visits to the Mondragon Cooperative Complex. At Mondragon, visitors are exposed to the vast potential of worker cooperatives and gain a detailed understanding of the merits and challenges of operating a cooperatively owned firm in a highly competitive, globalized economy. For most interviewees, visiting Mondragon was a dramatic and crucial experience, referred to by some as "life changing." Most described the shock they experienced upon realizing Mondragon was not a collection of artisan, food, and craft producers, but rather a cluster of highly sophisticated firms in a range of modern industries. Many were also taken aback by the level of financial knowledge and sophistication among line workers in the factories and the conviction and commitment among senior management despite the salary ratio cap of five to one (a few cooperatives have permitted a higher ratio). Stephen Keil describes his experience:

> For me, it was really surprising . . . the fact that the everyday worker had such a good knowledge of the profitability or lack thereof of the business. In our country so many employees are hoodwinked by the leaders of the organizations to stay without any real knowledge of how the company is doing, with employers being cautious about not disclosing inside information to workers, suppliers, customers. There, everybody was treated with respect and trust. There was this wage solidarity . . . the limited ratio between the highest paid and the lowest paid. The fact that job security was an issue . . . they put a lot into reserves as the company made money . . . a good portion of it sat in reserves for a rainy day. Nobody got rich quick; everybody had a job for life. (Keil 2010)

Another important result of the Mondragon trips was the cultivation of strong bonds within the Evergreen group. As Stephen Keil put it, "We came away thinking about this more as a family business than as an experiment." This is especially important considering the fact that the Evergreen Initiative has brought together some unlikely allies with considerably different experiences, backgrounds, and perspectives. And the simple experience of spending several days together abroad strengthened relationships, group cohesion, and personal commitment to the project. As Jim Anderson noted, "Going to Mondragon, it's a powerful learning experience. They come back and ask what can we do as an institution to make this work? If you can establish a group like that you can make something happen."

The Mondragon Cooperative Complex

Mondragon is small city located in the Basque region, a semiautonomous zone on Spain's northern border with France. The Basque people have a strong nationalist orientation developed over centuries, which has thrived despite severe repression during the Franco era. One distinct aspect of the culture is the language, Euskara, which is spoken by a quarter of the Basque people (including more than half of those living in the province where Mondragon is located). The Basque region is mountainous, and, until the last few decades, Mondragon was relatively isolated, with limited roadways connecting the city to the outside world. In the 1940s, Mondragon had a geographically isolated population of a little more than eight thousand people, limited industry, few educated people, and intense class divisions. It was, in other words, an unlikely candidate for dramatic regional economic development—but Mondragon had a number of attributes that led it to an experiment in economic democracy.

Arizmendi's Leadership

Mondragon's story begins with its founder, the priest Don José Maria Arizmendiarrieta (known as Arizmendi). Born in a village fifty kilometers outside Mondragon, Arizmendi joined the Basque military in 1936 to fight Franco's forces during the civil war. When Arizmendi arrived in Mondragon in 1941, he had completed seminary but showed little talent for the pulpit. Eschewing themes of individual salvation, his sermons and writings stressed the need for dignity in work, the importance of cooperation and solidarity, and the need for education in technical knowledge and skills. Arizmendi's strong interest in social issues and movements led him to organize social support services, athletic leagues, and a medical clinic; each of these programs expanded a social base that would ultimately support investment in rooted institutions and give rise to the Mondragon Cooperative Complex.

While Arizmendi's leadership was instrumental to the creation of the Mondragon Cooperative Complex, it was by no means the only ingredient. Prior to the priest's arrival, Mondragon was a predominantly working-class town with a tradition of "political radicalism and social-class militancy" (Whyte and Whyte 1991, 26). During the Middle Ages, the Basque region engaged in seafaring, shipbuilding, iron mining, and steel fabrication, developing a strong tradition of craftsman's guilds. Beginning in the late nineteenth century, various Spanish regions experienced growing interest in cooperative organizations, but the Basque region was a particularly fertile birthing ground, with the labor movement, political parties, and Catholic Church there actively supporting the formation of cooperatives (Whyte and Whyte 1991). A producer cooperative broke with the craft/service-orientation model and operated between 1920 and 1936 as a firearms cooperative, supporting a thousand families at its height. But overall, in the first half of the twentieth century, entry into the middle and upper classes was heavily limited by inheritance and nepotism, consigning the vast majority of Mondragon residents to lifelong wage work.

The School and the First Cooperative

The first project leading toward the Mondragon cooperatives came in 1943, when under Arizmendi's leadership, a parents' association raised money and started a technical school. The association organized the school as a cooperative: each of the approximately six hundred contributors received one vote for the general assembly that in turn elected the school board. The Escuela Politécnica Profesional (Professional Polytechnic School) initially accepted teenage boys between the ages of fourteen and sixteen and expanded as students completed each level. The school was critical to the building of the cooperative complex, not only for the technical skills students gained, but also because Arizmendi used the school as a means to impart his social vision.

In 1956, thirteen years after the founding of the technical school, five of its graduates started the Ulgor, the first worker cooperative in Mondragon. Using a technique similar to the one they had used with the Polytechnic School (i.e., using personal and organizational contacts to publicize and gain support for the project), the group raised seed money from the local community. The firm, which initially manufactured paraffin stoves, became the model for future Mondragon cooperatives in terms of governance structure and organizational rules and norms.

Caja Laboral Popular: The Bank

The Caja Laboral Popular (Caja), established in 1959, was the first secondary cooperative within the Mondragon network. The principal members and cofounders included Ulgor; Arrasate and Funcor, worker cooperatives founded soon after Ulgor and under similar circumstances; and San Jose, a producer cooperative that was previously unrelated to the three worker cooperatives. Arizmendi was convinced that relying on private investors or private banks would either constrain or otherwise undermine the cooperative movement and that it was therefore necessary to create a cooperative financial institution. Structured as a credit union and established for the principal purpose of creating and expanding worker cooperatives, the bank acquired capital for financing projects by providing both savings deposit accounts and social security for members. As it expanded, the Caja became capable of coordinating transactions within the emerging cooperative network.

Ikerlan: The Research and Development Cooperative

In the 1960s and early 1970s, Mondragon carried out industrial research activity on an informal basis under Manuel Quevedo, an instructor in charge of shop operations. In 1974, Mondragon put forward a proposal for Ikerlan, an applied industrial research cooperative. By 1977, and with the support of several industrial cooperatives and the Caja, Ikerlan began creating the internal capacity to drive technological advancement, product design, and development processes within the collective of industrial cooperatives (and later, the entire Basque region). Arizmendi aimed to eliminate the need to import advanced technology, either physically or in the form of product patents, so as to further remove the dependence on private capital. Although Ikerlan was originally created to support the Mondragon cooperatives, in 1982 the Basque government began providing it significant funding to make services available to non-member cooperatives and private firms.[2]

The Cooperative Group

In the 1960s, Mondragon's leaders adopted a policy of creating a new spin-off firm whenever a product line in one firm matured to the point of self-sufficiency in terms of marketing and manufacturing. With the consequent expansion of interrelated firms, the leaders needed a way to maintain some coordination and mutual support among them. In turn, they implemented the idea of a cooperative group.[3] The characteristics of a cooperative group included a shared governance structure, pooling of profits and losses, movement of worker/owners between firms, and facilitated planning for future growth. Over time, all of the cooperative firms in the Mondragon complex became members of this organizational innovation.

Successes, Challenges, and Replication

By 2008, the Mondragon Cooperative Complex encompassed 243 companies, together holding 33.5 billion euros in assets, generating 16.7 billion euros in revenue, and employing 92,773 people. The Caja administered close to 14 billion euros, while Mondragon educational centers enrolled over 7,300 students, and 891 worker/owners served on its governing bodies. At present, Mondragon's worker cooperatives and secondary cooperatives are active in four different areas: finance (e.g., banking, social welfare, and insurance), distribution (commercial and agribusiness), industry (capital goods, consumer goods, construction, industrial parts, and enterprise services), and knowledge (e.g., a university, research centers, vocational training, and education centers).

This is not to say that Mondragon has not faced challenges. A strike in 1974 over the prevailing system of job evaluation and compensation took four years to resolve, though the event ultimately strengthened Mondragon's system of governance as well as the organization of its management and work. The strike also led to the incorporation of political parties and labor unions into the Mondragon decision-making process, effectively broadening the cooperatives' civic infrastructure and support base. With the recession of the 1980s, which was particularly severe in the Basque region (27 percent unemployment compared to 20 percent for Spain overall), Mondragon once again found it had to implement such internal changes as reformulating compensation and employment policies to accommodate changing economic conditions, restructuring key firms and cooperative groups to enhance market competitiveness, and improving systems of unemployment compensation and social support. As leaders conducted an exercise in balancing technical solutions with member buy-in, the Caja played an integral role in providing cooperatives with subsidies to weather the difficult times.

Despite concerns that the market liberalization of the 1990s would undermine Spanish industrial competitiveness, Mondragon has thrived over the last twenty years; indeed, the cooperative has enjoyed its most pronounced growth during this period. In response to the challenge of internationalization that accompanied Spain's entrance into the European Union, the Mondragon Cooperative Complex has employed a number of strategies. These include significant investment in external cooperative strategies, such as mergers and spin-offs, joint ventures, and research and design partnerships (Clamp 2000, 562). Also, its global operations adhere to a set of basic principles: preserve jobs, sustain profitability of firms, comply with local labor practices in overseas operations, and, when possible, develop substitute technologies that enable the return of manufacturing operations from overseas to the Basque region (Clamp 2000). Consequently, Mondragon has become one of the most competitive firms in the Basque region, which, in turn, now dominates Spain's industrial output. In 1988, Mondragon employed 20,818 people and had sales of 1.2 billion euros, while that year the Caja administered 1.3 billion euros. Over the next twenty years, total employment expanded by 346 percent; the collective sales of the complex jumped by an overwhelming 1200 percent, and the Caja's holdings grew by 953 percent (Mondragon, "Historical").

In sum, the Mondragon experience has disproved the long-held belief that cooperative enterprises inevitably fail or devolve into privately held companies. It demonstrates to the contrary that cooperatives can thrive in a capitalist economic system, particularly if equipped with effective mechanisms for internal governance, training and education, technical assistance, and strategic planning. Perhaps most importantly, Mondragon shows that, when organized within a network of cooperative firms and support organizations, worker cooperatives can achieve economic democracy. Unfortunately, few leaders have replicated Mondragon's success, though many have tried. Many scholars and practitioners have concluded that Mondragon's success is due to a unique set of circumstances that cannot be replicated. Civic leaders in Cleveland, Ohio, however, are proving otherwise.

Cleveland's Evergreen Cooperative Initiative

Combining the procurement spending of rooted institutions with the creation of environmentally responsible worker cooperatives, the Evergreen Cooperative invests in neighborhoods around Greater University Circle. The rooted institutions' procurement spending is redirected from firms in outlying areas to local worker cooperatives, so the public dollars serve to catalyze local economic development. Rather than subsidize the profits of large corporations that may relocate overseas, public investments to support rooted institutions are dollars that benefit local communities.

A particularly challenging area for past worker cooperatives, especially for individual firms, has been start-up and expansion. Using rooted
institutions' procurement needs as a primary economic driver affords the
Evergreen Initiative more stability than it would have, if it were to rely
solely on privately financed businesses as the customer base. In terms of
financial planning and management, Evergreen has drawn lessons from
Mondragon's move to maintain independence from private capital and
achieve significant scale through the creation of a cooperative bank. It
has used start-up capital from the Cleveland Foundation, the city, and
the rooted institutions to seed the Evergreen Development Fund, managed by Shorebank Enterprise.[4] In addition to making direct contributions, its leadership team has solicited grants and other investments
from external sources. They use this initial capital to secure additional financing to provide start-up and working capital for the new businesses.
After a firm in the cooperative breaks even, 10 percent of its profits go to
the development fund to support the creation of additional businesses.
So far, the fund has raised $10 to $12 million, which is anticipated to
leverage up to $40 million.

Evergreen, like Mondragon, is creating a network of firms to share
services and maintain mutual agreements regarding governance and
operations. The leadership team is designing an organizational entity
to act as a holding company. The entity, led by representatives elected
by the workers, will establish governance and management policies and
perform planning functions for the Evergreen network. Finally, the
leadership team is taking proactive steps to avoid a phenomenon known
as "cooperative selfishness" whereby cooperative members tend to vote
against creating ownership positions for new employees and instead hire
traditional wage laborers as the firm expands. Mondragon's cooperatives
resisted this tendency by placing limits on nonowner employees at 10
percent of the firms' workforce. Evergreen is considering such strategies.

Evergreen's Worker Cooperatives

Each worker cooperative in the Evergreen Initiative is designed to employ approximately fifty worker/owners. Initially, each worker is hired
for a six-month probationary period. After the successful completion
of a performance review, the employee is offered the opportunity to become a co-owner of the firm. The membership cost to "buy into" the
firm is $3,000, paid by levying fifty cents an hour from the employee's

wages. The payment scheme enables a full-time employee to become fully vested in the company after three years. Additionally, a portion of the firm's profits are invested in a patronage account to facilitate wealth development for worker/owners. The expectation is that, after seven to eight years, each employee will own roughly $65,000 in assets. Rather than focus on the firm's rate of return, Evergreen's business plan emphasizes asset accumulation by its worker/owners. Performance reviews for the first two firms, the Evergreen Laundry Cooperative and Ohio Solar, were completed in March 2010. All of the employees were accepted as new worker/owners and will begin paying the membership fee until they are fully vested.

Evergreen consists of three worker cooperatives. The Evergreen Cooperative Laundry, which launched in the fall of 2009, is located in a former torpedo factory. Its chief executive officer, Jim Anderson, together with the facility's operating manager, worked with equipment suppliers and architects to maximize the facility's energy efficiency. The team also developed the business plan for the laundry after closely observing an existing industrial laundry operated by a large hospital and gaining the management's input on the strength of their proposal. At full capacity, the facility can process twelve million pounds of laundry annually, and the laundry is steadily working its way up from a present level of 15 percent of full capacity. Like other Evergreen businesses being developed, the laundry is designed to handle the needs of medium and large organizations. Although some of the rooted institutions were not able to enter into contracts with the laundry cooperative because of existing long-term contracts, the laundry has executed contracts with nearby nursing homes. With ten workers employed as of February 2010, the firm expects to grow to fifty members within four years. While the laundry has struggled to meet the initial projections for revenue delineated in the business plan, it is continuously exploring sales strategies and opportunities in adjacent lines of business.

Like the laundry, Ohio Solar launched in the fall of 2009 and employed ten workers as of February 2010. Initially developed to specialize in solar panel installation on the roofs of rooted institutions, Ohio Solar quickly expanded into weatherizing buildings so it could offer year-round employment to its employees. The cooperative uses power-purchasing agreements to lease roof space for its solar operations; it pays for equipment and sells electricity from its generators back to the institution at a fixed rate for the period of the contract. While the nonprofit status of many rooted institutions precludes their access to tax credits, the cooperative is eligible for such incentives, enhancing its profitability. Both the solar and the weatherization divisions have experienced early success. In a city with an "outstanding weatherization track record," it was able to partner with "the largest and most effective" executing agency for the utility-funded weatherization program. The cooperative's hiring of local residents and worker ownership gave them "staying power and legitimacy" in the eyes of the Cleveland Housing Network, which signed them on as a preferred contractor. Recently, the cooperative gained licensing and city approval to do federally funded HVAC work, which will expand its scope.

Two more worker cooperatives are expected to launch in 2011. The first is Green City Grocers, a five-acre greenhouse, which, at full capacity, is expected to produce four million heads of lettuce and three hundred thousand pounds of herbs annually. Cleveland has already provided about two-thirds of the projected $15 million needed to build and capitalize the greenhouse; the city has also worked with Evergreen to apply to the U.S. Department of Housing and Urban Development for funds for brownfield remediation on the project site. The other cooperative still in the works is a community newspaper, unique among the Evergreen firms in that it is not designed to serve the needs of the rooted institutions but rather the residents in neighborhoods surrounding University Circle, as Evergreen aims to strengthen its connections and legitimacy. Evergreen's leadership team is considering the development of worker cooperatives to perform building rehabilitation, recycling, home care, janitorial services, records retention, and medical-kit assembly.

During the next five years, Evergreen plans to start ten worker cooperatives that will each employ, on average, fifty worker/owners when operating at full capacity, for a total membership of five hundred worker/owners. However, if Ohio Solar is any indication, Evergreen may exceed these expectations. The Evergreen leadership team anticipates that the solar panel installation and weatherization business could employ upward of one hundred people in the next three to four years, a doubling of their original goal. Although creating the opportunity for five hundred worker/owners is a significant accomplishment, the long-term goal is to have a significant impact on the six adjacent neighborhoods and, eventually, the entire city. The Evergreen leadership team has taken on, as its most pressing challenge, growing the initiative from ten businesses to one hundred, employing roughly five thousand worker/owners. If this vision is realized, roughly 10 percent of the residents surrounding University Circle would become Evergreen worker/owners.

Remaining Questions

As noted by numerous observers of worker cooperatives, one of Mondragon's defining features is its memberships' Basque ethnic, linguistic, and cultural identity and predominantly working-class affiliations. In contrast, Evergreen is grappling with a very different internal dynamic on issues of race and class. To date, almost all of the worker/owners are low income and African American, while members of the leadership team and cooperative managers are largely middle class and white. The leadership team acknowledges the need to achieve diversity throughout the organization to build a strong sense of collective identity.

The project raises many questions: First, in this effort to realize investment that emphasizes environmental sustainability and promotes justice, can historical patterns of marginalization be changed? Second, if divisions along race and class are, in effect, inevitable, what are alternative foundations for collective identity? Can the members of Evergreen achieve a sense of solidarity based on their shared commitment to principles of economic democracy? Can the Evergreen leadership team focus more squarely on the skill sets residents possess and match those skills to viable business opportunities?

Currently, the Evergreen leadership does not include leaders from the neighborhoods surrounding Greater University Circle, though its neighbors are not without sociopolitical infrastructure or capacity to participate (Thompson 2006).[5] In contrast, Mondragon's cooperatives were driven entirely by local leaders (Arizmendi, while born elsewhere in Basque country, lived the majority of his life in Mondragon) and resources. This dynamic also calls into question the long-term viability of the initiative. Can an experiment in economic democracy move beyond its status as a philanthropically driven project guided by a benevolent team of outside leaders? What will happen when these leaders exit? Lastly, Mondragon's cooperative complex began with a school that socialized generations of leaders—how will Evergreen inspire and prepare its next generation of leaders?

Other questions surround the economic future of the project. How will the relationship between the Evergreen cooperatives and its institutional partners evolve? Will the worker cooperatives capture money from streams other than procurement spending? The Democracy Collaborative has discussed the possibility of including institutional investments from sizable endowments in the Evergreen Development Fund to support business creation as well as partnerships to support to worker training, management education, business development and planning, and technological research and development. While the presence of the school and the industrial research center were critical to the success of Mondragon, such considerations have yet to be incorporated into U.S. cooperatives like Evergreen. Beyond providing immediate gains, such partnerships might ensure long-term viability by developing human capital along with internal capacity for technological expertise and innovation. Mondragon's experience indicates that such investments facilitate the development of a manufacturing and advanced industry base and the attainment of significant scale.

Cooperative Economic Development

It is useful to consider the Mondragon and Evergreen model side by side, identifying strategic considerations of interest to progressive organizations and coalitions in other cities. Undeniably, the success of Mondragon results in part from factors unique to the region and its people; also, undeniably, Evergreen remains in its earliest stages of development. Both cases, however, are instructive. The three strategic considerations we culled from them are geography, networks, and endogeny; each may contribute to a promising place-based cooperative economic development initiative.

Geography

Both Mondragon and Evergreen are place-based cooperative economic-development initiatives. Such initiatives are sensitive to place insofar as they respond to the needs of the people who live there and relate to the rooted institutions that constitute their economic base. Prior to the establishment of the cooperatives, the town of Mondragon depended on a single employer. The majority of residents worked for this dominant firm, where they remained without opportunities for social mobility. The challenge in Mondragon, therefore, was to develop and diversify a local economy to improve living conditions and economic opportunities for its people. Similarly, Cleveland's rooted institutions are the dominant employers and residents struggling to make ends meet have little influence over the local economy. Both initiatives responded to existing circumstances by leveraging rooted institutions to create new sociopolitical structures for asset building and direct participation and control over the local economy.

The geographic focus of the Mondragon and Evergreen initiatives not only allowed the cooperatives to design programs to meet the specific needs of area residents, but also enabled organizers to draw upon a shared history, culture, and identity, nurturing a sense of trust and commitment among participants. In the case of Mondragon, the Basque identity is well-known as a binding force among its membership. Evergreen's participants are more diverse in terms of race and class, but there are place-based commonalities that enhance coherence during turbulent moments. For instance, the Cleveland Foundation highlighted the shared challenges and opportunities faced by rooted institutions as a strategy for winning their trust early on. At a later stage, during an episode at the laundry cooperative where management grappled with issues of employee behavior, Katherine Hall played a bridging role between the management and the locally hired workforce. As a Cleveland native, she was able to complement her professional expertise as a diversity and human resources specialist with a cultural intelligence that enabled her to relate to area residents vested in the future of the Evergreen cooperatives.

Finally, both Mondragon and Evergreen were deliberate in defining the geography of their initiatives. While establishing the Polytechnic School and the first worker cooperatives, the Mondragon Cooperative Complex limited itself to the town of Mondragon. A limited geography was manageable and enabled a sufficient diversity of knowledge, skills, and perspectives while also promoting a sense of common purpose.[6] However, as subsequent phases required a broader base of participants and resources, the complex expanded to neighboring areas. The Caja connected a producer cooperative from a neighboring town to three Mondragon worker cooperatives to effectively expand the base of bank deposits and the amount of available capital. On the other hand, Ikerlan, the applied industrial research cooperative, connected Mondragon with the entire Basque region, starting in the 1980s when it received Basque government funding in exchange for offering its services to nonmember cooperatives and private firms in the region.

Likewise, the success of Evergreen is partly attributable to its limited geographical scope. By defining the boundaries of the initiative to include rooted institutions as well as the surrounding neighborhoods, Evergreen synergistically brought together an identified need and institutional resources. This move, especially, carries implications for historically marginalized communities, which in American urban contexts are often surrounded by large institutions as a result of the communities' inability to fend off "undesirable" land uses. By limiting the scope of the initiative to six neighborhoods, the cooperatives and support organizations have also been able to generate a meaningful impact on the target area.

Networks

Cooperative businesses, even when well-positioned geographically, tend to struggle when operating independently in a capitalistic economy. Consequently, scholars and practitioners have acknowledged that networks are one of the most important considerations for developing and supporting worker cooperatives. The network generally consists of a leadership team, worker cooperatives, support organizations (often organized as secondary cooperatives), and a flagship institution. Some entities play multiple roles.[7] Those interested in creating place-based cooperative economic development initiatives in cities might consider establishing a network using these four steps: (1) establish a leadership team, (2) build institutional partnerships, (3) develop the governance structure for both individual firms as well as the network, and (4) plan the development and phasing of support organizations.

The leadership team develops and guides the initiative and provides capacity and commitment, both of which are critical for engaging institutional partners and support organizations. An effective leadership team has deep knowledge, a diverse set of skills, and a range of perspectives and relationships.[8] Inevitably, of course, the composition and structure of the leadership team will vary based on local conditions. In Cleveland, the Evergreen leadership team is made up of skilled professionals with expertise in management, public policy, finance, business development, and human resources and who live outside the initiative's geographic boundaries. Its organizational structure is highly centralized and makes a wide range of decisions. The strength of this approach is that tight coordination minimizes the possibilities for fundamental mistakes at the early stage. On the other hand, such an approach may compromise efforts to gain legitimacy among local residents and to develop leadership among worker/owners. A more decentralized approach would include leadership and decision making by worker/owners at the level of the individual firm.

Each institution encompasses significant political and financial capital, which can be leveraged through partnerships to support the development of the cooperative network. For each partnership, the leadership team may consider the interests of the partnering institution, the plausibility of the project proposal, and realistic expectations of the institution's role in the partnership. Beyond building relationships between the leadership team and institutions, the team may also facilitate relationships between key individuals within various institutions. The governance structure for both individual firms and the cooperative network as a whole may develop in phases, with the leadership team eventually ceding authority to individual cooperatives and supporting organizations (at the broader level) and management and worker/owners (at the firm level). Within the cooperative network, governance tasks include clarifying roles and relationships among the leadership team, cooperative firms, support organizations, and partner institutions, as well as defining a set of shared principles and practices among all member parties. Depending on the power dynamics between the various members of the cooperative network, democratic governance and accountability may prove to be a difficult challenge, with implications for the norms, practices, and policies of individual firms. Within cooperative firms, governance tasks include clarifying roles and relationships among employees, managers, and representative boards as well as establishing protocol for operations, management, hiring, firing, compensation, investments, and strategy. For instance, individual firms will have to specify terms such as pay differentials (between highest- and lowest-paid workers), the permitted percentage of wage laborers, profit and loss sharing, debt to capital ratio and contributions to member capital accounts, a common loan fund, and a social-programs fund. Balancing the need for worker/owner control with operational efficiency may prove challenging, but meaningfully engaging worker/owners in cooperative governance, as well as in the larger cooperative network, is essential to nurturing a culture of collective ownership.

Finally, in planning the development and phasing of the support organizations, a cooperative network can create new secondary cooperatives or incorporate existing organizations that can provide resources and support services to the cooperative network. A variety of support organizations help worker cooperatives to succeed in an economy dominated by private enterprise. Educational organizations provide skills training, democratic workplace preparedness, management, and leadership as well as research and development capacity. Financial support organizations, meanwhile, help worker cooperatives access significant investment capital by combining traditional capital sources with resources from community members (prosper.com and Kiva.org). In turn, business development organizations can support new and existing firms by providing technical assistance, evaluation, and planning services. Lastly, research and design organizations can conduct independent research to enhance the efficiency of existing cooperative firms and identify new product areas and market opportunities for firm expansion.

Endogeny

The third strategic consideration for parties interested in instigating a place-based cooperative economic development initiative is endogeny, or growth from within. Cooperative initiatives that consider endogeny explore import-replacing opportunities by appropriating existing internal assets. This strategy promotes the diversification of local economic activity, beginning when civic leaders identify ways to produce goods or services locally. If local production is feasible, the imported good or service is replaced, the local economy grows, and the firm that now produces the good or service may also begin to export to other markets. Beyond the local production of consumer products and services, this strategy also entails increasing the number "of firms that buy from and sell to one another" (Whyte and Whyte 1991, 59). As import replacement continues over time, it results in a diversification and expansion of the local economy, complete with "increasingly skilled workers and technical and professional people" (59). One of the key benefits of such an approach is the protection it affords against sudden changes in the national or international economy, which can prove devastating to specialized local economies. Further, as observed in the industrial clusters of northern Italy, a diversity of interrelated industries, firms, and people within close proximity produce knowledge spillovers that seed ideas for new products and methods of production (Piore and Sable 1996).

In the Evergreen Initiative, leadership initiated the process of endogenous economic development by identifying opportunities for import replacement inherent in the procurement spending of rooted institutions. Consequently, the Evergreen Cooperative Laundry was designed to handle the needs of local rooted institutions that were contracting services to firms located in outlying cities and regions. Ohio Solar likewise emerged as an import-replacement strategy, responding to opportunities resulting from the fact that the rooted institutions sourced their energy through external entities. By leasing rooftops, installing solar panels, and selling generated energy to the institutions at a fixed rate, Ohio Solar intervened in a process that would have transferred local dollars (many of them public) to the coffers of utility companies. In Mondragon, such import-replacement policies came at a later phase of development as the complex spun off firms that specialized in goods and services that had previously been imported for use in the production of other goods and services, as well as for consumption. Additionally, Mondragon benefited from the presence of cooperative groups, which facilitated knowledge transfer among interrelated firms by providing coordination and mutual-support functions. In replacing previously imported goods and services, Mondragon eventually became so efficient at production that they were able to export these goods and services.

Endogeny requires the effective use of local assets to implement import-replacement and diversification strategies. Beyond the ability to identify local sources of demand for imports, import replacement also requires strategic deployment of local inputs, including labor, capital, equipment, and facilities. The Evergreen Cooperative Laundry established a local procurement chain by drawing on available industrial land and building stock along with a local workforce. Similarly, in establishing Ohio Solar, Evergreen not only secured a power-purchasing agreement, it also brought in locally available inputs, including the rooftops of large institutions and a willing workforce. As Evergreen tries to expand fivefold over the next five years, it is likely to face challenges in its next stage of diversification and expansion, which will necessitate a more democratic engagement of local assets.

Conclusion

A place-based cooperative economic development strategy may profoundly transform a place along a developmental course of economic democracy. The experience of the Mondragon cooperative illustrates that worker or producer cooperatives can thrive in a capitalist economic system if equipped with effective mechanisms for internal governance, education, technical assistance, and strategic planning. Cleveland's Evergreen has taken this one step further, organizing a network of green cooperative firms and support organizations in an American city with the leadership and partnership of rooted institutions.

Notes

1. Following the economic recession of the 1970s and 1980s, the employee shared-ownership program proliferated and became the dominant business model for American firms that aspired to cooperative principles. But despite its popularity, the shared-ownership model fell short in that it failed to hand over decision-making power to worker-owners. Recently, the United States has seen a renewed interest in worker cooperatives as a means for stabilizing local economies and creating jobs, particularly in manufacturing. As an example, the United Steel Workers union and the Mondragon Cooperative Corporation established an alliance in 2009 to build manufacturing worker cooperatives in the United States based on the Mondragon model.

2. Nonmember cooperatives and private firms pay 50 percent more than Mondragon members for contracts.

3. The first cooperative group, named Ularco, consisted of the first cooperative firm, Ulgor, as well as two other firms, Arrasate and Copreci, which made machine parts and tools for Ulgor.

4. Shorebank Enterprise is the nonprofit arm of Shorebank, the largest community bank in the country. Shorebank was founded in 1973 "to demonstrate that a regulated bank could be instrumental in revitalizing the communities being avoided by other financial institutions." In 2000, Shorebank broadened its mission to include "investing in people and their communities to create economic equity and a healthy environment." Shorebank managed a loan fund, identified and accessed capital for investment into the cooperatives, and assisted with the financial management of the businesses once firms began operating.

5. As documented by J. Phillip Thompson (2006), Cleveland was home to black civic coalitions in the 1970s and 1980s.

6. Here, the tradition of metalwork and various crafts may have played a role in nurturing a diversity of knowledge, skills, and perspectives in the town.

7. In the case of Mondragon, Arizmendi played a strong leadership role, while the Caja served as both an anchoring institution and a support organization. Additional support organizations included the Polytechnic School, which specialized in education and training, and Ikerlan, which focused on technological research and development. The Evergreen model expanded

on the traditional understanding of a cooperative network by incorporating foundations and government into the leadership and partnership roles. The Cleveland Foundation has played an especially important role within the leadership teams and among institutional partners. Other institutional partners include Cleveland Circle's rooted institutions and the city of Cleveland, while Evergreen support organizations include the development fund and the community newspaper.

8.   The leadership team may benefit from internal capacity in economic development finance and planning, business development and planning, cooperative firm development, training, business management, community organizing, policy development, and advocacy. Strong relationships with rooted institutions, community organizations, the banking community, foundations, the business community, government, and organized labor can be valuable.

References

Anderson, Jim. 2010. Personal interview. February 9.

Clamp, Christina A. 2000. "The Internationalization of Mondragon." *Annals of Public and Cooperative Economics* 71 (4): 562.

Howard, Ted. 2010a. Personal interview. February 11.

———. 2010b. "The Evergreen Cooperative Initiative," The Democracy Collaborative, February 11. *democracycollaborative.org.*

Keil, Stephen. 2010. Personal interview. February 9.

Mondragon Corporation. "MONDRAGON Corporation: Historical Evolution." *www.mondragon-corporation.com/language/en-US/ENG/Economic-Data/Historical-Evolution.aspx.*

———. "MONDRAGON Corporation: Humanity at Work." *www.mondragon-corporation.com/language/en-US/ENG.aspx.*

Pierce Lee, India, and Lillian Kerr. 2010. Personal interview. February 10.

Piore, Michael, and Charles Sable. 1986. *The Second Industrial Divide: Possibilities for Prosperity.* New York: Basic Books.

Stropkay, Mary Ann. 2010. Personal interview. February 9.

Thompson, David. 1994. "Cooperative Principles Then and Now (Part 2)." *Cooperative Grocer,* no. 53 (August). *www.cooperativegrocer.coop/articles/index.php?id=158.*

Thompson, J. Phillip. 2006. *Double Trouble: Black Mayors, Black Communities, and the Call for a Deep Democracy.* New York: Oxford University Press.

United Steel Workers. 2009. "Steelworkers Form Collaboration with MONDRAGON, the World's Largest Worker-Owned Cooperative." Press release. October 27. *www.usw.org/media_center/releases_advisories?id=0234.*

Wheeler, John, and Margaret Carney. 2010. Personal interview. February 11.

Whyte, William Foote, and Kathleen King Whyte. 1991. *Making Mondragon: The Growth and Dynamics of the Worker Cooperative Complex.* Ithaca, NY: Cornell University Press.

PART II

Engaging Equity

3

Concentrating Investment

A Strategy for Sustainable Development in Kansas City, Missouri

Leila Bozorg

Introducing the Green Impact Zone

In late March 2009, Congressman Emanuel Cleaver II of Missouri's Fifth District hosted a meeting at the offices of the Mid-America Regional Council in downtown Kansas City. At that meeting, Congressman Cleaver presented his idea, soon to be known as the Green Impact Zone of Missouri, for attracting and maximizing the impact of federal stimulus dollars available through the American Recovery and Reinvestment Act, also known as the Recovery Act. Familiar as he was with the traditional disbursements of federal funds, the congressman feared that stimulus dollars would get spread thin, "like peanut butter," throughout his congressional district without making a strong impact where needed most. Particularly aware of the economic and environmental distress experienced by communities on the east side of the city, Congressman Cleaver designated a 150-block area in the southeastern section of the city's urban core as the target of the Zone. The idea behind the Zone was to concentrate and coordinate resources and investment from and between city departments, the private sector, and other partner organizations committed to improving the lives and livelihoods of targeted communities. The congressman also aimed to provide a model for other cities and regions in their efforts to use the Recovery Act to promote sustainable development.

Important to this idea is understanding what "sustainable development" really means for Kansas City and how it can be realized.

My first drive through the Zone was illuminating as I began to explore this question. On the one hand, there was obvious distress: foreclosed homes, abandoned schools, curbside dumping, sagging roofs, and vacant lots. On the other hand, there were signs of vitality: a man shoveling snow outside a church, neighbors talking with each other, a community garden with a colorful hand-painted sign, a recently renovated home.

As I researched the history of the neighborhoods in the Zone, it became clear that the streets themselves testify to the area's historical complexity: Troost Avenue marks the boundary between racially segregated areas; Paseo Boulevard recalls the legacy of George Kessler and the City Beautiful movement in Kansas City; the Bruce R. Watkins Expressway (Highway 71) marks a community's struggles with displacement; and Prospect Avenue—where it crosses the East-West Brush Creek corridor—is a reminder of a city's long and varied efforts to control flooding. This East-West corridor, which connects west to J. C. Nichols's Country Club Plaza (and the wealthier inner-ring suburbs on the Kansas side of the Missouri-Kansas state line) and east to the Blue River, tells a story of two types of political leaders: one, the notorious "Boss Tom" Pendergast, whose concrete company paved the creek in the 1930s, contributing to the massive 1977 flood that killed twenty-five residents, and the other, Emanuel Cleaver II, who as a city council member in 1987 introduced "the Cleaver Plan," which committed funding for the Brush Creek Flood Control and Beautification Project. Unfortunately, the project stalled before extending to the Blue River, leaving some communities vulnerable to future flooding. Construction resumed in 1998, after a flood killed an additional eight people, and was at last completed in 2004. Promoting east-west construction of the Brush Creek project was one of Councilman Cleaver's most significant contributions to the city.

When Cleaver, now a congressman representing Missouri's Fifth District, announced his idea for the Zone in 2009, many of his constituents understood the plan to be a continuation of his commitment to the Brush Creek Corridor, which has symbolic weight as a space crossing the racial and economic divide of Troost Avenue. But the Zone was about more than symbolism. The congressman was jumping on an opportunity that had not yet presented itself during his time as a city council leader. In 2009, the new administration had signaled a move toward establishing and strengthening place-based programs and made available federal funds to promote both the economy and the environment. The congressman aimed to leverage this opportunity to present new ideas and strategies for addressing perennial urban challenges not only around economy and the environment, but also around issues of equity.

The Recovery Act, announced on February 17, 2009, was President Obama's direct response to the economic crisis. It committed $787 billion to stimulating the economy through the creation and maintenance of jobs and through planned investment in long-term economic growth. Unlike its New Deal predecessor, the Emergency Relief Appropriation Act of 1935, the Recovery Act did not call for the creation of a new federal agency like the Work Projects Administration. Instead, it aimed to achieve its primary goals through existing agencies by funding "shovel ready projects." While the Recovery Act itself offered little in the way of innovation, its dual emphasis on job creation and energy efficiency motivated many community leaders, local governments, and energy-sector companies to begin organizing around the opportunities that were to become available.

This was the context from which the Zone emerged, and the Recovery Act itself emerged within a larger context of federal decisions that signaled a new wave of both federal investment and political will to address economic, equity, and environmental concerns faced by people and places nationwide, especially in cities. One such decision came two days after the Recovery Act became law, when the president issued the executive order establishing the White House Office of Urban Affairs, tasked with taking a "coordinated and comprehensive approach to developing and implementing an effective strategy concerning urban America" (Orszag et al. 2009). By August 2009, members of the Senate Banking, Housing, and Urban Affairs Committee introduced a piece of legislation called the Livable Communities Act, which established an Office of Sustainable Housing and Communities within the U.S. Department of Housing and Urban Development and an Interagency Council on Sustainable Communities. The administration's position on how to address these new priorities appeared in a memo written in April 2009 by Peter R. Orszag (Office of Management and Budget), Melody Barnes (Domestic Policy Council), Adolfo Carrion (Office of Urban Affairs), and Lawrence Summers (National Economic Council). The memo, addressed to the heads of executive departments and agencies and titled "Developing Effective Place-based Policies for the FY 2011 Budget," argued that place-based programs can "leverage investments by focusing resources in targeted places and drawing on the compounding effect of well-coordinated action" (Orszag et al. 2009).

Using place-based policies to address urban challenges is by no means a new idea. However, now that urban policy makers and practitioners aim to engage a confluence of priorities that fall within "sustainable development"—including economic, equity, and environmental concerns—opportunities exist for place-based policies and the initiatives they inspire to be applied in new ways. The questions facing this effort include the following: How can civic leaders and residents implement programs that merge old and new priorities, particularly equity and environment, which have traditionally taken a back seat to economy? Where, in practice, does the idea of improving the welfare of people intersect with the idea of improving and strengthening a wider neighborhood? While the Zone's relative newness does not allow for an analysis of its overall impact, examining it can help answer these questions, and important lessons emerge from its early experiences with organizing and implementation. As a strategy for sustainable development, the Zone offers important insight into new directions, methods, and processes for urban policy and practice.

To maximize understanding of the Zone as an idea-in-practice and the lessons it offers, I reviewed not only the current initiative but the history of policies and decisions that created the problems that this place-based program aims to solve. I collected data from twenty-five personal interviews, publicly available meeting notes and performance reports, local press coverage, and grant applications. I completed my research within a year of the Zone's inception; the project, inevitably, has subsequently moved forward in ways that this research cannot account for.

Because urban policy has historically concerned the question of people versus place, this chapter begins with an overview of that debate. I then introduce a short discussion on spatial justice and sustainable development, and on the three *E*s (economy, equity, environment) that are central to the current urban agenda. The history of urban policies and plans that contributed to an unjust geography in Kansas City are then discussed, followed finally by an analysis of the Zone's early evolution and its proposed strategy for promoting sustainable development.

People versus Place Debate

The debate over whether to target assistance and programs to distressed people or to distressed places has a long history in urban policy. During the civil rights movement and its ensuing urban unrest, housing economist Louis Winnick wrote a seminal piece titled "Place Prosperity vs. People Prosperity: Welfare Considerations in the Geographic Redistribution of Economic Activity" (1966). Winnick laid out a perceived tension between two policy goals: "the ideal of improving the welfare of deserving people as individuals, regardless of where they live, and the ideal of improving the welfare of groups of deserving people defined by their spatial proximity in 'places'" (Bolton 1992, 187). These two ideals have corresponding and seemingly conflicting implications for government policies: either the government promotes the direct transfer of payment to individuals, usually through assistance in moving out of declining or distressed areas, or it invests in a geographically defined area through giving grants to local government, subsidizing business, or targeting education and worker training in an area (187). Winnick's essay came down against place-based policies, arguing that they are "ineffective at redistribution . . . [and] too much of [the redistribution] goes to the wrong people; the unemployed are often not the main beneficiaries" (187). Many economists continue to stand by a version of this position today.

The case in favor of place-based policy goes back to the 1960s as well, when President Lyndon B. Johnson created the National Advisory Commission on Civil Disorder, which issued the Kerner Commission Report in 1968.[1] The report "provided careful, detailed findings regarding the status of African Americans in cities at the time—their income and employment status, their educational opportunities, their access to health care, their relation to the public welfare system and to the criminal justice system, and their access to political power" (Boger and Wegner 1996). With little explanation, the report recommended that this range of problems would be best addressed through a set of place-based programs (Fainstein and Markusen 1996, 143).

Since the Kerner report, the question of people versus place has reemerged several times. On the brink of Reagan's inauguration, the President's Commission for a National Agenda for the Eighties delivered a report titled *Urban America in the Eighties* that criticized the past decade's place-based policies and programs for inefficiently and ineffectively using federal funds, thereby coming down against place-based policies in favor of direct assistance to individuals. In the early nineties, with the election of President Clinton, the debate resurfaced as policy makers developed place-based empowerment zones, now arguing that people-based policies had done little to improve the condition of urban poverty. President George W. Bush took neither a people- nor a place-based approach; the neglect of his administration, some authors have implied, is characterized by then Housing and Urban Development secretary Alphonso Jackson's infamous line, "being poor is a state of mind, not a condition" (quoted in Drier 2004). In stark contrast to Jackson's idea, defenders of place-based policies often cite the reality of racial concentration in cities, pointing especially to the "coincidence of place and poverty" as reason enough to devise policies sensitive to this coincidence (Fainstein and Markusen 1996, 146).

Social movements such as the environmental-justice movement have exposed this "coincidence" on a larger scale, pointing to the pattern of injustices, such as the siting of toxic facilities near lower-income neighborhoods that occurs in many urban areas.[2] The environmental-justice movement and theorists of urban planning like Edward Soja have striven to link these issues more directly to urban decision-making. Soja considers such distributional inequalities to be "the most basic and obvious expression of spatial injustice," arguing:

> Distributional inequalities arise with regard to all basic needs of urban life, ranging from such vital public services as education, mass transit, police and crime prevention, to more privatized provisioning of adequate food, housing, and employment. The end result is often self-perpetuating interweaving of spatial injustices that, at least after passing a certain level of tolerance, can be seen as a fundamental violation of urban-based civil rights and legal or constitutional guarantees of equality and justice. (2010, 47)

John O. Calmore, a law professor and civil rights leader, goes so far as to suggest that policy has a role in redressing past injustices rather than simply ensuring that they are not perpetuated. Spatial equity, as he defines it, is "a group-based remedy that focuses on opportunity and circumstances within black communities and demands that both be improved, enriched, and equalized" (Calmore 1996, 315). Thus, spatial equity can address the fact that many of the inequalities faced by African

American communities resulted from "past discrimination by state and private actors who often operated in tandem" (311).

Why have concerns of equity remained relatively removed from the urban policy dialogue? Crucially, according to Fainstein, equity and justice are difficult to achieve without support from other levels of governance:

> To be sure cities cannot be viewed in isolation; they are within networks of governmental institutions and capital flows. . . . Justice is not achievable at the urban level without support from other levels, but discussion of urban programs requires a concept of justice relevant to what is within city government's power and in terms of the goals of urban movements. (2006, 4–5)

This point reinforces the importance of multilevel commitments to these issues and, in a sense, calls for an understanding of the systems that reinforce injustice. This mirrors calls from the sustainable-development arena, which similarly recognizes that a systems-level understanding of cities and metropolitan areas is crucial for promoting sustainability.[3] And, it is the emerging sustainable-development agenda that most recently placed the question of equity into the urban policy and practice arenas.

Sustainable Development

In 1996, urban-planning scholar Scott Campbell published an article entitled "Green Cities, Growing Cities, Just Cities?" in which he argued that the popular formulation of sustainability is "vulnerable to the same criticism of vague idealism made thirty years ago against comprehensive planning" (1996, 435). Campbell asked, "How could those at the bottom of society find greater economic opportunity if environmental protection mandates diminished economic growth?" (437). But who are these targeted populations? They are the same populations whose needs urban planners and policy makers have continually attempted to meet. What makes the current federal policy agenda different, however, is that it is tied to the idea of sustainable development where equity has a central position. Wheeler, a professor of landscape architecture, notes:

> Equity is by far the least developed of the Three Es [economy, equity, environment]. To be sure, it has long been the focus of many commu-

nity activists, labor unions and social justice organizers. However, these constituencies often have relatively little power, and equity concerns frequently take a back seat in planning and political discussions. (quoted in Baxamusa 2008, 20)

Moreover, the equity and advocacy planning traditions that emerged in the late 1960s and early 1970s responded to the overly technical approaches of the era's top-down planning. Although scholars tend to characterize these traditions as reflecting only the issues of their time, they are relevant to the current moment in important ways: first, in their aspiration to fight for the interest of less powerful segments of society, and, second, in their failure to truly empower those segments of society by speaking or acting on their behalf. The equity and advocacy planning traditions certainly pushed for more equitable outcomes, but often did so through exclusionary processes.

Questions thus remain about the most appropriate levels for engagement to achieve sustainable development in cities. This situation is further complicated by the comprehensive nature of sustainable development, which requires a nuanced and systems-based view of urban processes. In developing the Zone in Missouri, Kansas City's leaders attempted to implement a place-based strategy for sustainable development by simultaneously engaging civic leaders at regional and local levels. Before examining the initiative's early experiences with organizing and implementation, it is important to be grounded in Kansas City's unique history.

Kansas City's Production of an Unjust Geography

Spatial (in)justice [results] from [both] the external creation
of unjust geographies through boundary making and political
organization of space . . . [and] internally from the distributional
inequalities created through discriminating decision making by
individuals, firms, and institutions. —Edward W. Soja (2010, 9)

Kansas City, Missouri, has always held a peculiar position in the American landscape. Founded at the confluence of the Kansas and Missouri Rivers at the approximate center of the United States, Kansas City is unique in its Western orientation as a once-frontier city, its economic ties to the industrial North and East, and its Southern heritage as a slaveholding state. Over the course of its development, Kansas City came to be known as a "Northern town with a Southern exposure" and the "easternmost Western city."

After expelling the Shawnee Indians and growing to economic importance in the 1830s, the City of Kansas was incorporated in 1853. The city did not experience significant growth until the post–Civil War era, when the Hannibal and St. Lawrence Railway extended across the Missouri River. With the introduction of the rail line over the Hannibal Bridge in 1869, the city boomed, becoming the center of the region's commercial and industrial activity (Schirmer 2002, 11) and enjoying a significant increase in population and a major real estate boom between 1880 and 1887 (Brown and Dorsett 1978, 37). The subsequent boom and bust, ending at the end of the nineteenth century, created a significant drop in property values and led to the city's first set of official control measures: deed restrictions for the newly created subdivisions of Hyde Park and Kenwood.

When Kansas City first envisioned Hyde Park in 1886, its developers had a reasonable fear that the open space around a nearby ravine would attract informal settlements, as it had in similar neighborhoods. To ensure quality and separation from such informal "infringement," city planners hired landscape architect George Kessler, who designed a subdivision protected physically by a ravine and socially by rules within the deed restrictions, thereby regulating the quality of buildings in the subdivision and the class of its inhabitants (Schirmer 2002, 15).

Throughout this period, Kansas City remained a relatively integrated city, though four enclaves of African American settlers did develop over the course of the nineteenth century (Serda 2003, 71). The first was Hell's Half Acre, the site of worker housing for African Americans employed to build the Hannibal Bridge. A second enclave developed in Church Hill in the 1880s. Many families chose to live in Church Hill to be near churches, which doubled as community centers, and many of the enclave's African American residents worked as servants in nearby homes of the city's elite and middle class (Schirmer 2002). A third enclave, called Belvidere Hollow, developed between two ravines located in the North End, which housed many low-wage workers. The fourth enclave developed on the east side of the city after the real estate bust left developers with a surplus of homes they were willing to sell at modest prices. When these homes became available, many African American households settled on the east side between Troost and Woodland Avenues, from Twelfth to Twenty-fifth Streets, including part of Vine.

Historians have argued that these early enclaves did not emerge out of any particular racially discriminating practice or ideology, and that a significant number of whites lived in these neighborhoods (Schirmer 2002, 32; Gotham 2002b, 30). However, the real estate bust, the growing anxiety among whites over property values, the city's ensuing beautification projects, and the development of differentiated land use, which uprooted many black families, all contributed to the reconfiguration of African Americans' residential patterns (Schirmer 2002, 39).

Meanwhile, both the success of the Hyde Park deed restrictions as a mechanism for controlling use and the beautification projects that introduced the Parks and Boulevard System caught the attention of a prominent suburban developer, J. C. Nichols, who would substantially contribute to racial segregation and the production of an unjust geography in Kansas City.

J. C. Nichols and Race-Restrictive Covenants

By the end of 1910, Nichols had assembled more than one thousand acres of potential building sites in Kansas City. His first developments were housing subdivisions, and, with the assistance of other financial backers and Kessler's landscape designs, Nichols later developed what would become the Country Club District (given its proximity to the Kansas City Country Club), the site of today's Country Club Plaza (Worley 1993, 6).

Nichols's restrictive covenants, with their requirements for the size and cost of homes as well as restrictions that prevented "negroes" from owning or renting them, actively excluded African Americans from neighborhoods (Gotham 2000; Schirmer 2002).[4] These practices coincided with the influx of Southern blacks into Kansas City during the Great Migration, which fed directly into an exclusionary ideology pushed by real estate developers. By 1917, the Supreme Court had made racial zoning ordinances unenforceable, signaling some national attention to issues of race and the organizing of space. Kansas City's restrictive covenants evaded this ruling, however, and continued to contribute to the increasingly racialized landscape (Gotham 2000, 623). The city did not pass its own ordinance against racial zoning until 1923.

Racial tensions in Kansas City grew dramatically in the 1920s.

Growing white anxiety over integration, fueled by the real estate industry, created such contention over the character of some neighborhoods that, between 1921 and 1928, white residents targeted African American households in a series of bombings, predominantly on the east side (Schirmer 2002, 101). Middle-class African Americans began to develop an explicit race consciousness, with "race men" and "race women" proposing to shape race awareness among the city's white populations through protest and political independence (148). Leaders who emerged in this early period included D. A. Holmes, the pastor of the Vine Street Baptist Church, and a young entrepreneur named T. B. Watkins, whose stepson, Bruce R. Watkins, would become Kansas City's first African American city council representative in 1962.

By the time the Supreme Court finally declared racial covenants unenforceable, in 1948, they were in nearly every Kansas City Suburb and newly developed residential area (Gotham 2000, 624). These covenants served to keep African American residents out of white neighborhoods and also contributed to the growing suburbanization of white populations, particularly in the context of an emerging federally supported housing industry. The complete production of an unjust geography through the racial reorganizing of space would not be fully realized in Kansas City until the middle of the twentieth century, with the introduction of urban renewal, its construction of public housing, and building of expressways.

Urban Renewal, Public Housing, and Expressways

Urban renewal, the infamous federal program now associated with the large-scale displacement of poor, often minority communities, grew out of a set of three housing acts. The Housing Act of 1937 endowed local housing authorities with the legal power of eminent domain. This was followed by the Housing Act of 1949, which provided municipalities with federal funds that could be used for local redevelopment, particularly in areas deemed "slums." Finally, the Housing Act of 1954 broadened the program's scope and dubbed it "urban renewal." To qualify for federal funding available through the housing acts, municipalities had to ensure an adequate supply of housing for displaced populations (Gotham 2001, 302). It was through the implementation of this resettlement process that Kansas City's racial landscape began to take on its current form.

Projects funded through urban renewal were considered quite successful, as the city received numerous accolades for its transformation of slums into a "New Kansas City." But this transformation resulted in the displacement of thousands of residents, both African American and white. Instead of providing housing for the displaced, as the law demanded, the Land Clearance for Redevelopment Authority, created by the state of Missouri in 1953, illegally refused throughout the 1960s to provide financial assistance to residents seeking replacement housing. When the federal government mandated action in the 1960s, Kansas City's relocation specialists "maintained separate lists of available homes 'for Blacks' and 'for Whites,'" which steered displaced residents into different parts of the city.[5] Meanwhile, through 1964, the Housing Authority of Kansas City, Missouri, continued to segregate the recipients of public housing by race: white public-housing units were located north of Independence Avenue, and African American units south of Independence Avenue and east of Troost Avenue (Gotham 2001, 303–4).

Between 1889 and the end of the 1960s, then, Kansas City instituted a small set of deed restriction that later snowballed into race-restrictive covenants. Policies and practices associated with urban renewal, public housing, and downtown redevelopment not only destroyed important African American neighborhoods, but also spatially reorganized people by race. The most influential actions that resulted in spatial segregation, however, were those of the Kansas City Missouri School District, whose policies intentionally created a dividing line along Troost Avenue, a dividing line further solidified by the real estate and finance industries through blockbusting and redlining (Gotham 2000; Schirmer 2002).[6]

School Segregation and the Emergence of Troost Avenue

Though African American and whites were relatively integrated residentially during the years of early African American migration in the mid- to late 1800s, the education system remained strictly segregated because of the Jim Crow laws that followed the 1896 *Plessy v. Ferguson* Supreme Court ruling. When the 1954 *Brown v. Topeka Board of Education* ruling outlawed school segregation, the state of Missouri left desegregation to local authorities. The Kansas City Missouri School District subsequently abolished the use of "explicitly racial" attendance zones but continued the practice of segregation through neighborhood attendance zones established through the city's comprehensive 1947 Master Plan.

The school district then spent the next two decades making constant north-south shifts to its attendance boundaries while keeping the east-west boundary along Troost Avenue.

Meanwhile, the local real estate industry used this "cognitive racial boundary" to transform the racial makeup of the bordering neighborhoods by instigating "white flight" through the practice of blockbusting (Gotham 2002a, 93). One such advertisement read:

> Colored in Your Block?
> Want to Sell and Get All Cash?
> For Prompt Appraisal Estimate
> Call Bill Williams, Ch. 1–9063.
> Chas Curry Realtors.

Between 1950 and 1970 the dramatic racial transition of neighborhoods east and west of Troost Avenue resulted in a new concentration of African Americans east of Troost Avenue. The social implications of the east-west divide that resulted are still felt throughout the city, and Emanuel Cleaver II has attempted to address them since his early days in Kansas City politics.

Emanuel Cleaver II

Emanuel Cleaver II arrived in Kansas City in 1974 as a young activist from Texas charged with establishing a new chapter of the Southern Christian Leadership Conference, the American civil rights organization with close connections to Dr. Martin Luther King Jr. During his early time in Kansas City, Cleaver also earned his master of divinity degree from St. Paul School of Theology and started his pastoral career with the St. James United Methodist Church. Cleaver won election to the city council in 1979, representing the city's fifth district. In 1991, when Kansas City's population of voting age was 26.5 percent African American, Cleaver was elected as Kansas City's first African American mayor. He was reelected in 1995 and left Kansas City office in 1999 with a 71 percent approval rating. In 2005, he won election to the U.S. Congress to represent Missouri's Fifth District.

As a faith leader and political leader in Kansas City, Cleaver continually worked to reduce the effects of segregation's legacy and its resulting spatial inequity in the city. In addition to founding his church east of Troost, he established the Cleaver Family Young Men's Christian Association (YMCA) on Troost and Seventieth Street. In 1987, as a council representative, he passed "the Cleaver Plan" through the city council, raising $51 million for cultural and economic development in the city. The plan included the Brush Creek Flood Control and Beautification Project. In a Brush Creek Community Partners newsletter, Cleaver notes how "the Brush Creek project wasn't just a flood control plan; it was laced with sociology as well, [as] some of the most affluent parts of the city [west of Troost] were connected to low-income parts [east of Troost] by water and greenery" (*Brush Creek Bulletin* 2004).

Later, as mayor, Cleaver commissioned a study to create the city's first comprehensive plan since 1947, eventually known as the Kansas City Forging Our Comprehensive Urban Strategy (FOCUS). Cleaver's FOCUS plan was momentous in both content and process, engaging residents and professionals throughout the city, but it was also significant because it would finally upend the 1947 plan, which had enforced racial segregation in the city throughout the civil rights era, specifically through its use of the neighborhood unit to influence school districting. The city council completed FOCUS between 1994 and 1999—while significant pieces were implemented, much of it was ultimately shelved as a consequence of political turnover in the city.

Cleaver's early work in Kansas City could only begin to counter the planning practices and municipal decisions that, over decades, had sustained a racially hypersegregated Kansas City. The various challenges facing the city today are exacerbated by its sprawling geography: the city hosts a population of 451,572 spread over 318 square miles, with six council districts occupying parts of four counties. From a local-government perspective, the long-standing practice of giving each of these six districts an equal distribution of city funding, while fair in process, is insufficient to counter the unjust landscape that continues to be part of the city and region. Thus, with the announcement of the Recovery Act, Congressman Cleaver saw an opportunity to take on these same challenges with new resources and strategies that would capitalize on assets from throughout the region, while concentrating funding and programs in the area that was for decades the target of disinvestment. In effect, he argued that "sustainable development" would never be fully achieved in the region (or in his congressional district at large) without a strategy that addressed spatial equity.

The Green Impact Zone

During a recent press conference, when asked why the particular neighborhoods[7] were chosen as the target of new federal funding, the congressman explained:

> The truth of the matter is if we had tried to do this over the entire Fifth Congressional District [of Missouri], it would have included Kansas City, Missouri, Sugar Creek, Independence, Raytown, Grandview, Raymore, Peculiar, Lone Jack, Belton, and Lee's Summit. And had we tried do something like this, we would have a speck here and a speck there, and afterwards, the taxpayers would question what happened to their money. As a result, we've chosen one of the toughest parts of the city. The *Kansas City Star* labeled one of the tracts the murder factory.[8]

Cleaver's comments reiterate the spatial focus within Kansas City and shed light on the strategy behind this place-based initiative. The Zone's boundaries were eventually drawn along Troost Avenue to the west, Fifty-First Street on the south, Prospect and Swope Avenues on the east, and Thirty-Ninth Street on the north. This area contains parts of six neighborhoods: Ivanhoe, Manheim Park, Blue Hills, 49/63, Troostwood (which is located within the 49/63 neighborhood), and Town Fork Creek. Of these six neighborhoods, only Manheim Park falls completely within the Zone's boundaries.

Everyone I interviewed felt that concentrating investment in these neighborhoods was appropriate, given the intensity of poverty and other challenges within the urban core. When I asked how the Zone's boundaries were decided, however, I heard a variety of explanations. First, I was told that the boundaries included the 64130 zip code, which had recently received negative attention in the *Kansas City Star* as the "Missouri Murder Factory." I also learned that the boundaries included equal parts of the third and fifth council districts, two districts where Congressman Cleaver believed he would win support from council representatives (Melba Curtis and Sharon Sanders Brooks in the third district, and Cindy Circo and Terry Riley in the fifth district). Next, I was told that the boundaries included neighborhoods with some of the area's strongest neighborhood groups, such as Ivanhoe Neighborhood Council and Brush Creek Community Partners, and that they encompassed the Brush Creek Corridor, an area of particular focus during Congressman Cleaver's tenure as mayor and councilman. Last, some interviewees explained that such "shovel ready" projects as the Bus Rapid Transit system and the Troost Bridge project were within the proposed boundaries and could function as activities upon which the congressman and the Zone might build. In describing her understanding of the boundary-making process, an interviewee, who requested anonymity, explained:

> A lot of stimulus money got spent nationally on things that were shovel ready even if they weren't good. Well, Cleaver knew all that and about how things usually get divided up . . . in a way everyone would be happy but nothing would change; so he said what if we could focus money to transform a neighborhood. Not an easy idea politically; but he started floating the idea with political allies here, centered on that zone . . . eventually the boundaries were shared and negotiated.

Delineating the boundary of the Zone was not the only tough decision Congressman Cleaver tackled. During a time when city governments around the country were spearheading their respective efforts to attract stimulus funds, the congressman asked the Mid-America Regional Council to administer the initiative for Kansas City. This was widely considered a risky move as, in effect, it would necessitate transferring some of the local government's decision-making power over the application process for stimulus funds to a regional body. Nonetheless, the congressman was able to garner unanimous support of city council representatives within weeks of the first meeting in March. The city council subsequently passed a resolution that permitted the use of Recovery Act funds for the Zone.

Prior to Cleaver's request, the Regional Council had some experience working on very localized development issues, but nothing to the extent of the Zone. It had substantial capacity for securing and administering federal grants and for transportation and sustainability planning. These capacities theoretically put them in a strong position to apply for and administer Recovery Act grants while also engaging local development professionals. David Warm, the Regional Council's executive director, also noted how "being a public agency, but not a government, would allow [the Regional Council] to operate more nimbly and flexibly than a lot of governments" (Warm 2010).

While the project was to be administered from the regional level, the Regional Council's leadership and Congressman Cleaver's staff recognized that in order for the project to achieve any success at the local level the "neighborhood leadership needed to be at the forefront." Margaret May, executive director of one of the Zone's most active neighborhood associations, Ivanhoe Neighborhood Council, recalled:

> One of the things that Congressman Cleaver and [the Regional Council] made clear from the beginning was how important the community leaders were to this initiative—that we were, in effect, the leaders of this initiative . . . and they have been very serious and sincere about that and making it happen to the maximum extent possible. (May 2010)

Because of their minimal experience working directly with neighborhoods, the Regional Council relied on three local organizations considered to have the most administrative capacity: Ivanhoe Neighborhood Council, Brush Creek Community Partners, and Blue Hills Community Services. The leadership of these organizations assisted the Regional Council in organizing and convening a wider group of neighborhood-based organizations that eventually evolved into the official group of neighborhood partners, called the Neighborhood Leadership Committee. This group included five volunteer-run neighborhood associations, four community development corporations, and an advocacy organization.[9]

Just as the early process of partnership building and priority setting got underway, Congress recessed for its spring break, giving Congressman Cleaver time to promote and speak more publicly about the Zone. He led a group of fifty community members, advisers, partners, architects, planners, and local representatives on a bus trip to Greensburg, Kansas, to learn from the "greening" initiative that the town had undertaken following a devastating 2007 tornado. As a result, the Zone immediately caught both national and local attention, and expectations about what the initiative would deliver, and when, were set up.

For my interviewees, central among these expectations was the notion that every home in the Zone would be weatherized within one year. Such unrealistic expectations were a major challenge during implementation, particularly given that it was still unclear how much funding the initiative could expect. Regulation around public workers also conflicted with expectations, as the Davis-Bacon Act slowed down the Department of Energy's Weatherization Assistance Program, which would provide most of the funds.[10] Nonetheless, many interviewees acknowledged that the congressman needed to raise attention to attract federal funds. As Bob Housh from the Metropolitan Energy Center explained:

> The hype has a purpose too. If you don't raise the expectations, you're not going to get the kind of backing that you need to get something like this happening. So it's just a balance between getting people interested and raising expectations and raising support when you raise expectations. The hype to some extent is a necessary evil; you have to have it to get people on board. (2010)

From the beginning of March to the end of April 2009, Congressman Cleaver's staff and advisers, along with the Regional Council's leadership, convened a series of meetings for neighborhood leaders, representatives of city departments and agencies, private-sector leaders (like Kansas City Power and Light), and representatives from the local architecture and planning community (like BNIM architects).

Through this outreach process, a second group of partners formed, consisting primarily of organizations and agencies seen as potential implementation partners, as their work revolved around the programmatic areas and strategies being developed by the Neighborhood Leadership Committee and a newly formed coordinating council.[11] Once the committee defined the programmatic areas—which included housing and weatherization, employment and training, public safety and community services, neighborhood outreach, energy and water conservation, and infrastructure—corresponding committees were formed. The programmatic areas, although developed by the Neighborhood Leadership Committee, corresponded to particular categories of Recovery Act funds expected to be available through various federal agencies, including the Department of Justice, Department of Energy, Department of Transportation, and Department of Housing and Urban Development. The initiative hoped to acquire and coordinate funding from these agencies to maximize community benefit.

In addition to developing programmatic areas, the Neighborhood Leadership Committee and the Regional Council developed an "Initial Plan," which consisted of a vision, a set of guiding principles, and an overall strategy for the initiative. The vision articulated the long-term goal of creating a "sustainable community"; the guiding principles laid out a set of values establishing how the initiative planned to approach its work; and the strategies called for engaging the community in a process of "evidence-based" community building, which would require systematic data collection and analysis. As part of this strategy, the Regional Council reached out to the University of Missouri, Kansas City's Center for Economic Information, and the Department of Urban Planning, Architecture and Design to gather data about the Zone's economic and environmental infrastructure. Together, they formed a data committee and began a rigorous analysis of the Zone.

From May to August 2009, the committees met to develop strategies and prepare grant applications; they sought the Byrne Justice Assistance Grant from the Department of Justice, the Pathways Out of Poverty Grant from the Department of Labor, and the Transportation Investment Generating Economic Recovery (TIGER) Grant from the Department of Transportation. By this time PolicyLink, a national advocacy organization, joined the process to assist in designing and planning Zone activities, particularly those related to building the administrative and organizing capacity of local neighborhood associations. This was a crucial activity, given that five of the ten neighborhood partners were organizations led by volunteer staff. Margaret May articulated this staffing challenge:

> You can't depend on people working as volunteers to be able to be consistent in doing the kinds of things it takes to really rebuild a neighborhood. . . . [T]he state of readiness is important. . . . I [have tried in the past] to advocate with the city that the other neighborhoods did not have the opportunity through a three-year operating grant [that we received from the Kaufman Foundation]; . . . that [grant] gave us a head start. It would be a mistake—just as it would have been a mistake in 2000 when we first made a strategic plan—to expect [much] from us, to expect the other neighborhoods to be able to do what Ivanhoe is doing. But we should provide an opportunity for them to develop the way *they* want to develop. (2010)

PolicyLink later awarded the Regional Council $15,000, which was combined with funding from the city to create a $39,000 capacity-building fund for the neighborhood associations within the Zone. A small fraction of this fund went to neighborhood associations, and the Regional Council allocated the remainder based on the percentage of the Zone each neighborhood association covered. Ivanhoe Neighborhood Council, occupying the greatest percentage of the Zone, received the most funding. However, unlike some of the other neighborhood organizations, Ivanhoe had a paid staff and relatively strong capacity, so its greater allocation created some tension among civic leaders in the Zone. The controversy exposed what would soon become a significant organizing challenge, namely, that the early planning and visioning process relied on leaders with unequal levels of capacity to generate participation from their neighborhoods, risking the perception that the decision-making process and outcomes would be skewed toward the interests of higher-capacity neighborhoods; all at a time when the initiative sought to bring leaders together to start thinking about their neighborhoods as a broader place with a shared set of interests.

By July, the Regional Council decided that effective organization and implementation of the anticipated resources required staff who would work in the neighborhoods. Unfortunately, the stimulus dollars for which the Zone was applying could not be used to fund organizing activities, so the Regional Council and the congressman's staff sought city funds. Councilwoman Cindy Circo of Kansas City's fifth district, who took the trip to Greensburg and whose district lies partly within the boundaries of the Zone, allocated $1.5 million of her district's public-works dollars into a general fund, which allowed the Regional Council to hire Anita Maltbia, a former assistant city manager, to serve as the Zone's director beginning August 1, 2009. Together, Ms. Maltbia and the Regional Council hired a staff of six: one assistant director, four community ombudspersons, and one office administrator. The staff started their two-week training during the last week of September 2009, about six months after the March meeting when Congressman Cleaver had first presented the idea of the Zone. Though developing more slowly than originally anticipated, the Zone was underway.

In September 2009, before the new staff began their training, the director of the White House Office of Urban Affairs, Adolfo Carrion Jr., visited the Zone along with Shaun Donovan, secretary of the U.S. Department of Housing and Urban Development, and John D. Porcari, deputy secretary of the Department of Transportation. By that time, the initiative had yet to be granted any federal stimulus dollars, but the event thrust the Zone farther into the national spotlight as a potential model for sustainable development.

By March 2010, the Zone was able to attract more than $100 million in federal stimulus dollars into the region to support projects. In

November, Kansas City Power and Light was awarded the Smart-Grid grant from the U.S. Department of Energy, along with $24 million in federal funds. In February, the U.S. Department of Transportation approved the Regional Council's application for the competitive $50 million TIGER grant, with $26 million going to the Zone for public improvements. In April 2010, the U.S. Department of Energy awarded $20 million in Energy Efficiency and Conservation Block Grant competitive funds to EnergyWorks Kansas City, which will assist property owners in the Zone and six other neighborhoods to identify and finance energy retrofitting.

While the Zone was successful in securing these grants, other applications were denied early on, including the Byrne Justice Assistance Grant from the U.S. Department of Justice, the Department of Labor's Pathways Out of Poverty Grant, and the Neighborhood Stabilization Program II from the U.S. Department of Housing and Urban Development. Because these Recovery Act dollars were for social programs that more directly affect the day-to-day lives of residents, the Zone staff faced the challenge of having to focus on projects that involved long-term infrastructure upgrading, while fewer resources were available for projects that more closely identified with the immediate social needs identified in the neighborhoods, like job training, public safety, and the provision of social services.

Further compounding this challenge was the fact that the Regional Council had yet to develop a larger community visioning process. In early December 2009 the Zone staff and the Regional Council organized the first "Community Expo." Rather than serving as an opportunity to facilitate a deeper dialogue between neighborhoods about shared experiences, fears, and hopes for the future, the expo introduced residents—through entertainment, workshops, and presentations—to the wide range of organizations whose services and products aligned with the Zone's vision; all giving the impression that funding for the programs, rather than a vision developed and owned by the community, would drive the Zone's priorities. This sequencing paradox also suggested that the purpose of organizing residents would be less to create a set of community-identified goals and performance targets, and more to engage residents in meeting predefined goals and performance targets.

The Zone: Key Strengths

March 2010 marked one year since Congressman Cleaver first presented his idea for the Green Impact Zone of Missouri, imagining it as a national model for sustainable development through concentrated place-based investment. The Zone aimed to achieve these goals by targeting various streams of stimulus funding to implement economic and environmental interventions, from weatherization to community policing to workforce and infrastructure development. While the confluence of challenges facing neighborhoods within the Zone could not have been solved in a year's time, the initiative shows great promise and has already helped to secure more than $100 million in competitive Recovery Act dollars for the Kansas City region.

Perhaps the most obvious strength of the Zone is that it represents a serious governmental commitment to solving problems on various levels. From the federal to the regional to the local level, the creation of the Zone required immense political cooperation and coordination. The establishment of the White House Office of Urban Affairs and the Livable Communities Act signaled the intent to introduce the concept of sustainable development into the federal urban-policy agenda. In turn, Congressman Cleaver seized the opportunity of the moment by mobilizing constituents to create the Zone and tapping the Regional Council to assume its leadership. Although the Regional Council had limited experience administering such a complex and localized initiative and no precedent to follow, it accepted the challenge. By engaging the leaders of community-based organizations early on and asking them to drive the initiative, the Regional Council and Congressman Cleaver demonstrated their commitment to involving leaders at all levels of governance.

The Zone built a wide platform of support in a short period of time, in part because of the congressman's reputation. Another reason, however, is the coalition-building process, through which the Regional Council reached out to organizations and institutions—particularly those with systems capacities—while the neighborhood leaders with the greatest administrative capacity reached out to their local networks. As a result, the initiative engaged a diverse set of rooted institutions, including a utility company, a university, community-based organizations, and a variety of public agencies. Together, these institutions compiled and submitted numerous grant applications with clear and measurable goals. Joanne Bussinger from Blue Hills Community Services remarked:

> [One] success of this initiative so far is that it's brought all kinds of diverse people and organizations to the same table to have the same conversation, and I've been pretty amazed at how collaborative people have been and how excited they are to try and engage these communities to make something happen. (2010)

The Regional Council administers and coordinates the initiative but aims to empower and build the capacity of neighborhood-based groups and leaders to guide the direction of the Zone. The Zone's stated intent to engage the "community in a discussion of the kind of neighborhood [they] want and what needs to be done to create and sustain that neighborhood"—reaffirms the importance of grassroots organizing. Bob Housh, executive director of the Metropolitan Energy Center, also noted,

> It's *really* important for the neighborhood associations to be involved in the planning of this, because—and we talked about the "usual suspects"—unfortunately it's the organizations that are used to doing things with these communities, but it's always those organizations doing something on behalf of the communities, rather than *with* the communities. (2010)

Another key strength is the initiative's identified priorities: housing and weatherization, employment and training, public safety and community services, neighborhood outreach, energy and water conservation, and infrastructure. This range of programming reflects the central tenets of sustainable development (economy, equity, environment) and recognizes the necessity of engagement. In addition to creating committees for each program, a coordinating committee has been established to ensure efforts are streamlined and mutually reinforcing.

Finally, the initiative motivated the creation of links among various service providers throughout the city, as well as coordination among city departments. The city is beginning to evaluate its administrative capacity, modernize processes, and eliminate regulatory barriers within its control. Kimiko Gilmore in the city manager's office explained:

The city coordination is starting to happen. There is now a monthly meeting of all the city folks from departments that have anything to do with the Green Impact Zone, or anything to do with anything that could have to do with the Green Impact Zone; and out of those meetings there have been a lot of "aha" moments about what each department is doing and how they related and can coordinate. And it's not that we don't work together at all, but when you get to the boots on the ground level, you're just doing your job . . . but now I think those synergies are being made at those meetings. (2010)

These strengths—political leadership and cooperation, a commitment to equity, an emphasis on engagement at the local level with simultaneous participation from institutions at the regional level, and coordination across public departments—serve as the pillars of a place-based strategy that is well positioned to accomplish sustainable development. Many of these features set the Zone apart from place-based programs of the past. Where such programs typically have a narrow focus, such as economic investment or affordable housing, the Zone aims to address interrelated issues. Furthermore, the initiative relies on new relationships between institutions and organizations throughout the neighborhood, city, and region. It is a multilevel approach led at the regional level but focused on the local.

The Zone: Early Challenges

While the Zone was an innovative and strategic response prompted by the Recovery Act, the political expediency it required posed enormous challenges. First, the formation of the Zone was so swift that its boundaries were decided with little consultation from members of the target communities. Because the boundaries eventually incorporated parts of four neighborhoods and all of a fifth, collective action was initially stymied. While there was enormous trust in Congressman Cleaver given his history and commitment to justice in the city, in practice the Zone itself came to life without input from neighborhood leaders and residents. Additionally, the rush to apply for funds impeded a more inclusive visioning process. While the Zone intended to engage the community "in a discussion of the kinds of neighborhood residents want and what needs to be done to create and sustain that neighborhood," the committees that made up the initiative in its early phases were themselves developing the vision and setting the programmatic priorities. And although these committees had participation from community-based leaders through the Neighborhood Leadership Committee, this measure proved to be insufficient for ensuring wider resident buy-in and awareness in the early phases.

Compounding the problem of successfully engaging a broader set of local residents in the early planning stages was the fact that many of the expectations that were raised were unrealistic, particularly given the regulatory environment. The most obvious example was the expectation that the initiative could weatherize every home in the Zone within a single year. It is important to note, however, that in proposing this idea, Congressman Cleaver made several key assumptions that actually conformed to conventional wisdom about the U.S. Department of Energy's Weatherization Assistance Program (Brandin 2010).[12] Unfortunately, as the U.S. Department of Energy acknowledged in a 2010 report, many of the agency's own assumptions about the ease and expediency with which weatherization could take place were negated with the introduction of new regulatory requirements under the Recovery Act, such as the requirement that recipients of weatherization funds pay laborers at least the prevailing wage, as determined under the Davis-Bacon Act. Adjusting to this new requirement created an unexpected time lag, and, in the case of Kansas City, the weatherization program did not get the information needed to determine the prevailing wage until mid-summer 2009.

Another local regulation slowed the process of using neighborhood stabilization funds. As Cliff Pouppirt from Blue Hills Community Services explained: "The neighborhood stabilization program out of [the Recovery Act allowed] us to purchase homes that have been foreclosed and rehab them for homeownership; the challenge with this program is that our city has required us to presell the home, which makes the program move much slower than other places" (2010). Many interviewees discussed how these regulatory challenges were intensified by the fact that Kansas City, like many large cities, intentionally separates its development programs; housing, employment, safety, and transportation programs are each managed independently. This phenomenon has implications for both place-based policies, which demand programmatic coordination within a particular geography, and sustainable development, which requires a systems approach.

The Zone: Implications for Urban Policy and Planning

The Recovery Act promised both job creation and a push toward a more energy-efficient future, to be achieved through "shovel ready projects." This had a number of implications for the types of projects that would receive funding. As an entirely new initiative—one that packaged existing projects with proposals for new projects—it was not clear at the time of its inception whether the Zone would be more or less likely to win competitive grants.

What is clear is that the Recovery Act and many of the Obama administration's actions brought new attention and resources to cities while promoting the idea of integrated, place-based, and sustainable development. The creation of the Office of Sustainable Housing and Communities at the Department of Housing and Urban Development (HUD), the funding made available through its Regional Planning Grants, the introduction of the Promise Neighborhoods program from the Department of Education, and Choice Neighborhoods from HUD are just a few examples. Such programs promise to engage regions throughout the country in efforts to advance the livelihoods of people while strengthening place, thereby promoting all three *E*s of sustainability. However, the sequencing paradox that the Zone's staff faced when they were awarded more infrastructure-focused grants and fewer grants that touched on the more immediate social needs of target communities is no small consideration for urban policy makers.

Nonetheless, the Zone experience to date sheds light on both old and new challenges as regions begin to experiment with the idea of sustainable development. The old challenges include issues of competing and conflicting regulatory restrictions and the "silo mentality" that affects all levels of governance, from the federal level down to the local and neighborhood levels, where rooted institutions often fail to coordinate their services even when working for the same target population. Although regulatory challenges lie outside a single initiative or organization's immediate capacity to change, they point to crucial considerations for governing bodies at the municipal, state, and federal levels. This is particularly important because the success of initiatives like the Zone depends on the coordination of public and private sector resources, and the ability of governing bodies at various levels to evaluate and minimize regulatory barriers to promote sustainable development goals without risking the benevolent intent of such regulations.

Some of the new challenges the Zone sheds light on have to do with asking institutions, particularly regional levels of governance, to take on new roles. This becomes especially important in light of the fact that many regional councils and metropolitan planning organizations contributed significantly to today's spatial segregation. Ironically, the same Regional Council now charged with implementing the Zone defended the construction of the Bruce R. Watkins Expressway in the 1960s and 1970s that displaced many African American residents and dismantled neighborhoods in its path. Nonetheless, federal funding is now available for regions to take on a new role in promoting sustainable development, and, in Kansas City, the Regional Council has committed to engaging and empowering some of the region's most distressed communities.

At a national scale, redirecting the work of regional councils and metropolitan planning organizations will be a difficult task. Many regional planning councils do not have deep knowledge about the challenges facing inner cities and lack the ability and capacity to effectively solve neighborhood-level problems (Leavy-Sperounis 2010). Furthermore, such organizations are generally one step removed from city governments; those same city governments, especially in small cities, lack resources and civic leadership (Hoyt and Leroux 2007). However, two partnerships configured in response to the Zone point to ways to ameliorate this dilemma. Both PolicyLink and the University of Missouri at Kansas City play key roles in helping the Regional Council build the kind of knowledge necessary to accomplish sustainable development. In PolicyLink, the Regional Council had a partner with knowledge and experience on issues of race and equity, which enabled them to design an approach intended to benefit the region's most marginalized population. The university is a strong rooted institution with a track record of engaging neighborhood leaders and residents in the Zone. As a result, the university had accumulated local data and knowledge to offer valuable insights about the area and its people. Creating opportunities for bringing these partnerships into the fold will be crucial to success at the regional level.

A final daunting task, in terms of implementing place-based strategies that simultaneously promote the three *E*s (economy, equity, environment), is simply measuring their success. While indicators do exist for evaluating the success of poverty alleviation and sustainable development, none is designed to assess the process of implementation, which is critical to issues of equity. To be certain, a holistic view of sustainability cannot be understood solely in terms of process or outcome. Setting and tracking benchmarks will require participation at all levels of governance—from those who are closest to the ground to those crafting national urban policy—regarding what is important to measure, what success looks like, and who intended beneficiaries of place-based programs are. In practice, the Zone, more than anything else, speaks to the urgency of including engagement as the fourth *E*, as our nation moves toward just, green investment in cities.

Notes

1. In July 1967, President Johnson issued Executive Order No. 11,365 to create the National Advisory Commission on Civil Disorder, which was tasked with investigating "the origins of the recent major civil disorders in our cities, including the basic causes and factors leading to such disorder," and proposing "methods and techniques for averting or controlling such disorders" (Boger 1996, 6).

2. See Chapter 6, by Mackres and Song, for more on the environmental justice movement.

3. The concept of sustainability first emerged in 1987, at the World Commission on Environment and Development, from which emerged a document called the Bruntland Report. Its main concern was with what it called "sustainable development," which it defined as "development that meets the needs of the present without compromising the ability of future generations to meet their needs." The report was later adopted at the United Nation's Conference on Environment and Development, held in Rio de Janeiro in 1992.

4. Urban historian Sam Bass Warner was one of the first to note that while Nichols's work in Kansas City was considered a "city planning triumph," it simultaneously created a "social disaster" due to his rigid use of racially restrictive covenants (Worley 1993, 8). However, as a founder of the Federal Housing Administration, the Urban Land Institute, and the National Association of Homebuilders, Nichols is recognized nationally for his contributions both to Kansas City's development and to the real estate development field more generally (Gotham 2000, 625).

5. It wasn't until 1973 that the U.S. Department of Housing and Urban Development realized how the Land Clearance for Redevelopment Authority "[violated] federal regulations and civil rights statues in its relocation program" (Gotham 2001, 304).

6. Blockbusting was a practice of the real estate and development industries that deceitfully triggered white households to sell their homes at a loss by implying that the presence of racial minorities in their neighborhood would depress property values.

7. The Zone consists of five neighborhoods, an issue discussed later in this chapter.
8. Press conference with Ray Lahood, secretary of the Department of Transportation, February 17, 2009.
9. The original neighborhood partners include Ivanhoe Neighborhood Council, Historic Manheim Park Association, Troostwood Neighborhood Association, 49/63 Neighborhood Association, Blue Hills Neighborhood Association, Town Fork Creek Neighborhood Association, Blue Hills Community Services, Neighborhood Housing Services, Swope Community Builders, and Brush Creek Community Partners.
10. See also Chapter 5, by Brandin and Levitt, for more on the Weatherization Assistance Program. The Davis-Bacon Act is a U.S. federal law that establishes the requirement for paying workers on public works projects no less than the local prevailing wages and benefits paid on similar projects.
11. The original group of other partners included Kansas City Power and Light, Kansas City Area Transportation Authority, City of Kansas City (Missouri), Metropolitan Energy Center, University of Missouri–Kansas City, Full Employment Council, Kansas City Police Department, Kansas City Crime Commission, and Missouri Gas Energy.
12. These attributes were highlighted in a report that discussed the implementation challenges faced by cities throughout the nation. The report explained: "[The Weatherization Program had] an existing programmatic infrastructure, including processes and procedures which had been in place for many years; the techniques for weatherization tasks were well known and comparatively uncomplicated, and the requisite skills were widely available; performance metrics were relatively easy to establish and understand; the potential benefits for low income citizens were easily recognized; and, the potential beneficial impact on energy conservation was obvious" (U.S. Department of Energy 2010).

References

Baxamusa, Murtaza. 2008. "The Third E: Equity + Redistribution as Conditions of Sustainability." *Projections: MIT Journal of Planning* 8: 16–24.

Boger, J. C, and J. W. Wegner. 1996. *Race, Poverty, and American Cities.* Chapel Hill: University of North Carolina Press.

Bolton, Roger. 1992. "'Place Prosperity vs People Prosperity' Revisited: An Old Issue with a New Angle." *Urban Studies* 29 (2): 185.

Brandin, B. 2010. "Capitalizing on a Third Wave of Federal Investment: Reenvisioning an Energy Efficiency Retrofit Strategy for Oakland, California." Master's thesis, Massachusetts Institute of Technology.

Brown, A. Theodore. 1978. *K.C.: A History of Kansas City, Missouri.* Boulder, CO: Pruett Publishing, 1978.

Brush Creek Bulletin. 2004. Volume 6, Issue 5. Kansas City, MO.

Bussinger, Joanne. 2010. Personal interview. January 11.

Calmore, J. O. 1996. "Spatial Equality and the Kerner Commission Report: A Back-to-the-Future Essay." In *Race, Poverty, and American Cities,* edited by John C. Boger and Judith W Wegner, 309–42. Chapel Hill: University of North Carolina Press.

Campbell, Scott. 2003. "Green Cities, Growing Cities, Just Cities? Urban Planning and the Contradictions of Sustainable Development." In *Readings in Planning Theory,* 2nd ed., edited by Scott Campbell and Susan F. Fainstein, 435–58. Malden, MA: Blackwell Publishing.

City of Kansas City, Missouri. FOCUS KCMO Comprehensive Plan (1997).

Dean, Deletta. 2010. Personal interview. February 16.

Dreier, Peter. 2004. "Urban Neglect: George W. Bush and the Cities." *Shelterforce Online,* October, 137.

Fainstein, Susan. 2006. "Planning and the Just City." Presented at the Conference on Searching for the Just City, GSAPP, Columbia University, New York, NY.

Fainstein, Susan S., and Ann Markusen. 1996. "The Urban Policy Challenge: Integrating across Social and Economic Development Policy." In *Race, Poverty, and American Cities,* edited by John C. Boger and Judith W. Wegner, 142–65. Chapel Hill: University of North Carolina Press.

Frisch, Michael. 2010. Personal interview. January 5.

Gilmore, Kimiko. 2010. Personal interview. February 4.

Gotham, Kevin. 2000. "Urban Space, Restrictive Covenants and the Origins of Racial Residential Segregation in a U.S. City, 1900–50." *International Journal of Urban and Regional Research* 24 (3): 616–33.

———. 2001. "A City without Slums: Urban Renewal, Public Housing, and Downtown Revitalization in Kansas City, Missouri." *American Journal of Economics and Sociology* 60 (1): 285–316.

———. 2002a. "Missed Opportunities, Enduring Legacies: School Segregation and Desegregation in Kansas City, Missouri." *American Studies* 43 (2): 5.

———. 2002b. *Race, Real Estate, and Uneven Development: The Kansas City Experience, 1900–2000.* Illustrated edition. Albany: State University of New York Press, 2002.

Housh, Bob. 2010. Personal interview. February 1.

Hoyt, Lorlene, and Andre Leroux. 2007. *Voices from Forgotten Cities: Innovative Revitalization Coalitions in America's Older Small Cities.* Report sponsored by PolicyLink, Oakland, CA; Citizens' Housing and Planning Association, Boston, MA; and MIT School of Architecture and Planning, Cambridge, MA.

Leavy-Sperounis, Marianna. 2010. "Manufacturing Recovery: A Networked Approach to Green Job Creation in Massachusetts Gateway Cities." Master's thesis, Massachusetts Institute of Technology.

May, Margaret. 2010. Personal interview. January 6.

Orszag, Peter R., Melody Barnes, Adolfo Carrion, and Lawrence Summers.

2009. "Developing Effective Place-Based Policies for the FY 2011 Budget." Memorandum, August 11. Washington, DC.

Pouppirt, Cliff. 2010. Personal interview. January 11.

Schirmer, Sherry Lamb. 2002. *A City Divided: The Racial Landscape of Kansas City, 1900–1960.* Columbia: University of Missouri Press.

Serda, Daniel. 2003. "Re-constructing Place and Community: Urban Heritage and the Symbolic Politics of Neighborhood Revitalization." PhD dissertation, Massachusetts Institute of Technology.

Soja, Edward W. 2000. *Postmetropolis: Critical Studies of Cities and Regions.* Oxford, UK: Wiley-Blackwell.

———. 2010. *Seeking Spatial Justice.* Minneapolis: University of Minnesota Press.

U.S. Department of Energy, Office of Inspector General, Office of Audit Services. 2010. *Special Report: Progress in Implementing the Department of Energy's Weatherization Assistance Program under the American Recovery and Reinvestment Act.* OAS-RA-10-04. February 19.

Warm, David. 2010. Personal interview. March 10.

Winnick, L. 1966. "Place Prosperity vs. People Prosperity: Welfare Considerations in the Geographic Redistribution of Economic Activity." *Real Estate Research Program, University of California at Los Angeles, Essay in Urban Land Economics in Honor of the Sixty Fifth Birthday of Leo Grebler,* 273–83.

Worley, William S. 1993. *J. C. Nichols and the Shaping of Kansas City: Innovation in Planned Residential Communities.* Columbia: University of Missouri Press.

4

Network Organizing

A Strategy for Manufacturing Recovery in Lawrence, Massachusetts

Marianna Leavy-Sperounis

Green Jobs and Massachusetts's Gateway Cities

As the economic crisis bore down on cities across the United States during the summer of 2009, the *Boston Globe* reported a particularly crippling effect on the small city of Lawrence, Massachusetts:

> Nowhere is the recession's destructive power felt more than in Lawrence. This city of 70,600—one of the nation's first planned industrial centers, its seal bearing the word "industria" and the image of a bee—has 5,217 jobless residents. The unemployment rate in June was 17.3 percent, the highest in Massachusetts. . . . Almost double the state unemployment rate of 8.7 percent. Higher even than battered Michigan's 15.4 percent, the highest of any state.

More alarming than the numbers was the author's assessment of their impact: "The numbers are staggering and psychically punishing for a city that thought it was on its way back" (Schweitzer 2009).

Joaquin Santana is one Lawrence resident who was fortunate enough to keep his job during the crisis. He moved to the United States from the Dominican Republic in 2005 and came to Lawrence, joining the city's majority Latino and immigrant community. Soon after his arrival, Santana became a member of Lawrence CommunityWorks, Inc., a grassroots community development organization that counts six thousand Lawrence residents among its members.

As of March 2010, Santana was working for Sodexho, a national food service provider. But having been raised in the sun-drenched city of Santo Domingo, Santana had a longtime interest in solar power and wished he could find a job in the clean-energy sector. A year earlier, he had heard at CommunityWorks that green jobs might be coming to Lawrence. "I was talking with Annery Butten," he recalls. "She's in charge of Family Asset Building. . . . She told me they were going to be offering [green-job training] courses, so I let her know I was interested. But the courses never materialized" (Santana 2010).

The program that CommunityWorks had hoped to implement is known as Pathways Out of Poverty, a state grant program to foster green workforce development in Gateway Cities, a group of eleven, once-thriving industrial cities across Massachusetts.[1] While Lawrence's unemployment rate is the highest in the group (18.2 percent), the others are not far behind: Brockton (12.8 percent), Fall River (18.1 percent), Fitchburg (13.3 percent), Haverhill (11.1 percent), Holyoke (12.7 percent), Lowell (12.2 percent), New Bedford (17.8 percent), Pittsfield (10.4 percent), Springfield (14.5 percent), and Worcester (10.8 percent) (Bureau of Labor Statistics 2010).

Located outside the greater Boston area, the Gateway Cities have struggled to reinvent themselves since the 1960s, when the state's manufacturing base began to move south and eventually offshore in search of cheaper labor. As the knowledge- and technology-based economy grew and public policy began to favor new suburban development over investment in older communities, the Gateway Cities struggled to adapt. Their relative geographic isolation from the state's economic mainstream around greater Boston contributed to high unemployment and low tax revenue. The departure of large companies and middle-class residents from such cities had, to varying degrees, depleted their political infrastructures, weakening both civic participation and government accountability (Hoyt and Leroux 2007).

By the 1980s, these cities had become home to the state's growing immigrant communities, with high rates of poverty. In response, state legislators created the Gateway classification and, since then, have periodically targeted them for investment by way of revitalization funding; this investment, unfortunately, has been inconsistent and insufficient to generate long-term growth.

In 2007, a renewal of political cooperation at the state level to invest in the Gateway Cities led the Massachusetts Department of Environmental Affairs to target them for Pathways, its first green-jobs creation program.[2] In Lawrence, CommunityWorks took the lead on a Pathways application and formalized partnerships with a group of local organizations to propose a clean-energy workforce training program. With only five grants to distribute among the eleven cities, however, state officials opted to fund a program in the neighboring city of Lowell, passing over the Lawrence bid in the interest of achieving a greater statewide distribution of funds. Officials assumed that the resources provided to Lowell would extend to Lawrence, given the cities' proximity. According to Mary Beth Campbell, workforce development director with the Massachusetts Clean Energy Center, both the Lawrence and Lowell applications were high on the list of contenders, but the CommunityWorks application ranked just below that from Jobs for Youth, a Boston-based organization serving Lowell (Campbell 2009).

Green jobs have not yet come to Lawrence, and Santana's hope for training in solar installation has yet to be realized. "I've given up," he says, but then qualifies his statement. "No, I haven't totally given up. I am going to keep working in my job and see. I'll keep looking and if a job shows up, then—" He pauses before making his final point. "I would really like to work in clean energy" (Santana 2010).

How to link the entrenched need for employment in the Gateway Cities with investment in the burgeoning clean-energy economy is among the most pressing issues for recovery. How can state and federal stimulus programs best serve cities that suffered not only chronic poverty and unemployment, but also a lack of planning capacity, in the decades leading up to the Great Recession? What specific challenges do these cities face in their attempts to capitalize on available funds? What are the historic roots of these challenges? And how can planners and policy makers help cities overcome such challenges?

Massachusetts: A Leader for Green Jobs?

Massachusetts provides a useful context for analyzing the country's current emphasis on green-jobs creation. With key industry clusters, a robust innovation economy, and healthy export ties, the state appears well positioned to take a leadership role in the American clean-technology economy. Political cooperation to lead the effort also appears strong. In 2008, the Massachusetts House and Senate passed the Green Jobs Act with unanimous support, dedicating $68 million over five years to leverage resources in academic research, technological entrepreneurship, and workforce development to spur growth in its clean-energy sector.[3] The state also boasts a commitment to a reduction in the use of toxic chemicals, a strong record of attracting public and private investment, and a supportive regulatory environment. These conditions—along with leading university research, a well-educated workforce, and a strong advocacy community—provide fertile ground for Massachusetts to promote workforce and community development efforts through clean technology (*Clean Tech* 2007). In 2007, the Pew Charitable Trusts reported that Massachusetts was among twelve states with large and growing clean-energy economies. From 1998 to 2007, a decade when overall job growth in the state decreased by 4.4 percent, clean-energy jobs—which include work in clean energy, conservation and pollution mitigation, energy efficiency, environmentally friendly production, and training and support—grew by 4.3 percent.[4] Massachusetts ranks among the top ten states for employment in four of the five key clean-energy job categories (Pew Charitable Trusts 2009).

It remains to be seen, however, just how well green jobs will meet the needs of the communities most devastated by the recession. During a visit to Boston in 2008, Van Jones, then the White House special advisor for green jobs, enterprise and innovation, noted, "The Massachusetts model, if it includes green pathways out of poverty, could set the template for the other forty-nine states. Washington State has already got off to a good start, California is trying, but there's no comprehensive model that includes low-income people and pathways out of poverty" (Jones 2008). If Massachusetts is a potential leader in green-jobs creation, and if the Gateway Cities are potential hubs for clean technology development and manufacturing, then much can be gained from understanding the experience of the city of Lawrence in its attempts to access, leverage, and implement public program funds.

Lawrence and Lowell: Urban Twins?

Many factors will influence the growth of clean-energy industries in American cities, but an analysis of the green-jobs planning process in Lawrence reveals important information, especially when compared to how that process played out in the neighboring city of Lowell. Situated as they are, a few miles apart along the Merrimack River in northeastern Massachusetts, the two cities conjure up a two-of-a-kind image in the minds of many outside the region: both were designed by and for the textile industry; both were powerhouses during the Industrial Revolution; both were battered by the effects of deindustrialization; and both are now home to large immigrant communities. A 1997 *Boston Globe Magazine* article introduced them in the following way: "They've been mentioned in the same sentence for 150 years now. Sometimes, they're uttered in the same breath: Lowell-and-Lawrence, two old textile cities nine miles apart that share a river, a congressman, a Thanksgiving football rivalry, and a boom-and-bust history. It's easy to think of them as urban twins" (Powers 1997).

Despite relatively low levels of green-jobs development in either place, however, planners and city officials in Lowell have a higher degree of leadership capacity and ability to engage multisectoral partnerships. While Lowell appears poised to capitalize on a range of public and private investment opportunities, Lawrence stagnates. Why would these two cities, perceived as so similar, have such different capacity to plan for green jobs? And what are the implications for jobs programs, like Pathways, that target the Gateway Cities?

First, there are physical and demographic differences. At only six square miles, Lawrence is half the size of Lowell and, with a population of 71,234, it is one and a half times more dense. Lawrence's population is younger than Lowell's. It is also poorer: Almost a quarter of Lawrence families have an income below the poverty level, although the percentage in Lowell (15.5 percent) is high as well, more than double that of the state as a whole (7.1 percent). Lowell's largest racial or ethnic group is white (62.5 percent) and the second-largest group is Asian (17.9 percent), followed by Latino (15.8 percent). In contrast, more than two-thirds of Lawrencians are Latino (U.S. Census Bureau 2006–2008).

Residents of both Lawrence and Lowell have high rates of employment in manufacturing, educational services, and health care. In Lawrence, however, 36 percent of people over the age of twenty-five have less than a high school diploma, compared to 22 percent in Lowell and 12 percent statewide.

The types of rooted institutions, especially institutions of higher education, also look different in these two cities. While Lowell boasts the presence of the University of Massachusetts (the UMass Lowell campus of the state university system) and a downtown location for Middlesex Community College, for many years Lawrence had only a satellite campus of the regional community college, Northern Essex. In 2003, however, Cambridge College, which focuses on working adults, established a Lawrence campus; it is the city's first four-year college. Moreover, since 2002, M.I.T. faculty, students, and staff have worked with city hall and a variety of organizations through the MIT@Lawrence partnership, though M.I.T. does not maintain a physical presence in the city.

These present-day differences have historical and physical origins. Although both cities were founded to support the country's growing textile industry, Lawrence and Lowell had very different original physical and social designs. In a sense, these designs predetermined the capital that would accumulate in Lowell and not in Lawrence, as well as the local leadership capacity that would emerge in Lowell, but not in Lawrence. These factors help to explain the relative absence of rooted institutions to support long-range planning, which today challenges Lawrence's ability to access, leverage, and implement just green investment.

The regional cooperation between Lawrence and Lowell—which the state assumed, when planning for Pathways, would spread the benefits of funding programs—is weak at best. In a context where resources are scarce, Lowell and Lawrence sometimes find themselves playing a zero-sum development game: instead of fostering a collaborative environment, the Gateway Cities classification seems to feed competition between such cities, limiting the potential investment in Lawrence and leaving the region less well-off as a whole. As an unintended consequence, such programs may perpetuate place-based inequalities instead of alleviating them, leading already struggling cities to suffer the most egregious effects of the recession.

However, despite disadvantages in Lawrence, an innovative network organizing strategy developed by CommunityWorks to enhance civic engagement can be applied in the area of green-jobs creation. In the end, this chapter proposes a place-based, networked, and regional approach to green-jobs creation that can support Lawrence and its neighboring Gateway Cities. The insights, however, will prove useful to cities and regions throughout Massachusetts and beyond.

Efforts to Create Green Jobs in Lawrence

In the fall of 2008, Eric Mackres, a graduate student working with the MIT@Lawrence partnership, gathered Lawrence civic leaders to launch a citywide strategy for creating green jobs. Meeting participants formalized the group as the Lawrence Green Jobs Working Group, a multisectoral partnership to foster the creation of green jobs in Lawrence. After an uncertain beginning, the working group merged with the newly formed Green Jobs Advisory Council of the Merrimack Valley Workforce Investment Board. But by the time the groups merged, limited leadership capacity had already begun to stymie efforts at green-jobs creation in Lawrence; in the absence of strong leadership and effective communication, members of the original working group found their work challenged by groups that should have been at the table. For example, CommunityWorks took the lead on the Pathways Out of Poverty Grant application and organized a partnership that included Groundwork Lawrence, MIT@Lawrence, Northern Essex, and three local clean-energy firms to serve as advisers on curriculum development. But as CommunityWorks staff prepared the application they discovered that the Workforce Investment Board was submitting a separate, competing grant request (McCann 2010). Ultimately, both applications lost to Lowell's.

One challenge was posed by limited demand. Construction companies and home improvement contractors already seemed to have the ability to perform energy-efficiency retrofits without a skill upgrade or the creation of new jobs. Area manufacturers were not generating new workforce demands either (Carberry 2010). Without a clearly articulated demand for workers, strong municipal leadership, or private investment, the citywide effort to create green jobs failed to gain momentum. The true cost of Lawrence's perennial disadvantages would become all the more evident as Lowell's strategic process progressed.

Efforts to Create Green Jobs in Lowell

In Lowell, meanwhile, a citywide strategy for green-jobs creation began as early as 2002, when staff at the UMass Lowell Center for Family, Work, and Community led a sustainability workshop for the city. About sixty people participated in the workshop and produced an action plan, leading to a chapter on sustainability in the city's master plan. Local academics and government officials spearheaded the creation of the Green Building Commission dedicated to green design, construction, and development advocacy and practice throughout Lowell.

In Lowell, the green building commissioners act as direct advisers to city hall. They include representatives of local banks, the Lowell Planning Board, UMass Lowell's Toxic Use Reduction Institute and Center for Family, Work, and Community, Northeastern University, Harvard University, and local companies involved in real estate development, construction, plumbing, architecture, biotech, and sustainable business planning. Among their activities, they work with UMass Lowell and

Lowell-based Middlesex Community College to develop education and outreach programs focused on clean-energy fields such as waste reduction, recycling, building materials and techniques, energy efficiency, air quality, and site and building design.

While Lawrence failed because of a lack of coordination, Lowell's experience highlights the benefits of strong municipal leadership. After clean energy was identified as an emerging industry for the city, Lowell began actively recruiting firms in environmental engineering and other forms of green technology (Park 2010).[5]

Leadership alone will not guarantee jobs for residents, but its value is demonstrated by the city's success with winning the Pathways grant. David Turcotte, a UMass Lowell alumnus and senior program manager with the Center for Family, Work, and Community, explained: "When Jobs for Youth came into town to apply for Pathways, they organized a stakeholder meeting with the various players in workforce development in the city. I attended the meeting with some members of the Green Building Commission. We voted and provided a letter of support for their application" (2010). A diverse range of organizations also partnered with Jobs for Youth on their application.[6] No one knows whether the city's written support of the team's application was the deciding factor that secured Lowell's ranking over Lawrence, but the city's initiative demonstrates its leadership capacity, a critical factor in capturing limited state resources.[7]

Another key advantage for Lowell was the presence of UMass Lowell, which houses the United States' only accredited undergraduate program in plastics engineering and is a school with considerable strengths in green chemistry and nanotechnology. According to Aaron Clausen, an associate planner with the city's Division of Planning and Development, the university enables smaller businesses to expand their capacity by functioning as partners on various projects (2010). UMass Lowell also employs some of state's leading experts in clean technology.

A final advantage of Lowell over Lawrence is the former city's emphasis on the essential role of locally embedded planning and development institutions such as the Lowell Financial and Development Corporation, established in 1975 to finance economic revitalization in the city's downtown. In 2009, when the U.S. Department of Energy launched the Energy Efficiency and Conservation Block Grant program, Lowell budgeted $100,000 of its $954,000 grant allocation to capitalize a financial incentive program to encourage energy efficiency and renewable energy improvements in commercial buildings. The city selected Lowell Financial to manage the program, and the city might not have supported the program without it—with its impressive combination of qualifications, including a close relationship with the city's planning department, experience managing revolving loan funds, and capacity to help building owners leverage additional funds.

Affirmation of Lowell's promise to lead in green-jobs creation came on April 21, 2010, when the White House announced the twenty-five winners of the national Ramp Up to Retrofit grant program and Lowell was the only Massachusetts city selected. The city proposed to develop a carbon-neutral Park and Preservation District with help from the state's historic preservation office and the National Park Service.

"We Have the River in Common—But It Diverges There"

The differences between Lowell and Lawrence detailed above—differences in rooted institutions, in leadership patterns, in capacity for green-job creation—are not accidental, but the product of a long and complicated history.

Patricia McGovern is a former state senator who hails from Lawrence. She represented the city in the Massachusetts State Legislature from 1981 to 1993 and became the first woman to chair the powerful Massachusetts Senate Ways and Means Committee. Having lived in the region for her whole life, she knows both Lawrence and Lowell well. The differences between their efforts to create green jobs, she says, are deeply entrenched: "We have the river in common—but it diverges there" (McGovern 2010).

Physical and Social Design

Incorporated in 1826 and 1847, respectively, Lowell and Lawrence are both planned cities, constructed by textile manufacturing companies to harness the power of the Merrimack River. Lowell was named for Francis Cabot Lowell, a Yankee entrepreneur who traveled to England as a young man and memorized the design of the British power loom. In 1813, Lowell and his associates formed the Boston Manufacturing Company, and they developed the first American textile mill in Waltham, Massachusetts, the following year.

Determined not to replicate the degradation and squalor he saw among English factory workers, Lowell envisioned a labor force of young women who would work no more than four or five years in the factories and live under the watchful eye of a housemother. He died only three years after the development of the Waltham mill, but his social vision for American manufacturing communities lived on. Partners at the Boston Manufacturing Company named their next project, the city of Lowell, in his honor (Schinto 1995, 75–77). The city quickly emerged as a major hub for New England textile production (Gittell 1992, 9).

The first twenty years of the "Lowell Experiment" (1826–1846) strongly influenced the plan for Lawrence. In the 1830s, men from some of New England's most elite families had begun to quietly purchase adjoining plots of land, totaling three and half square miles from the town of Methuen and two and half square miles from neighboring Andover. In 1845, they formalized themselves as the Essex Company, named Abbot Lawrence their president, and combined their parcels of land to create the city of Lawrence. Developers took to the Merrimack River, as they had in Lowell, and built the Great Stone Dam, a great feat of engineering for its time.

Despite the financial and perceived moral success of Lowell, the plan for Lawrence incorporated critical differences. The most explicit of these was the prioritization of profit: Lawrence would be a moneymaker, with an emphasis on productivity and profit (Gittell 1992, 9). Lawrence's mills were built larger than Lowell's and there were more of them.[8] When Lowell began it had just two mills; Lawrence was built with eleven. The Essex Company also reduced the amount of space separating the mills (Schinto 1995, 79). McGovern's description of the plan for Lawrence captures the profit-extraction motive that informed the city's founding: "By the time they got to Lawrence, they said, 'Let's just build the mills.' They were far less interested in social experimentation. They took six square miles, which is small. And they said, 'You're Lawrence'" (McGovern 2010).

Without the paternalistic, mixed-income vision of industrial society that had guided the creation of Lowell, Lawrence was designed to be a machine, churning out the world's largest supply of wool, a simple exporter of wealth to the region; Essex Company shareholders never intended for the money produced by Lawrence to stay in the city. In a sense, it was the orphaned twin, less a city and more an industrial artifact, and its design would have long-lasting implications for the city's economic viability. As Fred Carberry, who had served as director of Lawrence's Department of Planning, describes: "The city of Lawrence was designed to be very compact for a reason: To allow tens of thousands of workers to make their way back and forth to the mills on foot. And now we're in a different age and that compact design is our limiting factor" (2010).

Concentration of Capital

The respective plans for Lawrence and Lowell significantly influenced whether or not affluent neighborhoods were formed. McGovern explains how a middle class emerged in Lowell but did not in Lawrence: "In Lowell, even if the center began to deteriorate, they could keep a middle class. In Lawrence, there are very few outlying areas to keep a middle class, so when the city started to decline, the middle class just left. In was too hard to keep a socioeconomically diverse group within the city. It was too small" (2010). The lack of economic diversity in Lawrence, relative to Lowell, persists today. While median household income in Lowell ($50,944) is roughly 75 percent of median income across the state ($64,684), in Lawrence ($32,007) it is less than 50 percent (MassInc, 2010a, 2010b). Lawrence has maintained small pockets of middle-class wage earners in the Prospect Hill, Tower Hill, and Mount Vernon neighborhoods, but when the city's principal owner—the Essex Company— left town, it left little capital behind. The overall Lawrence tax base has remained low, and the city has struggled to generate revenue.

Lowell, in contrast, maintained an organized elite, concentrated largely in the Belvidere neighborhood. This group would go on to drive the city's efforts at reinvention and revitalization when its manufacturing base began to deteriorate. Bankers, members of the university, and a cultural identity fostered by civic leaders would provide channels for future federal and state investment.

Leadership Capacity

Paul Marion, a Lowell native, published poet, and now executive director of community and cultural affairs at UMass Lowell, has spent years studying Lowell's history and evolution as a cultural hub; he is, in many ways, the city's resident storyteller. One story he tells, relating to the diverging paths of Lowell and Lawrence, is of the "Mogan-Tsongas nexus" (Marion 2010). Patrick Mogan moved to Lowell from the town of Norwood when he married into a political family in the city. He began his career in the city as a teacher and went on to become a school principal and eventually the superintendent of schools. Along the way, he acted as a community organizer and the city's unofficial long-range planner: "Mogan was all about grassroots empowerment. He had an intellectual integrity and expansiveness that was inspiring. It drew people to him and his vision" Marion 2010). His vision was one of Lowell as a self-sustaining place, one with a rich history to leverage into economic and social benefit. Investing in the next company or industry, whether it was textiles, shoes, or electronics, would never guarantee an escape from the boom-and-bust cycle. Instead, he argued, the city needed to invest in the things that could not be taken away: the state forest, the rivers, the architecture, and the social history. His vision gave rise to a diversified plan for the city's economy, attracted attention and validation from elite schools like Harvard and M.I.T., and led to creation of the Lowell National Historical Park, established in 1978, which showcases the city's mills and industrial heritage. "The National Park became one manifestation of Mogan's philosophy," says Marion. "He set in motion an epochal transformation of the city" (Marion 2010).

Where Mogan developed academic and cultural assets and pursued a grassroots path to community empowerment, Paul Tsongas sought political and financial capital through a top-down approach. A Lowell native and son of a Greek immigrant, Tsongas graduated from Dartmouth College and Yale Law School, became a Lowell city councillor in 1969, and went on to serve as Middlesex county commissioner. Beginning in 1974, he served two terms in the U.S. House of Representatives for Massachusetts' Fifth Congressional District and, in 1978, defeated a Republican incumbent to win a seat in the U.S. Senate. He held this seat until 1984, when he retired due to illness. Tsongas reentered the national political scene in 1992 with an unsuccessful bid for the Democratic presidential nomination. He succumbed to non-Hodgkin's lymphoma in 1997. In 2007, his widow, Niki, ran for and won the Fifth District seat that he once occupied.

Despite their differences, Tsongas and Mogan were allies as Tsongas went about securing federal and state money to support Mogan's vision of economic development. In particular, Tsongas negotiated federal legislation for the Lowell National Historical Park and played a key role in the 1991 designation of the University of Lowell as a campus in the University of Massachusetts system (Sperounis 2010).[9]

In the Lawrence story, no one has promoted a vision for the city or been able to secure public resources in the way that Mogan and Tsongas did in Lowell. Since 1895, of the eleven individuals who have served in the U.S. House of Representatives representing Massachusetts' Fifth Congressional District, seven have been residents of Lowell, but only two have come from Lawrence. Marion observes, "Even with Pat Mc-Govern, Lawrence has struggled" (Marion 2010). Although not equivalent in status to that of a U.S. senator, McGovern's position as the state senator representing Lawrence could theoretically have been more powerful than that of U.S. senator in its ability to secure resources for her hometown. But the fact that McGovern brought Lawrence Heritage State Park to Lawrence, while Tsongas's reach enabled him to secure funds for a national park, testifies to the true power of Tsongas's leadership. Rooted institutions like historical parks and academic campuses provide much-needed infrastructure to support development activity, and in the Lawrence-Lowell case, they also illuminate the importance of leadership capacity.

Though there have been strong civic leaders in Lawrence, the vacuum created by the Essex Company's departure led to a patronage system in local government, preventing the recruitment and nurturing of talented professionals. As a result, Lawrence planning and politics were often reactionary in character, such as attempts in the 1980s by predominantly Irish American city officials to keep out a growing Latino population through the exclusion of affordable housing.

Bill Traynor, co–executive director of CommunityWorks, was born and raised in Lawrence and graduated from the University of Lowell; he also taught there during the five years that he worked as a community organizer in Lowell before returning to his hometown in 1999. He describes the lack of vision in Lawrence in the early 1980s:

> The mayor ran on the platform that they were not going to take any more public money. His perspective was that public money was forcing the city to build affordable housing. In this negative political climate, there was no one group of people saying, "Hey, wait a second, there's a path and we need to stay on this path in the long term." (Traynor 2010)

Traynor contrasts this scene with his memory of Lowell's political environment, where a powerful and well-organized regime ran the city. They had a vision and, to some extent, the means to promote their vision. "There were disagreements," says Traynor, "but when the time came to vote and move things forward, it happened" (2010). At this time, the elite included Tsongas, the president of the University of Lowell, the owners of the city's pro-growth newspaper, the *Lowell Sun,* and bankers who either owned or ran banks in the city. They have had successes, like the national historical park, as well as failures, like the 1993 collapse of the high-tech giant Wang Laboratories. Through it all, however, Lowell's leaders maintained a robust political infrastructure and influential rooted institutions to channel public and private investment.

Planning and Rooted Institutions

Perhaps the largest variable distinguishing Lowell's planning environment from Lawrence's is the Lowell Plan, a gathering of civic leaders and businesspeople that has guided the city for three decades. Today, the Lowell Plan counts thirty-four board members, including the city manager, the mayor, the assistant city manager for planning and development, the superintendent of schools, chairs from the university, the president of the community college, and the publisher of the *Lowell Sun.* Paul Marion explains the group's purpose:

> The Lowell Plan has its critics, but it's been an incredibly effective community tool. Every month for thirty years, they have brought influential people in the community around the same table for a continuing dialogue about the city. Paul [Tsongas] would say, 'The Lowell Plan is a Chamber of Commerce that works." (2010)

The group does not take public money so as to avoid any conflicts of interest with city hall (Cook 2010). As a result, it institutionalizes the type of public-private partnership that many cite in explaining Lowell's success.

Jim Cook is executive director of the Lowell Plan. He explains the city's path toward a more diversified economy: "Wang was good for us, but when they went bankrupt in ninety-three, we were in trouble. It's taken a lot of work, but I think we're stronger now than we were then" (2010). What is remarkable here is not so much Lowell's experience with a boom-and-bust economy but the fact that it rebounded, emerging from upheaval with vigor and keen insights.

As the companion organization to the Lowell Plan, Lowell Financial has provided capital to finance a vision for a revitalized Lowell. Cook, who oversees both groups, explains that banks had essentially (but unofficially) redlined neighborhoods in the city in the 1970s: "Lowell was in bad shape. No bank wanted to lend money. At the time Paul Tsongas was in Congress, so in 1975, he and a banker, George Duncan, got together and said, "We have to turn this around'" (2010). With seed funding from nine Lowell banks, Tsongas and Duncan established Lowell Financial, a tax-exempt revolving loan fund to provide secondary financing for the rehabilitation of buildings in downtown Lowell. Tsongas knew the presidents of all the Lowell-controlled banks and could pressure them to come to the table. But, as Cook notes, Lowell Financial also served the banks' interests by protecting the value of their downtown properties. The fund's focus changes every year, but it continues to provide a consistent institutional and financial basis for long-range, strategic planning in the city.[10]

The consensus among interviewees—from Traynor at the local level, to Carberry and Cook at a regional level, and to McGovern at the state level—is that Lawrence has lacked an effective plan for decades and that leaders have been unable to form any sort of multisectoral partnership analogous to the Lowell Plan. Cook recalls that in the mid-1990s, Lawrence officials established the Lawrence Strategy, using the Lowell Plan as a model. They excluded public officials from serving on the board, however, exacerbating tensions between public and private entities in the city. "It actually split the community even further," Cook said (2010).

The longtime absence of partnerships to support strategic planning in areas like capital improvement, housing, and workforce development in Lawrence has taken a tremendous toll on the city's ability to position itself for the twenty-first century. Traynor offers his impression: "I've been connected to Lawrence for over thirty years and I've never seen a strategy, plan, or idea about how you move Lawrence into the next century. This is over a thirty-year period when it's been clear that cities like Lawrence have to reinvent themselves" (2010). In the context of the current economic crisis, Lawrence's lack of leadership and strategic-planning capacity places it at a distinct disadvantage. Bob Halpin has worked in the region for decades and served as president and CEO of the Merrimack Valley Economic Development Council from February 2000 to May 2010. He explains why employment challenges in Lawrence may not be specific to green jobs: "I'm not sure that the challenge in cultivating green employment in Lawrence is any different than any other sector. When it comes down to workforce, getting a green job is the same as getting any job. The hard skills and the soft skills, they're the same" (Halpin 2010). If cultivating green jobs is similar to cultivating employment in other sectors, the implication is positive for a city that has enjoyed recent success in workforce development. But Lawrence has not. For Lawrence to succeed in the modern economy—green or otherwise—then local, state, and federal policy makers will need to work together to build local capacity to implement a plan, leveraging both the city's internal assets and its connections to the region.

Manufacturing Recovery

The word "manufacturing" can refer not only to Lowell and Lawrence's once and potentially future role in the state's manufacturing economy; according to Merriam-Webster's online, the word also means "to produce according to an organized plan and with division of labor," and it underscores the planning necessary for residents of these communities to recover from decades of systematic disinvestment. Here, I offer three principles to guide recovery: an understanding of place, a regional scope, and a network organizing strategy.

An Understanding of Place

All Gateway Cities face distinct obstacles to development. A strong Gateway Cities program focused on green-job creation will aim to equalize the advantages among cities. The first step is to understand the unique histories, political economies, planning environments, and assets in these cities. In Lawrence, the state and federal government must work to support local planning capacity. The political climate under the Obama administration is conducive to this type of planning, which Shaun Donovan, secretary of Housing and Urban Development, describes as "the New Federalism."

> This isn't about returning to the old way of doing business—the one-size-fits-all approach in the development of public housing or urban renewal. It's about using new tools that help us partner with

local governments in ways that recognize the variations of place and the communities we all serve in one way or another. That is the New Federalism. (2009)

As evidenced by the Gateway Cities classification, grouping cities according to their economic history has value, but this approach may overlook gaps in local capacity. As Donovan makes clear, it is essential for states and the federal government to acknowledge "variations in place" and to use the individual, local challenges to development as the starting point for capacity building by way of partnerships.

A Regional Scope

Lawrence needs local planning capacity, but its economy is also an inherently regional one. Designed as an exporter of financial capital, the city today manifests its relationship to its region in the labor capital it supplies to surrounding communities. In 2006, Andrew Herlihy, then regional industry manager of the Merrimack Valley Workforce Investment Board, explained:

> Lawrence produces workers for the entire region, in literally every direction. Lawrence residents are working in everything from retail and landscaping in Methuen, to nursing homes in Andover, to manufacturing, warehousing and transportation in Amesbury and Newburyport, to the industrial parks in Wilmington and Haverhill. Hospitality businesses in Southern Maine are even looking to Lawrence for workers. We are a labor-exporting city. (*Our Money* 2006)

Regional planning poses a particular challenge in Massachusetts where state regulations largely limit planning to the municipal level. Although regional planning organizations operate throughout the state, a lack of strong institutional capacity has led to a climate of what might be called "competitive regionalism." With limited funds made available through programs such as Pathways, state officials strive for a regional distribution of money; without mechanisms to facilitate communication and coordination among cities, the impact of such programs is limited to the grant winner. Ironically, the Gateway Cities classification separates such cities from their regions. For example, though Gateway City mayors have formed a caucus to lobby collectively for state resources, those whose cities are in close proximity to each other have taken competitive approaches to planning (Halpin 2010). For Lawrence, this means that city officials do not plan jointly with their counterparts in neighboring cities like Lowell. Many communities will need capacity to address cross-jurisdictional and regional issues in order to strategically and collaboratively develop their economies.

A Network Organizing Strategy

How can the cities of Lawrence and Lowell better coordinate their efforts to create green jobs? What might a coordinated strategy look like? How do we recognize the variations in place and imagine productive partnerships between cities?

The network organizing strategy developed by CommunityWorks, which has provided the basis for $30 million of investment in the city over the last ten years, offers guidance on many of these questions. CommunityWorks first implemented its network organizing approach in 1999 by applying network theory in the community development context to create a "demand environment for change." Network members believe, for example, that community groups should be flexible, easy to join, and willing to change course; residents should have many rewarding ways to participate in public life, to get to know people, and to have fun with each other (Traynor and Andors 2005).[11]

Now with more than six thousand members in Lawrence—engaged in campaigns, adult education, real estate projects, and youth development programs—the strategy has attracted national attention. CommunityWorks staff and other members are careful to note, though, that this is not a model that can be exported and applied from one place to another. Rather, network organizing is a set of principles that groups can test and adapt to a range of environments; it will look different in each of them.[12] Several of these principles might prove helpful in creating green jobs in Lawrence and other Gateway Cities.

Engaging People as Agents of Change

In CommunityWorks' approach, the network's hubs and nodes are forums—such as a group of women saving money to start small businesses or a cadre of residents participating in a leadership development program—that serve different, but complementary, functions in advancing the aims of the network. The existence of multiple hubs and nodes is essential to the health of a network. In other words, a strong network cannot rely on one organization, a charismatic leader, or a booming company, but instead requires strong and weak links among its varied hubs and nodes.

The hubs and nodes of a green-jobs network might be organized by elected officials who advocate on behalf of the region at the state and federal levels and include real estate developers who support clean-technology incubation. There is a particularly pressing need for colleges and universities in Gateway Cities to function as hubs and nodes, taking more proactive roles in sparking and maintaining multisectoral partnerships.

These hubs and nodes are connected by human relationships. The network draws its strength not only from the strongest of its relationships—those between individuals and groups with long histories of connection and trust—but also from its weakest. Weak links provide new opportunities for people by giving them access to information and resources not normally within reach. Weak links also ensure that when a node or hub suffers a setback, it does not unravel the entire system. As an analytical tool, network organizing helps to reveal, from the inside out, the connections that civic leaders and residents may have overlooked. For Lawrence and Lowell, it affirms that the pieces needed to support green jobs are largely in place. No new institutions necessarily need to be created, but new relationships must be forged, existing groups must be strengthened, and the local government's capacity to lead and collaborate must grow. To begin, weak links could be forged between Lawrence's and Lowell's directors of economic development, between a green-chemistry researcher at UMass Lowell and a mill developer in Lawrence, or between a middle-school science teacher and the directors of the workforce investment boards of nearby communities.

These connections do not occur automatically, so CommunityWorks has formalized the role of individuals who actively connect people to each other in a network. They are called "weavers," and their primary responsibility is to be curious—about people's stories, interests, and relationships—and to help connect people to other people and activities in the network. In this way, network organizing actively engages people as agents of change. By activating otherwise latent relationships, weavers provide much-needed network stability. Similarly, groups that have demonstrated some degree of leadership, such as the Economic Development Council, UMass Lowell, and the Clean Energy Center, are potential weavers for a green-jobs network. Articulation of their roles as weavers will help to formalize the activity of engaging people and institutions as agents of change in this area.

Finally, network organizing emphasizes place-based assets. As in Mogan's vision for Lowell, it values and capitalizes on what exists, what can grow, and what cannot be taken away. In Lawrence, the assets that the city brings to the state's growing emphasis on green-jobs creation include a supportive environment for small businesses (Sidell 2010),[13] affordable building stock for commercial and residential use, easy transit and highway accessibility, dense walkable neighborhoods and commercial corridors, a highly organized CommunityWorks membership, high environmental-planning capacity at Groundwork Lawrence, a rich industrial history, a compelling story of renewal, and a large youth population.

Goals for Creating Green Jobs in Massachusetts

Under the current and disconnected approach to creating green jobs, many goals are difficult to accomplish. The adoption and adaptation of a network organizing strategy might enable civic leaders to realize two otherwise unattainable goals. One is a short-term opportunity for Lawrence mill owners to incubate small clean-energy companies, bringing to market the intellectual capital developed at UMass Lowell (Sidell 2010).[14] Capitalizing on the city's real estate assets and investing in a range of small companies, including those that produce clean-technology products and those that use clean processes to manufacture other products, can help the city avoid tying its future to the fate of any one company or industry. Subsidies from the state, along with federal support, will make such incubation financially feasible for local development teams. An entity such as an economic development council could serve as weaver, facilitating such connections.

In the long term, a network organizing strategy might also enhance the opportunity to develop and implement systems to give Lawrence's young people the skills to acquire green jobs. When I met with Joaquin Santana, I asked how he would advise planners and policymakers on green-job creation. He replied: "My suggestion is that they try to build consciousness among students, so that from now on, they learn about clean energy. This is the moment; the students are the future. If tomorrow, we run out of oil, they'll have the knowledge that other types of energy exist and the ability to make the most of them" (Santana 2010). Such opportunities will become more readily available as the flow of information, resources, and people improves. For example, networking Lawrence and Lowell might accelerate the implementation of curricula to track middle school students through clean-energy-oriented science and technology programs. These curricula could be "vertical," linking educational opportunities at all levels—middle school, high school, community college, and university. Young people who are not yet prepared for the university could first go to the community college to receive training in clean technology. Curricula could also be "horizontal," linking educators and young people to each other and to opportunities across communities. By creating direct connections among secondary schools and institutions of higher education, Lawrence students would have better access to UMass Lowell. In turn, university researchers would have improved access to Lawrence's assets.

Faculty at UMass Lowell are currently seeking funds to implement a vertical curriculum in local public schools that will track students in a course of science and technology studies from middle school to the university (Forrant 2010, personal interview).[15] Overlaying a horizontal network might provide new opportunities to students in Lawrence. Adapted to fields like nanotechnology, green manufacturing, and green chemistry, a vertical network—in which the schools in one community not only function as a node, but also have weak links to public educational nodes in other communities—will create points of entry and advancement for youths in the way Santana describes. In this scenario, the university functions as a weaver, facilitating crucial connections in the network.

Implementing a Network Organizing Strategy in Massachusetts

Participation at the local, regional, state, and federal levels is essential to the development of green-jobs networks supporting Lawrence, Lowell, and other Gateway Cities. Although a great deal can be accomplished through the private sector, no substitute exists for a city government that actively seeks connections with other communities; local and regional political cooperation is essential. Strong leadership from UMass Lowell and a willingness to connect university assets to opportunities outside the city, as well as a strengthened role for the economic development council (which will require significant state political and financial support), is also important. Finally, businesses—which benefit from regional agglomeration—must ally with regional entities in this effort.

To foster stronger cross-jurisdictional collaboration, especially among communities such as Lawrence that lack robust leadership and planning capacity, the state and federal government can make resources available to cities for evaluating their assets and determining how to connect to a regional strategy. Such a process could encourage cities with weak leadership and planning capacity to adopt nontraditional approaches to green-jobs creation.

Lastly, the state might consider issuing requests for proposals to fund coordination among geographically proximate Gateway Cities such as Lowell/Lawrence, New Bedford/Fall River, and Springfield/Holyoke.[16] Support for individual cities, combined with an articulation of shared agenda and performance expectations, could greatly enhance the vitality of these cities and their regions. Place-based policy making and program implementation will require the time and willingness to understand the histories of individual cities and to integrate state planning with local political, economic, and social systems. Although it is the nature of state and federal agencies to support cities that are already poised to succeed, the real job of the states and of the federal government is to help the cities that are least likely to prosper.

Conclusion

Pew Charitable Trusts finds that, at the federal level, investments in clean energy are likely to increase in 2010, when the government is slated to spend one-third of its clean energy stimulus funding (Pew Charitable Trusts 2009). Although the United States dominates in clean-energy venture finance and technology innovation, Pew finds that it falls behind other countries in manufacturing. Public subsidies to support small-scale manufacturing in clean technologies are as critical as subsidies to cash-strapped states for coordinating green-jobs creation among localities.

Recovering from the Great Recession requires a place-based, regional approach that does not naturally occur within our current system. Xavier de Souza Briggs, associate professor of sociology and urban planning at M.I.T., who is now serving as associate director for general government programs at the White House Office of Management and Budget, explains the need to align federal policy with local realities:

> You're going to see us take this notion of place-based policy and use it as a discipline, use it as a focusing device across agencies and within them across their programs. . . . If we can create real strategies that strengthen communities, both rural and urban, what's the most appropriate role for the federal investments and for regulations that shape local action? (Simon and Hersh 2009)

It is vital to invest in the future of the country's once-thriving industrial cities, which are now experiencing high rates of unemployment. By implementing place-based, regionally coordinated, and networked strategies for green-job creation in these communities, we can build the capacity necessary for a just and green recovery.

Notes

1. Pathways aimed to support "job training programs directed toward the clean energy industry that move training participants towards financial self-sufficiency" and targeted individuals in poor households. "Pathways out of Poverty," Massachusetts Clean Energy Center, *www.masscec.com/index. cfm?pid=11185&cdid=11277.*
2. Following implementation of the 2008 Green Jobs Act, the Clean Energy Center assumed control of the state's green jobs programs.
3. Under the Green Jobs Act, Massachusetts defines clean energy as "advanced and applied technologies that significantly reduce or eliminate the use of energy from non-renewable sources, including but not limited to: energy efficiency, demand response, energy conservation and those technologies powered in whole or in part by the sun, wind, water, biomass, alcohol, wood, fuel cells, or any renewable or non-depletable or recyclable fuel." Of the $68 million, $43 million came from the FY07 surplus and $5 million dollars per year came from the Massachusetts Renewable Energy Trust, now part of the Clean Energy Center ("Governor Patrick" 2008).
4. Pew Charitable Trusts defines "large and growing" clean energy economies as those in which the number of clean energy jobs exceeded the national average (Pew Charitable Trusts 2009).
5. Park is director of economic development for the City of Lowell.
6. Affiliates and partners on the grant include Community Teamwork (Lowell's

Community Action Program agency), YouthBuild, the Coalition for a Better Acre (a community development corporation), the Cambodian Mutual Assistance Association, the United Teen Equality Center, the Lowell Adult Education Center, the New England Consortium (a worker health and safety training organization based at UMass Lowell). The Institute for Environmental Education (New England's largest environmental workforce training organization, based in Greater Lowell) is a regional partner on the grant.

7. After the Jobs for Youth grant was awarded, the Massachusetts Board of State Examiners of Electricians issued a ruling that only licensed electricians could perform solar installation. This prompted the Clean Energy Center to revise the Jobs for Youth contract to permit weatherization-training activities, but that led to a significant delay in program implementation ("Massachusetts Electricians" 2009).

8. Lawrence's Wood Mill, for example, is almost one-third mile long. Its length is roughly equivalent to the height of the Empire State Building, which is 1,250 feet tall.

9. Sperounis is former executive vice-chancellor of University of Massachusetts, Lowell.

10. In the summer of 1978, Lowell received a $5 million Urban Development Action Grant from the federal government for job creation. Originally intended as a gift to Wang Laboratories to move their headquarters to Lowell, the city negotiated to provide the money as a loan at 3 percent interest, to be managed as a revolving loan fund by Lowell Financial. This allowed Lowell Financial to no longer depend solely on bank contributions (Cook 2010).

11. For further descriptions of Lawrence CommunityWorks and the network organizing approach, see Traynor and Andors 2005; Traynor 2008; Preer 2005.

12. CommunityWorks has consulted with groups in cities such as Denver (CO), Des Moines (IA), Hartford (CT), Louisville (KY), McAllen (TX), Oakland (CA), and Silver Spring (MD). Between 2003 and 2007, I had the opportunity to participate in several of these visits.

13. Sidell is a prominent developer and property manager in Lawrence.

14. Sidell is a member of the development team for the Union Crossing mill redevelopment project. He expressed keen interest in incubating clean technology start-ups at Union Crossing, but also voiced concerns about financial feasibility (Sidell, personal interview 2010).

15. Forrant is professor of history and codirector of the Center for Family, Work, and Community at University of Massachusetts–Lowell.

16. The state requests evidence of regional partnerships in some grant programs, but leaders in both Lawrence and Lowell said the state should require formal partnerships and provide direct subsidies in order to better facilitate collaboration between municipalities and between organizations in different cities.

References

Andors, Jessica. 2010. Personal interview. March 5.

Bureau of Labor Statistics. 2010. *Current Population Survey. www.bls.gov/cps/.*

Campbell, Marybeth. 2009. Personal interview. December 21.

Carberry, Fred. 2010. Personal interview. January 14.

"City of Lowell, MA: Energy Efficiency and Conservation Block Grant Application—Budget Justification." Internal document, city of Lowell, MA.

Clausen, Aaron. 2010. Personal interview. January 21.

Clean Energy Workforce Development Forum—Report. 2009. University of Massachusetts–Lowell, June.

Clean Tech: An Agenda for a Healthy Economy. 2007. Lowell Center for Sustainable Production, University of Massachusetts Lowell, December.

Cook, Jim. 2010. Personal interview. January 20.

Donovan, Shaun. 2009. "A New Federalism Focused on Place." Lecture at the Harvard Graduate School of Design, Cambridge, MA, October 26.

Forrant, Bob. 2010. Personal interview. February 12.

Gittell, Ross J. 1992. *Renewing Cities.* Princeton, NJ: Princeton University Press.

"Governor Patrick Signs Bills to Reduce Emissions and Boost Green Jobs." 2008. Office of the Governor of Massachusetts, press release, August 13. *www.mass. gov/governor/priorities/jobs/smartgrowth/governor-patrick-signs-bills-to-create-green.html.*

Green Building Commission, Lowell, Massachusetts. "About Us." *greenbuilding. lowellma.gov/about.*

Halpin, Bob. 2010. Personal interview. January 15.

Hoyt, Lorlene, and Andre Leroux. 2007. *Voices from Forgotten Cities: Innovative Revitalization Coalitions in America's Older Small Cities.* Report sponsored by PolicyLink, Oakland, CA; Citizens' Housing and Planning Association, Boston, MA; and MIT School of Architecture and Planning, Cambridge, MA.

Jones, Vanessa E. 2008. "Donning a Green Collar." *Boston Globe,* July 4. *www. boston.com/business/articles/2008/07/04/donning_a_green_collar/.*

Mackres, Eric. 2008. "Lawrence Green Jobs Initiative Launch Meeting, Background Information." *MIT@Lawrence,* December 4.

Marion, Paul. 2010. Personal interview. January 17.

"Massachusetts Electricians Board Would Restrict Solar Installation to Licensed Electricians." 2009. *Solar Power,* November 30. *www.solarpower. org/News/11300902-massachusetts-electricians-board-would-restrict-solar-installation-to-licensed-electricians.aspx.*

MassInc. 2010a. "Profile: City of Lawrence." Data from the U.S. Census Bureau, "American Community Survey (2006–08)." *www.massinc.org/Programs/ Gateway-Cities/About-Gateway-Cities.aspx.*

———. 2010b. "Profile: City of Lowell." Data from the U.S. Census Bureau,

"American Community Survey (2006–08)." *www.massinc.org/Programs/ Gateway-Cities/About-Gateway-Cities.aspx.*

McGovern, Patricia. 2009. Personal interview. December 15.

McMann, Heather. 2010. Personal interview. January 27.

Muro, Mark, John Schneider, David Warren, Eric McLean-Shinaman, Rebecca Sohmer, and Benjamin Forman. 2007. *Reconnecting Massachusetts Gateway Cities: Lessons Learned and an Agenda for Renewal.* Boston, MA: MassInc and Brookings Institution.

Osmer, Kelly. 2010. Personal interview. February 11.

Our Money, Our Future, Our Right to Know: The People's Guide to the Lawrence City Budget. 2006. Lawrence, MA: Lawrence CommunityWorks.

Park, Theresa. 2010. Personal interview. January 13.

"Patrick Administration Announces 'Pathways out of Poverty' Green Collar Job Training Grants." 2009. Executive Office of Energy and Environmental Affairs, Commonwealth of Massachusetts, May 28. *www.mass.gov/eea/pr-pre-p2/patrick-administration-announces-pathways-out.html.*

Pew Charitable Trusts. 2009. *The Clean Energy Economy: Repowering Jobs, Businesses and Investments across America.* Washington, DC: Pew Charitable Trusts.

Powers, John. 1997. "Of Mills and Momentum," *Boston Globe Magazine,* May 11.

Preer, Robert. 2005. "Making Connections: In Lawrence, a CDC Builds More than Homes and Businesses," *CommonWealth,* Summer.

Santana, Joaquin. 2010. Personal interview. March 27.

Schinto, Jeanne. 1995. *Huddle Fever: Living in the Immigrant City.* New York: Knopf.

Schweitzer, Sarah. 2009. "Lawrence Reels as Hope Recedes." *Boston Globe,* July 22. *www.boston.com/news/local/massachusetts/articles/2009/07/22/ hope_recedes_in_lawrence_where_unemployement_rate_is_highest_in_mass/.*

Simon, Harold, and Matthew Brian Hersh. 2009. "Shelterforce Interview: Xavier de Souza Briggs." *Shelterforce,* no. 158 (Fall). *www. shelterforce.org/article/shelterforce_interview_xavier_de_souza_briggs/ shelterforce_interview_xavier_de_souza_briggs/P0/.*

Sidell, Gary. 2010. Personal interview. February 17.

Sperounis, Frederick. Personal interview. February 1.

Traynor, William J. 2008. "Community Building: Limitations and Promise." In *The Community Development Reader,* edited by James DeFilippis and Susan Saegert, 214–24. New York: Routledge.

———. 2010. Personal interview. January 20.

Traynor, William J., and Jessica Andors. 2005. "Network Organizing: A Strategy for Building Community Engagement." *Shelterforce,* no. 140 (March/April). *www.nhi.org/online/issues/140/LCW.html.*

Turcotte, David. 2010. Personal interview. January 19.

U.S. Census Bureau. 2006–2008. *American Community Survey. www.census.gov/acs/ www/.*

PART III

Engaging Environment

5

Citywide Retrofits

A Strategy for Creating Green Jobs in Oakland, California

Benjamin Brandin and Kate Levitt

Introduction

In the summer of 2009, the city council in Oakland, California, unanimously passed an Energy and Climate Action Plan, committing to slash greenhouse gas emissions to 36 percent below 2005 figures by 2020. Meanwhile, the unemployment rate in Oakland is nearly twice the national average, with 18 percent of residents living in poverty, and the vast majority of the city's building stock is more than thirty years old and would benefit from energy retrofits. The gap between Oakland's environmental goals and its economic realities highlights the question faced by most American cities today—how to square a desire for economic progressivism with a lack of cash. As a city in a progressive region of California, and one that suffers from some of the most extreme economic inequalities in the nation, Oakland provides a compelling case through which to understand the nation's need to engage federal, state, and local leaders in the practice of just green investment.

We examine Oakland in comparison with Seattle, Washington, and Portland, Oregon, focusing on how these three cities are using different retrofit strategies to improve the energy efficiency of their building stock. We extract and share key lessons about retrofitting strategies to inform civic leaders and residents, in Oakland and in other cities, as well as the next generation of city planners, political leaders, and housing developers.

We begin by studying Oakland, a city with a storied history of federal involvement in local job creation. Our analysis illuminates how past investments inform the city's response to the American Recovery and Reinvestment Act, also known as the Recovery Act. Next, we compare

Oakland's energy-efficiency retrofit strategy with programs initiated in Seattle and Portland, and from this comparison we draw lessons to guide other cities' efforts. We recognize that every city has its own unique political, economic, social, and cultural climate and do not propose a single retrofitting strategy be applied to all U.S. cities; our aim is to provide lessons that civic leaders and residents might consider as they design their own local strategies.

The Federal Government as an Economic Agent

Between 1945 and 1970, the United States government funded two separate economic development initiatives in Oakland. The sole purpose behind the first wave of federal investment was to serve the World War II effort. New jobs were created, people migrated to fill them, and the new workers kept the war machine operating at full capacity. After 1945, shipyard closures deprived many workers of job security, especially minorities who had immigrated to Oakland during the war. This loss was compounded by the recent experience of the Great Depression, only a half decade earlier. Postwar housing policies that favored white home-buyers and the growth of suburban economic opportunities physically isolated Oakland minorities and further limited their access to new jobs.

Within a decade after World War II, President Lyndon Johnson launched the Great Society programs, including the War on Poverty, which led to a second wave of federal investment in Oakland. The Economic Development Administration spearheaded a pilot program to put Oakland's unemployed inner-city minorities back to work. The administration used an innovative approach to secure its employment objectives: all firms receiving government grants or business loans had to produce a business plan subject to agency approval and an employment plan explaining how they intended to recruit, train, and hire unemployed minority workers from Oakland. The administration's special representative in the city, Amory Bradford, explains in *Oakland's Not for Burning* that the task force performed exceptionally well at procuring agency funds, selecting and approving projects, and establishing the employment plan requiring firms to target minority unemployed workers for hire (Bradford 1968). But it failed in the implementation, struggling to keep beneficiary firms on schedule and to elicit the promised minority jobs. By 1970, Oakland stood in much the same place it had at the program's launch five years earlier.

Forty years later, in January 2010, Oakland's unemployment rate stood at 17.7 percent, compared to the national rate of 9.7 percent for the same month (Oakland Community and Economic Development Agency 2010; United States Department of Labor 2010). The high unemployment rate in the city is likely exacerbated by the stagnant growth of the national economy, but for years Oakland has experienced other problems, such as disinvestment and poverty. These deep-rooted realities hinder economic development that could benefit all Oakland residents, especially the least advantaged. A 2007 report produced by the East Bay Alliance for a Sustainable Economy and Oakland NetWork for Responsible Development found that 42 percent of city residents live in poverty and almost half of renters and homeowners spend in excess of 30 percent of their income on housing. In addition, poorer residents spend a larger portion of their income on housing, which means that their finances are far more constrained than those with greater earnings. Combined with the high unemployment rate, these problems illustrate a continuing need for meaningful economic development in the city.

The two prior waves of federal policies, dating back more than a half century, contributed to Oakland's current state of high unemployment and limited economic opportunity. Municipal funding through the Recovery Act represents a third wave of government investment, with the potential to reshape the city along new economic, social, and environmental dimensions.[1] Economic development lies at the heart of the Recovery Act, and President Obama has specifically spoken of his desire to advance what are known today as "green jobs."

Van Jones, the founder of Oakland-based organizations Green For All and the Ella Baker Center for Human Rights, argues in *The Green Collar Economy: How One Solution Can Fix Our Two Biggest Problems* (Jones 2008) that green jobs could simultaneously improve the nation's environmental and economic circumstances. However, more than thirty years before Jones began promoting this strategy, the federal government introduced a program built on two interrelated principles: increased economic equity and environmental improvement. In 1976, the U.S. Department of Energy launched the Weatherization Assistance Program to fit low-income homes with energy-efficient technologies such as air sealing, lighting, insulation improvements, and appliance upgrades. Based on the program's successful track record over the past thirty years, Congress allocated approximately $5 billion to it through the 2009 Recovery Act.

Along with the federal government, community-based organizations, policy think tanks, and planning consulting firms acknowledge the need for energy-efficiency retrofitting programs as a fundamental strategy toward national economic development and increased energy independence. To be effective on both fronts, however, such programs must greatly exceed the Weatherization Assistance Program's prior achievements. Later sections will show that the effectiveness of retrofit programs depends on affecting the entire city, not just select neighborhoods. Many cities are exploring energy-efficiency retrofitting strategies as a mechanism for simultaneously realizing social equality, economic growth, and environmental benefit.

Retrofitting the American City:
Energy Efficiency and Weatherization Benefits

Why is federal investment in retrofitting and weatherization important? Energy efficiency refers simply to technological building improvements that deliver more services for the same or reduced energy input. According to the International Energy Agency, maximizing energy efficiency is a key step for securing a sustainable energy future. Energy-efficiency advancements reduce the need to construct new power plants; they cut fuel costs and alleviate the nation's dependence on both foreign and domestic oil. They also offer huge environmental benefits by reducing greenhouse gas emissions and improving air quality.

In the United States, buildings account for roughly 40 percent of primary energy use, 38 percent of carbon dioxide emissions, and 72 percent of electricity consumption. Investing in energy-efficiency retrofits could reduce building energy consumption by 20 to 40 percent. In addition, these investments would amount to significant savings on energy bills and could pay for themselves over time (Ho and Rhodes-Conway 2009, 2). For example, the average American household could save between $300 and $1,200 each year (Hendricks et al. 2009, 1–2). This is especially important for low-income families, who spend four times as much of their income on energy than do average American households (Millhone 2009).

Additionally, energy-efficiency retrofits could spur the creation of a new green-job sector. The Center for American Progress has proposed an ambitious plan to retrofit fifty million residential and commercial buildings—40 percent of the nation's building stock—by 2020. Its aim is to generate as many as 625,000 jobs over the next ten years, employing some of the 2.4 million construction workers now unemployed (Bureau of Labor Statistics 2010). A national retrofit plan, what the center calls the "Rebuilding America" model, might also open the door for people lacking college degrees to access high-quality jobs in manufacturing energy-efficiency materials and parts, retrofit training, building energy auditing, and retrofit construction work. Stimulating the expected economic and employment gains would require the investment of billions of dollars over the course of a decade. If the U.S. retrofit market is to reach its full potential, the private sector must play a critical role as the primary financier. Though the federal government has supported residential retrofits of low-income homes for more than thirty years, the weatherization program requires more support if a national plan for energy-efficiency retrofits is to be realized. The program represents an important platform on which to build a national retrofit strategy, but, as the following section demonstrates, it alone cannot provide the necessary funding or service capacity to achieve the reach prescribed by energy-efficiency advocates.

The Weatherization Assistance Program

The Weatherization Assistance Program installs energy-efficient technologies in low-income family residences. Weatherization, the first level of home retrofitting, focuses on sealing the building envelope, improving the efficiency of heating, cooling, and electrical systems, and installing energy-efficient appliances ("Weatherization Assistance Program" 2009). The U.S. Department of Energy initiated the program in 1976 under Title IV of the Energy Conservation and Production Act to curb heating bills and conserve imported oil. Most Americans faced tighter budgets because of the increase in oil prices in the mid-1970s, but the spike in energy costs disproportionately affected low-income households, where rising heating bills dragged some families into debt and, in extreme cases, poverty. Legislators—particularly those from cold-winter climates—feared that some of their constituents might freeze in their own homes. These and other concerns led to the establishment of the Weatherization Assistance Program.

Early in its existence, the program focused primarily on emergency and provisional upgrades (United States Department of Energy, "DOE Weatherization Assistance Program: History of the Weatherization Assistance Program" 2010). These included caulking and weather-stripping doors and windows to prevent leakage and other economical modifications (Kaiser and Pulsipher 2004). Over time, administrators began incorporating more cost-effective measures, such as storm windows, attic insulation, and enhanced space- and water-heating systems, as well as home energy audits. Energy audits—analyzing individual homes to determine optimal weatherization improvements to reduce energy consumption—are now a benchmark of weatherization practice. To benefit low-income families in warmer climates, the program expanded to include measures to reduce cooling costs. In short, the weatherization program, even in times of budget cutbacks, continually expanded in reach and improved in efficiency to reduce the energy needs of low-income Americans who own or rent single-family, multifamily, or mobile residences (U.S. Department of Energy 2008b).

The program's long history and established infrastructure have made it an ideal candidate for investment money from the Recovery Act. The procedures have been in place for decades, the techniques are understood, and the results are measurable. In short, the program delivers immediate economic and environmental benefits (U.S. Department of Energy, Office of Inspector General, Office of Audit Services 2010, 4–5). Based on these factors, and because it was deemed a "shovel ready" activity, Congress assigned the program $4.7 billion in Recovery Act funds (Wald and Kaufman 2010).

Such a massive funding injection created pressure for program administrators to rapidly expand their services. The Weatherization Assistance Program had only received a combined $6 billion during its first thirty-three years (U.S. Department of Energy 2009). The program was expected to grow from approximately 140,000 to an average of 240,000 annual weatherization retrofits by 2012 (U.S. Department of Energy n.d.), but problems at the federal, state, and municipal levels have severely impeded progress. An early analysis of the program reveals that local administrators made minimal progress weatherizing residences. In fact, state grantees drew less than 8 percent of the nearly $5 billion awarded to the program. Accordingly, the slow activation of weatherization program grants translated into a minuscule number of retrofits. The ten highest-funded recipients weatherized just 3 percent of the planned combined units for those states (U.S. Department of Energy, Office of Inspector General, Office of Audit Services 2010, 8). According to the inspector general's report, program impediments include regulatory requirements, various state-level issues, and training mishaps.

The increased pressure to weatherize as many units as possible during a short period of time leads to the possibility of "wasteful, inefficient, and ... even abusive practices" on the part of the states and subgrantees as they struggle to meet weatherization targets (3–5). In sum, the program is failing to produce an economic return on the enormous public investment, and low-income households continue to suffer from the higher utility costs the Recovery Act promised to relieve.

Even if it can come closer to meeting its goal, the Weatherization Assistance Program alone cannot be relied upon to drive the entire retrofit market or meet total service demand. Broad-based retrofit strategies will require new marketing tactics and a more comprehensive system for retrofitting both residential and commercial properties. Additional obstacles, such as overcoming financial barriers, establishing good labor and workforce development standards, and monitoring and evaluating retrofit work, must also be considered when designing an effective citywide retrofit program. Furthermore, Recovery Act dollars meant to grow green jobs must leverage far more private-sector investment to lower carbon emissions and joblessness simultaneously.

Energy-efficiency proponents see citywide retrofit programs as a silver bullet capable of minimizing utility bills, generating green-job growth, restoring the environment, expanding business opportunities, and extending the reach of Recovery Act funding (Green For All 2010b). Such programs consist of three primary components:

1. A mechanism to recycle the monetary savings produced by energy-efficiency upgrades in order to fund additional retrofits
2. The development of high-road jobs that are accessible to all
3. A citywide, instead of neighborhood, impact
   (Ho and Rhodes-Conway 2009, 3)

Expanding on these core factors, a number of social, environmental, and economic-justice organizations, as well as organized labor affiliates, add a fourth component:

4. Programs that focus on low-income service delivery and job development

Based on our research—described in the following section—we suggest a fifth and final criterion of citywide retrofit programs:

5. Partnerships between local governments and community, business, and labor institutions

Ideally, local energy retrofit programs should complement the Weatherization Assistance Program by offering services to middle- and higher-income households, creating loan funds to expand and recycle retrofit capital, and performing deep retrofits—that is, work that extends beyond the typical suite of upgrades, like wall and floor insulation or heating- and water-system improvements. Seattle and Portland are both implementing citywide retrofitting strategies that embrace the five criteria listed above as they take advantage of the energy-efficiency opportunities created by the Recovery Act.

Emerging Strategies:
Comparing Seattle, Portland, and Oakland

We selected Portland and Seattle for this analysis for a variety of reasons: their strategic plans for growth are environmentally sound, they initiated their retrofit programs using Recovery Act funds, and they designed citywide programs. Further, Seattle and Portland are useful points of comparison because, as West Coast cities, they have climates similar to Oakland's; climate is important because retrofit programs must be tailored to regional weather conditions. Lastly, the three cities have similar population sizes. Evaluating Oakland's, Seattle's, and Portland's retrofitting strategies using the five components described previously reveals the strengths and weaknesses of Oakland's program relative to its counterparts, as well as the ways it can be improved in terms of job creation and increased scope.

An Appropriate and Robust Financial Model

All three cities used grants from the Recovery Act to establish loan funds to finance retrofit programs and to recycle the monetary savings achieved by energy-efficiency upgrades. A revolving loan fund is an unregulated pool of capital used to provide loans to small businesses and development projects, and loan repayments are recycled through the fund over time. Such funds typically are established to address capital supply gaps and stimulate local economic development; in this case, the funds fill the financing gap left by private investment. Debtors are responsible for repaying their loans to the fund, and repayments allow the fund to extend new loans. Over time, a revolving loan fund can produce waves of debt capital for a city (Seidman 2004).

The city of Seattle acquired seed capital from the Recovery Act's Energy Efficiency and Conservation Block Grant program in 2009 and will use these funds to obtain private support to fully finance the citywide retrofit pilot.[2] Seattle expects that $12 million could pay for 1,000 energy-efficiency home retrofits; this amounts to an average of $12,000 per home, almost double the $6,500 energy-efficiency provision limit of the weatherization program. The city hopes to grow the fund to between $20 and $40 million through additional grants, philanthropic gifts, and private equity investment. Ultimately, this plan allows Seattle to retrofit a minimum of 1,500 and a maximum of 3,300 residential units.

Seattle's revolving loan fund provides property owners with reasonable interest rates, longer amortization terms than private banks, and loans up to $20,000. The interest rates vary between 2 percent and 6 percent, determined by the borrower's income level, and the loans allow participants to amortize their debt over fifteen years. Property owners can access between $8,000 and $20,000 for energy-efficiency retrofits. However, to qualify for an energy-efficiency retrofit loan, borrowers must pay a $450 origination fee to a local community development financial institution that manages the loan accounts.[3] A lien on the property suffices as collateral for each retrofit loan (City of Seattle 2008; City of Seattle et al. 2009).

Like Seattle, Portland used Recovery Act funds to help start its retrofit pool, but the city also added its own money to the $2.5 million of federal seed capital, and city officials continue to consider other ways to supplement and enlarge the revolving loan fund. Issuing government bonds or assuming low-interest debt are two options city officials might consider as they broaden the program's financial reach, and socially conscious investors might also contribute to building the fund's lending power.

Portland's approach is different from both Oakland and Seattle because Portland's retrofitting program uses on-bill financing. In this system, the revolving loan fund enters into a loan agreement with participating homeowners, while the fund pays contractors directly for the retrofit work. The local utility company pays the aggregate costs of all energy-efficiency retrofits to the bank managing the fund, replenishing the fund and enabling the community development financial institution to issue new loans. After contractors complete all work and an energy advocate approves the upgrades, the utility begins charging the property owner an additional fee on her bill, representing the monthly payment, plus interest, the building owner must repay to settle the loan. The interest paid on the monthly retrofit charge guarantees a new and consistent form of profit for the utility. The reduction in energy costs offsets some of the cost for the efficiency upgrade, but because the utility produces less overall energy as a result of the retrofit, the interest it collects from customers improves the energy supplier's profit margin. In short, this model allows property owners to improve their energy efficiency without up-front costs. Utilities, meanwhile, benefit from the continued income stream without needing to boost energy production in the form of costly new power plants.

Oakland's retrofit program also operates via a revolving loan fund, but does so in a way different than either the Seattle or the Portland model. In January 2010, the city assigned approximately $2 million in Recovery Act Community Development Block Grant funds to Oakland's Housing and Community Development division, the municipal office that administers the retrofit program for poor and moderate-income homeowners. Oakland offers extremely flexible terms because it wants homeowners to engage in retrofits exceeding traditional weatherization, thus maximizing their investment (City of Oakland 2010). Homeowners can access between $6,500 and $30,000, and the revolving loan fund charges no interest and sets no amortization period over which the loan must be repaid. Oakland recovers its investment only when the property title changes hands; instead of having another monthly bill to pay, the property owner repays Oakland for the energy-efficiency upgrades when he sells the home.

The success of these programs will depend on their ability to manage, recycle, and procure additional loan capital over time. The three funds outlined here align their financing policies with their economic-development goals—providing no- or low-interest loans to homeowners for retrofitting. The low interest rates and flexible payback terms encourage homeowner participation. Higher loan thresholds will likely attract property owners because they enable landlords to finance retrofits and reap greater energy-efficiency gains, as in the case of Oakland. Consequently, these financing terms should foster retrofit market growth and contribute to job and business development.

However, revolving loan funds also exhibit weaknesses that retrofit program managers must monitor. The programs in both Portland and Seattle are designed to attract supplemental investment dollars; if they cannot acquire the philanthropic and private investment that funding program managers expect, their retrofitting programs will fail to have citywide impact. Portland has considered issuing government bonds or securing low-interest debt to increase program funds, but if the city takes on debt to finance its revolving loan fund, it could create problems in the future. Capitalizing a revolving loan fund with debt requires fund managers to charge program participants higher interest rates to ensure the fund can cover its own debt payments.

Oakland's revolving fund faces its own distinct challenges. First, the fund charges no interest on its retrofit loans. This will certainly attract people to participate in the program, but it deprives the fund of supplemental capital that could help expand the program and extend more loans. Likewise, loans will only be settled at the time of sale, suggesting that retrofitted homes will be priced at a value that, at a minimum, covers the loan the owners took out to make the efficiency improvements. Regardless, property owners must pay the city the total loan amount when they sell. There is no loan loss reserve fund, meaning the fund maintains no protection against losses or participants' failure to repay their loans. If homeowners do not replenish the fund by selling their homes or transferring their titles, Oakland has no an alternate means of recharging the fund.

This flaw in Oakland's payback mechanism only underscores the reality that, of the three programs, Oakland's underperforms in the possible total of retrofitted units. In one year, Oakland's program could retrofit between 67 and 307 low- to moderate-income homes based on its loan-option range. In contrast, Portland's pilot may retrofit 500 homes in the first year, and Seattle's program could reach as many as 250 to 400 units given its current financing. Slow payback periods and an inability to generate additional capital for the revolving loan fund seriously hampers the Oakland program's reach and could spell significant shortcomings in the long term. But without injections of additional capital, none of the three programs will succeed in retrofitting even a fraction of the intended residential units nor have a fraction of the economic and environmental impacts to which they aspire.

High-Road Job Development

In addition to putting unemployed construction hands back to work, retrofit program managers also focus on job creation in economically depressed communities, focusing on so-called high-road jobs: positions that provide family-sustaining wages and benefits to employees. Such jobs provide long-term positions for workers and open career-development pathways for poor, disadvantaged, or new workers. Community workforce agreements represent the most effective strategy to assure the development of high-road jobs. These agreements define the contracting, training, and employment policies intended to produce high-quality jobs for community members. They empower cities to set the economic-development terms of a program: which contractors can participate, which people employers can hire, and the types of benefits those workers receive. Each of the programs analyzed here professes a commitment to the creation of high-road jobs as an integral component; each of the three cities, however, applies a different approach to this responsibility.

In Seattle, the Residential Energy Efficiency Pathway program is a retrofit job ladder with four rungs, beginning with educational training for the least educated and least skilled, and rising up through succeeding skill levels to the highest level, where participants learn to conduct inspections, advanced diagnostic testing, combustion appliance safety, and twelfth-grade math. This four-step apprenticeship program is designed to prepare workers for a variety of positions in the energy-efficiency market.

The commitment to design and implement a well-articulated training program for novice energy-efficiency workers illustrates Seattle's focused approach to its retrofitting strategy and to green-jobs development. Currently, the city expects to generate 230 jobs from the existing building policies initiated by the program. The success of the Residential Energy Efficiency Pathway hinges on at least two factors. First, the program must provide low-income and low-skilled populations with a means of accessing the training ladder. And, after completing the pilot, the Green Building Task Force will need to evaluate, improve, and streamline the residential and commercial retrofit career pathways the program intends to develop (City of Seattle et al. 2009).

Seattle's retrofitting strategy exhibits a number of strengths. It acknowledges that workers possess different levels of education and abilities and provides them with multiple points of entry and opportunities for advancement. It also benefits from a city ordinance that mandates an energy-performance disclosure from owners of commercial and large multiunit residential buildings. Owners of the largest buildings began reporting energy performance in 2010, while midsized and smaller started reporting in 2011 and 2012, respectively. This policy is expected to increase the demand for retrofits and generate green jobs by recognizing building performance and identifying opportunities for energy-efficiency gains. On the other hand, Seattle's strategy rests on the ability of managers to attract additional fund capital to extend new loans. The retrofitting market might expand, but without adequate financing. Lastly, the Seattle strategy lacks a community workforce agreement and therefore may fall short with respect to minority training and hiring.

Portland's retrofitting strategy, by contrast, relies on a binding agreement to generate specific outcomes. Portland's community workforce agreement addresses six separate but related principles relative to workforce development: job quality, access, high-road employers, legal enforceability, democracy, and accountability. This comprehensive approach asserts control over the market to produce greater economic equity from the energy-efficiency retrofit market. In this way, Portland can serve as a model for other energy-efficiency programs.

The job-quality standards included in the Portland agreement center on wages, benefits, and upward mobility. In this case, contractors must pay workers any existing prevailing wage or 180 percent of Oregon's minimum wage, whichever is higher. Portland's strategy entails awarding points to employers that provide workers with benefits, such as health insurance, a pension plan, vacation time, or sick days. The community workforce agreement also stresses upward mobility as a key element of good job-quality standards. Further, the program has involved local unions and training providers from the outset to open up job pathways for retrofit workers. The agreement also emphasizes the importance of local hiring (80 percent of energy-efficiency retrofit workers must originate from Portland), the development of a diverse workforce, and high-quality training programs. Training programs must fulfill certain criteria to be designated a qualified training program, and a minimum of 20 percent of all contracts must be granted to minority business owners.

Portland's strategy will not succeed, however, without a supply of high-road employers. Program managers maintain a list of approved contractors, but contractors who wish to be added to the list must complete mandatory weatherization training in energy-efficient retrofitting. In addition, the community workforce agreement established an incentive-based structure to attract the most qualified efficiency contractors for the program, based on their energy retrofit experience, a positive service record, the hiring of local and disadvantaged workers, and a favorable reputation dealing with employees, city staff, and members of other organizations. Contractors sign legal documents agreeing to uphold the standards outlined in the agreement.

The market regulation achieved through the community workforce agreement assures that the Portland strategy balances disparate interests between private business and the public sector, between organized labor and nonunionized firms, and among the assortment of participating contractors. Following the pilot, the committee will begin regularly evaluating the program and realign its goals as necessary. Though the Portland pilot reports it will produce only thirty to forty jobs, the program's comprehensive and thoughtful approach sets the stage for much larger economic results (Clean Energy Works Portland 2009c).[4]

The Portland program displays a commitment to democratic input and engagement, places a value on accountability, and stresses the importance of implementing changes when appropriate. The community workforce agreement demonstrates how a diverse set of stakeholders can negotiate terms that promote collective economic benefits. However, such agreements cannot drive market growth. As in Seattle, Portland has a strategy that requires additional capital to generate jobs and stimulate market expansion. Also, the community workforce agreement imposes restrictions that could dissuade some independent contractors from participating in the program.

Oakland's retrofitting strategy, like those in the other two cities, promotes equity, opportunity, and high-road job development. The city is currently producing an application for qualified retrofit contractors. The criteria will dictate that a contractor comply with Alameda County wage standards, hire Oakland residents, and recruit workers from local green-jobs training programs, such as the Oakland Green Jobs Corps. With dollars from the Recovery Act, the city will reimburse contractors who hire Oakland job seekers or graduates of local training programs 80 percent of paid wages through the fall of 2010.

A Citywide Scale

Seattle and Portland intend to broaden their programs' reach to retrofit large multifamily buildings, but because the foci of the individual pilots differ, their building-targeting strategies and policies serve separate goals. In contrast, Oakland aims to use Community Development Block Grant funding to retrofit as many homes as possible, with the understanding that the loans will ultimately be recycled to finance future retrofits. Oakland established income criteria for homeowners to participate in the program, without addressing the age of homes, their condition, or appropriateness for retrofitting. Of the three cities examined in this study, only Portland explicitly evaluated the age of building stock as a targeting criteria for expanding its retrofitting strategy citywide.

As mentioned earlier, Seattle plans to retrofit 20 percent of the city's existing building stock by 2020. The pilot targets owners of single-family homes and condominiums in small multifamily buildings. Seattle will use an eighteen-month, five-thousand-unit energy performance and home rating pilot program. Seattle intends to use the Seattle Building Energy Disclosure policy lever to achieve two ambitious economic-development goals: grow the local energy-efficiency retrofit market and subsequently increase the program to a citywide scale. City officials believe that mandating that commercial and multifamily property owners disclose how much energy their buildings consume will induce them to invest in energy-efficiency retrofits. They also anticipate that building owners will discover that energy-efficiency upgrades provide the supplemental benefit of increasing overall property value. The model gambles on these beliefs, as it is very possible that property owners may conform to new regulation by disclosing energy-consumption information but not make building improvements. This conundrum boils down to the fact that building owners and tenants have different interests and are motivated by different incentives: landlords bear the responsibility of providing appliances, but tenants pay for the energy those appliances consume. Hence, building owners receive little direct return from their energy-efficiency investments. Seattle's program, therefore, will be of clear benefit to single-family homeowners, but it is far less certain how commercial property and multifamily unit owners will respond. Another factor could also impede scale: the disclosure requirement strictly applies to commercial and multifamily properties, highlighting a disconnect between the policy and those who stand to gain most from such an initiative. Mandating that single-family homeowners disclose their energy usage would likely require some political innovation, but it seems that one way to encourage energy retrofits would be to market them more strategically to single-family homeowners. Finally, the disclosure ordinance does not mandate that property owners cut energy usage, only that they disclose how much their buildings consume.

Portland has a different approach to reaching a citywide scale, a method that complements state legislation freeing the market of regulatory barriers. Portland's strategy focuses on the physical characteristics of the building stock. To qualify for retrofitting, Portlanders must live in a home constructed prior to 1993 and covering fewer than 4,500 square feet; focusing on older and smaller homes will yield greater energy-efficiency benefits for property owners. Bundling retrofits allow Portland to achieve economies of scale by compiling adjacent properties to be retrofitted simultaneously, streamlining the delivery of services and allowing larger contractors to participate in the program. To alert homeowners to the benefits of energy-efficiency retrofitting, Portland relies on community-based organizations with close ties to neighborhood residents.

Despite these smart strategies and others—including coordinated business and training support, and loan-targeting policies to concentrate retrofits in poorer areas—success in Portland is by no means guaranteed. If program managers activate the measures described above and streamline the process, then Portland could provide a model for other cities to follow. Like the Seattle strategy, however, Portland's must ultimately attract more capital; meeting the goal of retrofitting one hundred thousand homes will be nearly impossible without it.

As for Oakland, the city aims to perform energy-efficiency retrofits on as many homes as possible, using the $2 million it received from the Community Development Block Grant program of the Recovery Act. As the property titles of retrofitted buildings transfer to new owners over time, the loans will be repaid and new weatherization retrofit loans will be made to additional homeowners. Understanding the need to market its retrofitting strategy, the city has announced a request for qualifications to solicit bids for outreach services. The city expects subcontractors to perform specific duties: engaging in general outreach and referral, informing participating contractors of the city's intention to generate jobs via the program, and following up to ensure job quality and customer satisfaction (Green For All 2010c, 2). Some homes in

Oakland will be retrofitted in the first round, but subsequent rounds will depend on how long it takes the fund to recoup loans.[5]

In the absence of an expansion model, Oakland's Housing and Community Development staff can focus on developing a cadre of qualified contractors, promoting local hiring practices, ensuring quality service delivery, and evaluating the program. Prioritizing quality service delivery simplifies the program and enables managers to set manageable goals and strive to meet them. The limited reach of the Oakland program means that many low- to moderate-income homeowners will not be able to participate. As one way to expand the program's reach, Oakland submitted a federal grant proposal describing a plan to retrofit buildings operated by the Oakland Housing Authority and city schools.

Focus on Low-Income Service Delivery and Job Development

Each of the three citywide retrofitting strategies, in its own way, takes into account the needs of low-income families. Seattle's plan targets homeowners who do not qualify for the city's HomeWise program, which provides low-income renters and homeowners with weatherization grants. The city addresses the needs of low-income city residents through its workforce development strategy and recognizes that creating access for disadvantaged workers will be one of its larger challenges. Seattle's task force claims that in order to promote success the program must "increase the number of on-ramps ... for low-skilled, low-income residents to acquire clean energy workforce skills," but it does not explain how it will achieve this. The energy-efficiency career pathways articulate how an individual with no or few skills could climb an energy-retrofit job ladder, but its commitment to train low-income workers might be unrealistic if the task force fails to funnel people into such programs.

Oakland's strategy offers services exclusively to low- and moderate-income people. By incentivizing contractors to hire from local training programs like the Ella Baker Center's Oakland Green Jobs Corps, the city indirectly influences workforce development opportunities for Oakland workers—some from poor, disadvantaged, or minority backgrounds. Oakland's targeting policy and support for local job development deserve note, but the program's limited capacity will hinder its ability to make significant impacts with regard to energy efficiency and job creation.

Of the three cities, Portland has the pilot that best incorporates policies that promote low-income service delivery and workforce development. In that sense, Portland's strategy is a blend of Seattle's and Oakland's. The community workforce agreement sets baselines for job quality and access; it produces standards for contractors, rewarding those who deliver the best value. Portland's strategy sets the bar high, aiming to retrofit one hundred thousand homes over the next ten years. Achieving even a fraction of that number would mark a huge success, especially for disadvantaged homeowners and workers prioritized through the program.

Partnerships

Seattle enlisted fifty stakeholders, representing an array of perspectives from the private sector and community-based organizations, to participate on two task forces responsible for program policy design. Their commissions charge them with developing the financing, incentive, and mandate policies to reduce greenhouse gas emissions. This structure draws on the expertise of stakeholders and provides them with an opportunity to shape program policies reflecting the interests of their respective constituencies (City of Seattle 2008, 2). While the task forces will play an advisory role, a more effective approach might have involved these stakeholders helping the city to both define goals and design measures to meet them. Without a process that prioritizes constituent input, at least to the extent of granting task force recommendations increased weight in the decision-making process, the city of Seattle will control all decisions governing its retrofit program.

Community workforce agreements deny any single entity total control of a program, creating the opportunity for community-controlled economic development.[6] Portland's strategy, developed with twelve collaborators working with the city of Portland and the federal government, is an example of sharing control and responsibility among various partners. Though the city of Portland and Energy Trust of Oregon administer the strategy, different responsibilities are assigned to various program partners, assuring that various constituencies play active roles. Twenty-nine separate parties signed the community workforce agreement, so this legally binding document works as a "check and balance" instrument to facilitate efficient, equitable development of the retrofit sector in Portland.

Of the three retrofitting strategies considered, only Oakland launched its program without any business, community, or labor partners. A number of forward-thinking organizations, however, have declared themselves committed to expanding the energy-efficiency retrofit sector in Oakland and the larger Alameda County area, and the inability of the city to take full advantage of this resource represents a missed opportunity. Still, the program relies on a screening process for contractors, which allows the city to establish good relationships with quality companies who will be necessary allies should Oakland pursue a wider retrofit strategy in the future. The following section discusses and analyzes Oakland's efforts in greater detail and highlights practices that other Pacific-coast cities should consider in implementing a local retrofitting strategy.

A Citywide Retrofit Strategy for Oakland

In all the cases we have considered, the cities themselves assumed the lead role in establishing retrofitting strategies. In Portland and Seattle, the mayors led the charge, challenging city departments to craft policies to establish energy efficiency as an environmental boon and economic driver. Both mayors' offices sought support and input from a wide range of partners and built these relationships into the decision-making process, albeit in different ways. Both cities believe they have a strategy that can expand citywide, allowing thousands of residents to enjoy the rewards of cheaper energy, an improved environment, and increased economic opportunities.

Oakland's strategy also displays certain strengths. As noted above, Oakland's prescreening criteria for contractors will institute good relations with valuable retrofit contractors, and its support of local training programs casts the city in a facilitator role, coupling the local green-labor supply with employers. These actions represent a good start, but Oakland could do much more to maximize federal dollars. The failure to create a sustainable means for recycling program loans remains a central impediment to Oakland's success. The following section will explore what an improved strategy might look like in Oakland, which parties could help bring it to fruition, and what some of the potential outcomes and challenges might be.

On March 10, 2010, Oakland hosted a contingent of federal officials to publicize the local community benefits from Recovery Act dollars.

Oakland Tribune correspondent Kelly Rayburn reported, "[Mayor] Dellums said ... [t]he goal ... was not simply to receive money and spend it, but rather to leverage it with local government, non-profit and private-sector programs to help build sustainable economic opportunities" (Rayburn 2010). An effective citywide retrofitting strategy in Oakland will require the Community and Economic Development Agency, the unit charged with implementing the strategy, to do the following: restructure how the revolving loan fund recycles program loan payments; improve job opportunities for Oakland residents; involve city agencies and enlist the planning expertise, support, and capacity of local community and nonprofit organizations; prioritize low-income service delivery and job development; and analyze the local building stock and population demographics to determine development targets and phases.

Restructuring and Managing the Revolving Loan Fund

Oakland established a fund to recycle retrofit loans, but the payback mechanism cannot reasonably recover loans in a time frame sufficient to broaden the strategy citywide. The Portland and Seattle funds, with their discrete amortization periods, assure that new loans will become available at a faster rate. Oakland must establish a dependable loan amortization schedule that offers low interest rates to poorer residents while still ensuring that the fund can extend new loans. A restructured fund could also leverage private investment to subsidize growth; Oakland should follow Seattle's example and pursue investment from philanthropic and private sources, partnering with agencies like Enterprise Community Partners, a national affordable-housing nonprofit, to manage the retrofitting fund.

Using Policies to Promote Job Growth

Oakland should also consider adopting Seattle and Portland's policies regarding workforce development. To spur the growth of its energy retrofit market, Seattle enacted the energy disclosure requirement; theoretically, when property owners are informed of the energy their buildings consume and encouraged to make voluntary upgrades, the demand for retrofits (and retrofitting jobs) will grow. Portland established its community workforce agreement to ensure certain workforce development outcomes, mandating that contractors participating in the program abide by certain rules. Oakland might consider these different strategies and explore how it might adopt comparable policies to encourage job growth while managing job standards.

Oakland's prescreened contractor list has a function similar to Portland's community workforce agreement; also, the city's Green Jobs Corps support and integration of Recovery Act–financed contractor incentives echo the job-access mandates in Portland's community workforce agreement. However, while Oakland's strategy encourages contractors to hire locally trained workers, it offers too much leeway in terms of job quality and access. Program managers should continue to prescreen contractors based on their compliance with Alameda County wage standards, hiring of local residents, and recruitment from local green-job training centers. These are sound practices but fall short of the standards achieved by Portland's community workforce agreement, which sets a family-supporting wage, rewards contractors that provide benefits to workers, stipulates a minimum percentage of disadvantaged workers or local trainees that must be hired, and prioritizes contracts for minority-owned businesses. In Portland, the parties represented in the community workforce agreement can deny participation to union and contractor signatories that fail to comply with the agreement, and this affords great leverage to exact worker benefits and job-quality standards from contractors who are thereby held accountable for their hiring and work practices. Critics of community workforce agreement regulations argue that such restrictions constrain the energy retrofit market and hinder contractors from participating in the program. But this analysis ignores the fact that in Portland, there is a huge unmet demand for energy retrofits. Given this demand and the high numbers of unemployed workers, we conclude that many contractors would be eager to participate in the program.

Involving Multiple City Agencies, Community Groups, and Nonprofit Organizations

City agencies play a critical role in all three retrofitting strategies. In Seattle the lead is taken by the Office of Sustainability and Environment; in Portland, the Bureau of Planning and Sustainability performs administrative duties. In Oakland, the Housing and Community Development office directs the strategy. Only in Oakland did the city fail to consider how a broader strategy might include business and community partners. In Portland, Green For All helped craft a community workforce agreement that involved more than two dozen parties; similarly, Seattle engaged people from diverse backgrounds for its task forces. In contrast, except for promoting the Green Jobs Corps and defining program participation terms for contractors, Oakland has ignored the wealth of input and support that local organizations could provide. In one instance of collaboration, the Ella Baker Center for Human Rights joined with the Oakland Apollo Alliance, Laney College, Cyprus Mandela Construction Training Program, and Growth Sector Inc. to establish the Oakland Green Jobs Corps. The program trains workers for careers in Bay Area industries such as green construction, energy efficiency, and solar energy production. The collective expertise of these institutions could help the city draft job-quality and access standards for a retrofit community workforce agreement. The East Bay Alliance for a Sustainable Economy, a Bay Area nonprofit organization, issued a paper in 2007 delineating how the city could gain from a more developed green economy. But city officials involved neither East Bay Alliance nor Alameda Building Trades when developing its retrofitting strategy. To realize a more ambitious and effective energy retrofitting strategy, Oakland must coordinate with the building-trade groups that can do the work.

Prioritizing Historically Disadvantaged Groups

Along with other energy retrofit program supporters, we argue that these strategies should focus on low-income job development and service delivery. As noted above, Oakland's unemployment rate as of January 2010 was 18 percent, more than one and a half times the national average; almost one-fifth of Oakland residents earn incomes at or below the federal poverty level, and nearly half spend roughly 30 percent of their earnings on housing costs. Such statistics underscore why the city must make every effort to increase job growth targeted at less affluent populations and illustrate that an expanded energy retrofit program could ameliorate multiple problems facing low-income Oakland residents. Many of the potential partner organizations in the region have strong ties to underprivileged urban communities and could effectively conduct outreach efforts and market a citywide retrofitting strategy.

Analyzing Building Stock and Demographic Data

Energy-efficiency retrofitting experts believe that incorporating rental properties and bundling retrofits are two strategies that could induce larger contracting companies to enter the field. Including rental properties would greatly expand the total number of buildings that cities could retrofit, and the practice of grouping, or bundling, properties streamlines the process by creating economies of scale. It is nearly impossible for big contracting firms to profit from individual retrofits because of their higher operational costs, but bundling a group of buildings might stimulate interest.

To determine where to target its efforts, Oakland must first understand which residents would benefit most from the program and identify the housing stock most in need of upgrades. Portland set participation criteria and mapped those homes that fulfilled the city's specifications; it also mapped household income and race distribution by neighborhood, average gas-heating energy intensity, and total greater-than-median energy intensity to understand which residences would benefit most from energy retrofits. Such metrics show which populations live in the oldest housing stock and pay larger proportions of their income for energy. Our analysis of median home incomes and racial distribution in Oakland found valuable information about which areas a citywide retrofitting strategy might target first. The bottom line is that to maximize benefits for those most in need of help the retrofitting strategy should target flatland neighborhoods like West Oakland, where the high concentration of prewar structures and proportion of poor minorities make it an ideal place to test the possibility of bundling home energy retrofits.

Building out the program as proposed here requires Oakland to take a number of key steps: improve coordination among city agencies; solicit private, nonprofit, and labor partners to participate in new program design and task management; diversify the workforce development and program delivery strategies; and perform a more detailed analysis of the building stock to identify the build dates for single-family residences. Such improvements to the existing strategy are necessary for achieving the city's environmental goals while addressing the inequality that has plagued Oakland for decades.

Conclusion

The case of Oakland focuses our attention both on the past, where we can learn important lessons from previous waves of federal investment, and the future, as we consider practices to ensure equitable and sustainable development. The history of federal economic stimulus in Oakland's economy emphasizes how precarious such support can be: federal investments have proven to be time contingent and highly politicized, demanding extensive oversight from governing bodies at different levels. Nonetheless, federal funding is a primary source for financing green economic development programs in cities, as we have seen with the Weatherization Assistance Program, and therefore requires that municipalities implement well-planned strategies to engage leaders at both local and regional levels.

As of now, however, Oakland is like a number of cities that sought to use Recovery Act funds to establish energy-retrofit programs: lacking the capacity necessary to develop a sophisticated and scalable retrofit strategy. The city should not be faulted for its efforts; in the midst of the stimulus frenzy, several municipalities, including Oakland, have worked aggressively to secure competitive federal stimulus grants and initiate new programs. This funding comes with a strict timetable, along with use restrictions that create a difficult challenge outside of a city's traditional workflow. In this way the stimulus is both a boon and a burden for cities like Oakland, which struggle to maximize the available opportunities. Cities are under the federal microscope as never before.

Yet despite these challenges, local and regional leaders can take steps to facilitate more successful implementation of federal investment. As we have seen in Seattle and Portland, strong mayoral leadership can help prioritize green development, as can support from local politicians and city councils. In order to gain financial support for green initiatives that target equitable development, states and cities must also develop strategies to build deep connections with the communities they hope to serve. To deliver on the promise of improved employment opportunities and energy services for the populations in greatest need, cities like Oakland should partner with community-based organizations and civic groups as frequently and directly as possible. These partnerships will enable municipalities to better develop and target programs that pursue not only economic development and environmental improvement, but also social equality. For example, while Oakland officials have involved retrofit contractors and initiated training programs in exemplary ways, they can still tap into the potential of the area's many nonprofit organizations working on social, environmental, and economic-justice issues. We further recommend that cities prioritize communication with decision makers at the local, regional, and state levels to facilitate the most effective use of federal investments. Finally, refining loan mechanisms and reaching out to investors beyond the federal government will sustain these programs after the initial pilot phase. Only through such engagement can retrofit programs in cities like Oakland successfully scale up, develop sustainable financing mechanisms, and target populations with tailored services.

In the face of serious challenges, Oakland has begun the process, establishing a strong framework for retrofits, but this is truly just the beginning: more steps are needed to maximize the opportunities created by its own Climate Action Plan, the president's vision for the Recovery Act, and the clear need for new economic development to serve the city's least advantaged. History shows that federal investment in two successive economic development strategies failed to produce positive and lasting change in Oakland. The Recovery Act is different in that it grants Oakland the opportunity to initiate a range of projects to stimulate local economic growth. The energy-efficiency retrofit market is a budding industry with great potential, but cities, partner organizations, and local businesses will have to work together to unlock its promise of just green investment.

Notes

1. As of May 2010, Oakland garnered $205,746,401 of stimulus money. Another $217.5 million is currently pending. If Oakland received all of the pending awards, the total amount of stimulus funding would amount to almost a half billion dollars for a city with approximately four hundred thousand residents. City of Oakland, "Oakland Stimulus Grants," March 3, 2010, *www2.Oaklandnet.com/Government/o/CityAdministration/DOWD005832.*
2. The Energy Efficiency and Conservation Block Grant Program provides grants to U.S. local governments, states, territories, and Indian tribes to fund programs and projects that reduce energy use and fossil fuel emissions and improve energy efficiency.
3. Community development financial institutions provide credit and banking services to underserved communities.

4. The Center for American Progress estimated that for every $1 million invested in building efficiency retrofits, 12.5 direct and indirect full-time equivalent jobs would be created. It claims that this target aligns with other estimates produced by the Political Economy Research Institute, the National Association of Homebuilders, the Center on Wisconsin Strategy, and others. About two-thirds of jobs are created from energy efficiency installation and one-third are created for retrofit parts and material manufacturing (Hendricks et al. 2009, 9). Portland claims it will produce approximately 14 jobs per every $1 million invested in the program. It is clear that if cities are going to experience large job growth in the energy-efficiency sector, these programs will require much more private and public investment capital.
5. The brief analyses of Oakland's financing, high-road job development, and scale development plans are not the result of a lack of available information on the program; rather, they reflect its simplicity relative to the more comprehensive programs implemented in Seattle and Portland.
6. In this case I use "community" to mean collective participation by a number of stakeholders including but not limited to nonprofit organizations, the local utility, regional government entities, and the City of Portland.

References

Affordable Power Alliance. 2010. *Potential Impact of the EPA Endangerment Finding on Low Income Groups and Minorities.* Report prepared by Management Information Systems, Washington, DC.

Bradford, Amory. 1968. *Oakland's Not for Burning.* New York: D. McKay.

Bureau of Labor Statistics. 2010. "Employment Situation Summary," February 5. *www.bls.gov/news.release/archives/empsit_02052010.htm,* accessed February 19, 2010.

Center for American Progress. 2009. *Green Jobs/Green Homes New York: Expanding Home Energy Efficiency and Creating Good Jobs in a Clean Energy Economy.* Report sponsored by Center for American Progress, Center for Working Families, and Half in Ten.

City of Oakland. 2010. Oakland Stimulus Grants. City of Oakland, March 3. *www2.Oaklandnet.com/Government/o/CityAdministration/DOWD005832.*

City of Oakland, Community and Economic Development Agency, Housing and Community Development Division. 2010. "Housing Loans and Grants, Weatherization and Energy Retrofit Loan Program." *www.oaklandnet.com/government/hcd/loansgrants/werip.html,* accessed March 17, 2010.

City of Seattle. 2008. "Green Building Task Force Charter." August 26. *www.seattle.gov/environment/documents/GBTF_Charter_revdraft8-26-08.pdf.*

City of Seattle, Office of the Mayor. Office of Sustainability and Environment, and Department of Planning and Development. 2009. *Seattle Green Building Capital Initiative: Summary Report.* April 22.

Clean Energy Works Portland. 2009a. "Clean Energy Works Portland Pilot Application." Accessed online March 31, 2010.

———. 2009b. "Clean Energy Works Portland: Frequently Asked Questions." Accessed online April 18, 2010.

———. 2009c. "Clean Energy Works Portland: More Frequently Asked Questions." Accessed online April 3, 2010.

Green For All. 2010a. *Case Studies from the Green Collar Economy—City of Seattle Office of Sustainability Green Jobs Taskforce.* Oakland, CA: Green for All.

———. 2010b. *Clean Energy Works Portland: A National Model for Energy-Efficiency Retrofits.* Oakland, CA: Green for All.

———. 2010c. *Case Studies from the Green Collar Economy—Weatherization and Energy Retrofit Loan Program Summary for Oakland, CA.* Oakland, CA: Green For All.

Hendricks, Bracken, Benjamin Goldstein, Reid Detchon, and Kurt Shickman. 2009. *Rebuilding America: A National Policy Framework for Investment in Energy Efficiency Retrofits.* Washington, DC: Center for American Progress and Energy Future Coalition.

Ho, Stacy, and Satya Rhodes-Conway. 2009. *A Short Guide to Setting Up a City Scale Retrofit Program.* Oakland, CA: Green For All; Madison, WI: Center on Wisconsin Strategy.

Jones, Van. 2008. *The Green Collar Economy: How One Solution Can Fix Our Two Biggest Problems.* New York: Harper One.

Kaiser, Mark, and Allan Pulsipher. 2004. "WAP explained." *Energy Policy* 32 (16): 1843–60.

Millhone, John. 2009. *Weatherization—A Case Study.* Policy Outlook. Washington, DC: Carnegie Endowment for International Peace.

Oakland Community and Economic Development Agency. 2010. "Oakland CEDA—Labor Force." January. Accessed online April 9, 2010.

Rayburn, Kelly. 2010. "Stimulus in Action: Federal Officials Tour Oakland Sites." Oakland Tribune, March 1. *lee.house.gov/in-the-news/ stimulus-in-action-federal-officials-tour-oakland-sites-oakland-tribune-3110/.*

SBI Energy. 2009. *Energy-Efficient Home Renovations Market, Part 3: HVAC & Roofing.* November 1. Rockville, MD: SBI Energy.

Seattle Mayor's Office. 2009. *City of Seattle Mayor's Green Building Capital Initiative.* Report. Seattle, WA.

Seidman, Karl F. 2004. *Economic Development Finance.* 1st ed. Thousand Oaks, CA: Sage.

U.S. Department of Energy. 2008a. "DOE Weatherization Assistance Program: DOE and States' Roles in the Weatherization Assistance Program." July 8. Accessed online January 27, 2010.

———. 2008b. "DOE Weatherization Assistance Program: History of the Weatherization Assistance Program." July 16. Accessed online February 5, 2010.

———. 2009. "DOE Weatherization Assistance Program: 2009 Recovery

Act—Frequently Asked Questions about Weatherization." Accessed online December 9, 2009.

———. n.d. *Weatherization Assistance Program—The American Recovery and Reinvestment Act of 2009.* Fact sheet. *www1.eere.energy.gov/wip/pdfs/wap_arra_factsheet.pdf.*

U.S. Department of Energy, Office of Inspector General, Office of Audit Services. 2010. *Special Report- Progress in Implementing the Department of Energy's Weatherization Assistance Program under the American Recovery and Reinvestment Act.* OAS-RA-10-04. February 19.

United States Department of Labor. 2010. Bureau of Labor Statistics Data. April 9. *data.bls.gov/PDQ/servlet/SurveyOutputServlet?series_id=LNS14000000.*

Wald, Matthew L., and Leslie Kaufman. 2010. "Hiring Freezes Hamper Weatherization Plan." *New York Times,* February 24.

"Weatherization Assistance Program for Low Income Persons." 2009. *Federal Register* 65, no. 237, December 8, Rules and Regulations, Department of Energy, Office of Energy Efficiency and Renewable Energy, 10 CFR Part 440, 77210–19.

6

Community/Labor/Utility Partnerships

A Social-Movement Organizing Strategy
for Energy Efficiency in Massachusetts

Eric Mackres and Lily Song

Introduction

On July 14, 2009, hundreds of Boston residents filled the normally quiet halls of the Massachusetts Department of Energy Resources to attend the bimonthly public meeting of the Energy Efficiency Advisory Council. The council was a newly created body, charged with overseeing state-regulated utility energy-efficiency programs. A year prior, in June 2008, Massachusetts had passed the Green Communities Act, which established aggressive energy-efficiency goals, called for new approaches to meet them, and supported these initiatives with increased spending. In turn, the council had convened to develop three-year plans for energy efficiency to be implemented by every utility in the state. The council was meant to provide a forum for people to respond to the utility plans before the more rigid and formal regulatory process began at the Department of Public Utilities. But despite the theoretically collaborative nature of the council, at the time of the July meeting council members and meeting participants largely consisted of a small circle of technical experts from private and nonprofit energy-efficiency business, environmental advocates, and state representatives.

As the enormous crowd gathered in the meeting chambers, it was clear to council members that people had organized and come with a mission. The crowd included members of the Green Justice Coalition, a statewide coalition, led by the Boston-based Community Labor United, of environmental, workforce, and labor organizations, who viewed energy efficiency through a social-justice lens. Whereas the council played an advisory role within the state energy-efficiency regulatory space, Green Justice, which counted among its leaders the Tufts University professor and community activist Penn Loh, had come to assume an advocacy role within the council's collaborative planning process. For Green Justice, the council was a stage for engaging in negotiation as well as confrontation. Prior to the meeting, the coalition had successfully lobbied for time on the agenda for an "extended comment period." When their turn came, Green Justice members, all Massachusetts residents, testified before the council about why the issue of equity in energy-efficiency regulation was of personal importance to them. They told their stories, at great length and passionately. Mike Sherman, director of energy-efficiency programs at the Massachusetts Department of Energy Resources, recounted the event:

> People made a lot of personal statements about their situations, some
> of them very heart wrenching . . . [the] kind of things that impacted
> them, either looking for jobs and sustainable career paths or what sort
> of things had suffered because everybody is poor and trying to pay
> their energy bills was another thing. It personally makes connections
> but to my mind I don't think it changed a single thing about what we
> intended to do. . . . Thirty minutes of that was affecting; two hours of
> that was numbing. But at the end there were no alternatives to take
> away to consider so the whole event had essentially no effect. (Sher-
> man 2010)

Although they found the personal testimony compelling, council members like Sherman were unable or unwilling to transform their momentary insights into action.

The council members were used to engaging in technical conversations during the meetings and unaccustomed to dealing directly with the public on energy efficiency. For them, the event was both illuminating and disconcerting. By telling their stories, Green Justice members infused their practical knowledge into a process that typically emphasized technical knowledge; they brought up issues of equity and accountability that affected low-and middle-income ratepayers—pressing concerns that had been absent or buried in previous council's discussions. Green Justice's confrontational tactic here emboldened and unified its membership but increased tension with the members of the council.

As the council drafted its three-year plans for state-regulated utility energy-efficiency programming, Green Justice intended to make sure that certain participants, issues, or forms of knowledge were not privileged over others. Following the July confrontation, however, the council endorsed a version of the three-year plans without key pieces of Green Justice's proposals and sent it to the Department of Public Utilities for final approval. Marginalized within the council's planning process, Green Justice responded by filing for "intervener" status to formally challenge the council-endorsed plans at the Department of Public Utilities. High temperatures rose higher, but all was not yet lost.

Community Labor United, Green Justice's organizing entity, is a regional alliance of social-movement organizations that engages in large, organized campaigns to achieve social goals. Their confrontational tactics, in particular lobbying for an extended comment period and filing for intervener status in the three-year plan review process, fit the standard profile of social-movement organizing. At the same time, their stance toward elites and authorities, as seen in their willingness to both confront and work side by side with energy-efficiency experts and public officials, is not entirely oppositional. Also, they appear better ingrained in the policy arena of state-regulated energy efficiency than most social-movement organizations.

While Green Justice's achievements are remarkable, the details and significance of their interactions with the council remain less clear. This raises the question of how Green Justice, Community Labor United, and Penn Loh came to enter in the planning process for the three-year plans for state-regulated utility energy-efficiency programming in the first place. Why did they become involved? How did they prepare and what was their point of entry? What is the underlying logic to their approach? And what are the defining attributes of Green Justice and Community Labor United that enabled them to be effective in this venue?

Network Power

This chapter presents the case of Community Labor United to demonstrate how an organization can develop network power by using both social-movement organizing and collaborative planning techniques. We will define and establish some theoretical background for these concepts, then examine how well they conform to Community Labor United's experience.

Much of the practice and scholarship on building social movements has focused on injustice framing: the opposition to an "other" and the use of confrontational rhetoric, motivation, and identity (Tarrow 1998, Alinsky 1971, Piven and Cloward 1977). Consequently, in the rhetoric, history, and mythology of social movements, collaboration is a contentious term, commonly suggesting collusion with, and co-optation by, the enemy. In practice, however, collaboration need not be so self-compromising. Rather, a collaborative planning process, defined by "a variety of stakeholders in long-term, face-to-face discussions to produce plans and policies on controversial public issues," can help solve complex and intractable issues as well as transcend conflict or ambivalence (Booher and Innes 2002, 221). In fact, social-movement organizations often engage in and benefit from collaborative planning, including that undertaken (1) inside organizations and movements, (2) among organizations and movements, and (3) between organizations/movements and elites, authorities, and opponents (Piven and Cloward 1977). Through joint problem solving and action, "linked agents" are able to "alter their environment in ways advantageous to [them] individually and collectively" (Booher and Innes 2002, 225).

At the same time, collaborative planning processes can produce negative results for social-movement organizations and their constituents in the absence of attention to power dynamics among stakeholders. Marc Weiss, for example, has argued in *The Rise of the Community Builders: The American Real Estate Industry and Urban Land Planning*, that collaborative planning methods are biased toward economic development and the interests of the business community (Harvey 1989). Marxist economic geographer David Harvey has likewise asserted that planning is designed to protect the capitalist system by balancing all interests (Harvey 1989). More recent iterations of collaborative planning theory, however, have defined power in ways that extend beyond using resources to coerce. "Often the powerful player gets acquiescence but not results, or even results contrary to his intentions" (Harvey 1989). Less influential and resourced players may draw upon alternative sources of power, such as the power of action; the power of ideas and methods; or the power of deep structure.[1] In essence, *how* a social-movement organization approaches a collaborative planning process defines the possibilities of what they can achieve within it. By employing their strengths to level barriers to participation, equalize the power of different methods, and coordinate actions within a collaborative planning process, a social-movement organization can enable a new conceptual and relational structure for problem solving. This, in turn, can open up "new options that were not available to [stakeholders] individually or when they were in conflict mode with others" (Booher and Innes 2002, 225).

David Booher and Judith Innes, authors of "Network Power in Collaborative Planning," call the ability to better address problems through collaboration "network power." They identify three preconditions necessary to create network power: (1) "diversity of agents," (2) "interdependence of agents," and (3) "authentic dialogue." The first precondition follows from the premise that having a wider range of stakeholders with various interests and knowledge relevant to the issues at hand allows for a greater body of resources to draw upon in exploring options and finding solutions. The "interdependence of agents," on the other hand, speaks to the need for participants in a collaborative planning process to recognize the mutual value of working together. The awareness among participants that all have something others want, and all want something from the others, helps keep everyone engaged in the process. The final precondition, "authentic dialogue," ensures that the diverse and interdependent participants speak honestly and in an informed way about their interests and perspectives, and that all participants are listened to. Authentic dialogue can nurture learning, creativity, and reciprocity in the short term while facilitating mutual adaptations (complete with shared values, identities, meanings, and heuristics) and innovative solutions over the longer run. In sum, where there is a diverse network of people who are aware of and ready to capitalize on their mutual interdependence, authentic dialogue helps translate such ingredients into network power.

As we shall see in the Community Labor United case, social-movement organizations can incorporate collaborative planning approaches into their organizational repertoires to foster the three preconditions and generate network power. We will provide two interrelated instances in which Community Labor United created network power by combining social-movement organizing and collaborative planning approaches. In the first instance, Community Labor United used collaborative methods to bring progressive people, organizations, and movements together in the Boston area. In doing so, it built an unlikely alliance of social-movement organizations engaged in joint dialogue and action around issues of common concern. Thus Community Labor United's first manifestation of network power resulted from these diverse progressive social-movement agents coming together to "alter their environment in ways advantageous to [them] individually and collectively" (Booher and Innes 2002, 225). In the process of convening and becoming accountable to these diverse and interdependent agents, Community Labor United came to represent a subset of interests. Consequently, it was able to leverage this new position to gain access to the world of state-regulated utility energy-efficiency policy and planning. In the second instance, Community Labor United created network power in collaboration and in confrontation with outsiders: the energy-efficiency regulators and utility companies. The resultant network power expanded possibilities for energy-efficiency regulation and implementation.

Community Labor United's emphasis on building long-term alliances is significant because it enables the development of network power in an ongoing manner. This allows the group to better tackle a variety of issues, as the members become vested in the alliance, recognize their interdependence with other alliance members, and capitalize on their collective capacity. Short-term alliances, although valuable for dealing with particular policy issues, may not provide the benefits or challenges of creating shared meaning, identities, or innovations. As Booher and Innes describe, network power emerges as follows:

1. Diverse participants in a network focus on a common task and develop shared meaning and common heuristics that guide their action.
2. The power grows as these players identify and build on their interdependencies to create new potential.
3. In the process, innovations and novel responses to environmental stresses can emerge.
4. These innovations in turn make possible adaptive change and constructive joint action. (Booher and Innes 2002, 225)

In the following section, we describe how these steps have worked in the story of Community Labor United, beginning with the development of its internal deliberation and joint campaign planning and its use of that planning to create an alliance of progressive social-movement organizations in Boston. Next, we describe how Community Labor United balanced movement organizing with collaborative planning strategies in the regulatory process of the Energy Efficiency Advisory Council to create network power in partnership with social-movement outsiders. We conclude the chapter by highlighting the major components of Community Labor United's approach, considering the implications for other social-movement organizations across the United States, and discussing related challenges.

Community Labor United's Third Campaign

Community Labor United was founded in 2004 as a long-term, progressive labor-community alliance for the Boston area. It has a central focus on supporting the work of labor unions and community-based organizations. Community Labor United's founder and co-director, Lisa Clauson, described her goals for the organization:

> We set up Community Labor United to be a coalition of organizations. I also wanted it to be partner driven and not so much staff driven in terms of what campaigns to take on, what issues to move. . . . So I wanted to set up a structure where there was clear accountability across organizations. (2010)

Community Labor United, like similar labor-community alliances in other cities, was initiated by a regional labor council, in this case the Greater Boston Labor Council. Scholars have dubbed this regional community-labor coalition model, developed in California in the late 1990s, the Regional Power Building model (Dean and Reynolds 2009).

The Community Labor United member organizations represent a racially, ethnically, and geographically diverse swath of greater Boston. Its main leadership and decision-making body, the strategy committee, manages multiple interests to ensure the organization's legitimacy among members. It consists of equal numbers of community groups and labor unions, all of which are organizing groups that are always actively seeking new members.[2] The strategy committee is a standing body that evaluates and decides which campaign opportunities, research reports, and potential members to pursue.

Community Labor United has thus far run three campaigns. The first was a joint campaign between the painters union and community groups to win a union contract to paint Boston public schools and simultaneously provide jobs with good pay, training, and union membership to residents in nearby communities. In the second campaign, the Service Employees International Union partnered with community groups to organize security workers in downtown Boston office buildings to negotiate benefits, like foreclosure protection in the workers' communities.

Community Labor United's third and most recent campaign was the Green Justice Coalition, a multiphase, statewide, alliance led by community groups. Through the course of the campaign, Community Labor United has come to adopt an environmental-justice frame as their primary approach to messaging and organizing.[3] They have also built their coalition to include environmental, faith-based, and workforce development organizations across the state.

Each campaign that Community Labor United runs has its own leadership body made up of representatives from interested member organizations. An exploratory phase at the beginning of campaign development (described in detail below) allows Community Labor United to verify interest from its membership; member groups opt into a campaign when they recognize an interdependence of interests. Not all members are involved in every campaign. Green Justice, for example, has been largely led by community organizations and supported by unions representing the building trades from across the state of Massachusetts.[4]

Through national affiliations, Community Labor United is connected to organizations and networks acting at the regional level to shift the direction of economic development in their communities. Community Labor United is a longtime member of the Partnership for Working Families; Green Justice is a local affiliate of the Apollo Alliance. These two organizations are national alliances with regional chapters that, like Community Labor United itself, focus on building long-term relationships among various progressive constituencies and taking mutually beneficial action. The Partnership for Working Families focuses on building relationships between labor unions and community groups, particularly in low-income communities and communities of color. The Apollo Alliance promotes common frames and action among progressive movements to transition to a clean-energy economy that creates broad benefits for working Americans. These affiliations provide Community Labor United and Green Justice with technical and political support.

Membership Diversity and Interdependence

At Community Labor United's founding, Lisa Clauson established criteria for membership in the organization as well as guiding principles for selecting campaigns. The criteria allowed for recruitment of a diversity of organizations while limiting member organizations to a manageable number. It also ensured that members had some obvious shared identities and interdependencies to start with. These shared characteristics facilitate movement co-development and organizing between two diverse movements, processes that can be fraught with difficulties. Ms. Clauson explains,

> We decided it would focus in on groups that were organizing, [groups that] had a similar constituency of low- and moderate-income communities or workers, that were aggressively doing new organizing and not just maintaining the membership base, and where there was a commitment of senior staff to participate in the work. (2010)

Shared constituencies, methods, and commitment provided the interdependence and diversity ensuring the organization was quickly seen as valuable and legitimate by most members. These criteria enabled members to unite around three common characteristics: the definition of the problem (marginalization of low- and moderate- income people in economic and political processes), the approach to problem solving (empowerment of low- and moderate- income people through base building), and their identity (a group of base-building organizations drawing power from their memberships, committed to working together over the long term for common benefits). Interdependencies, such as common geography and issues of interest that no single group could successfully solve on their own, provided further incentives for the group to come together and stay together.

A Culture of Joint Deliberation

There is a long history of tension between labor unions and communities of color in the United States. This is especially true in Boston where, for example, disagreement on issues of integration and school busing resulted in physical violence between white and black working-class communities in the 1970s. Soledad Boyd, a senior organizer at Community Labor United and former organizer at City Life / Vida Urbana, described how this history has affected the development of working relationships within the coalition.

[Integration of workers from communities of color into unions] is not going to happen overnight. . . . You have got to realize that some of these folks, when they are looking across the table at a union guy, white union guy, they are looking and they're saying, whether it is the actual person, they're saying, "That's the kid that threw the rock at me when I was bused to South Boston High." They hear the voice, they hear the whole South Boston pathos or whatever and that is what they see. Those tensions run deep. "OK, they were throwing rocks at me when I was a kid. They were locking me out of the unions when I was a young adult." (2010)

One of the initial challenges that Community Labor United faced in trying to move beyond this dysfunctional past was to balance the need to build trust between its labor groups and its community organizations with the need to have a "win." A shared win early on was needed to prove Community Labor United's value, build momentum, and retain the commitment of its member organizations. In order to make progress on both of these needs, Community Labor United's organizations embarked on a series of meetings and activities to learn about each other and, simultaneously, to search for campaigns that would benefit both community and labor groups. This was the beginning of an internal deliberative culture within Community Labor United.

One of these meetings was a leadership institute run by Amy Dean, a founder of Working Partnerships USA, one of the first regional power-building coalitions. Lisa Clauson recounted her observations of the meeting:

Most of the community partners had no clue about the details of the different unions at the table, and some of them had little clue about each other as well. And definitely the unions at the table had no clue about the community partners and the type of organizing that they do. It was exciting to see how quickly people realized the self-interest that they do have in the overlap of issues that come and different approaches to it. (2010)

Clauson also described how storytelling was used as a departure point to establish self-interest and learn about points of commonality and difference. The storytelling became a starting point for developing relationships, allowing each side to recognize itself in the other. On one occasion, when members of the Brazilian Immigrants Center were describing the various ways in which employers exploit day laborers, Clauson noticed:

> The painters [union] immediately, kind of getting very excited about how that looks and how they are dealing with day laborers around what happens on the jobs and how they are undercutting the work of their union contractors, but a desire not to go after the worker but instead try to figure out ways to fold them into the union and make the work that they are doing union as well. The synergy across that was exciting to be a part of. (2010)

This meeting was followed by another, this time focusing on creating ideas for mutually beneficial campaigns. In evaluating potential campaigns, participants conducted power analyses, listed potential opponents, and discussed the implications for each of the involved groups. Speaking openly about their interests, participants began to approach their differences with respect, empathy, and a willingness to learn rather than to judge. Clauson described how the admission of differences led to working together.

> [T]here was a definite interest from . . . a couple of [community] groups to take on the Boston Redevelopment Authority [BRA] and how development gets done in Boston, and what a crazy process it is that there is no city council oversight, there is no planning department, it is just the mayor and the mayor's folks at the BRA who have such total control over the development process. It has very much not worked for them and their issues on affordable housing and land control issues. . . . [But the unions said], "Look, it totally works for us. We like the mayor, and the system works. Through this process the mayor forces developers to agree to building things union. And if you take on this campaign, we are going to be on the other side of the fight with you on it." That could have been a very divisive moment and it could have kind of torn apart the coalition before we even started, but there was just really good discussion of people understanding each other's self-interest, of understanding where organizations are coming from, and understanding that there are going to be issues on which we

do not agree ... but there is still enough value for each organization of what they can get out of this emerging coalition for them to stay in it. Even though their primary issue was not going to be taken on in the case of [those community groups], they still wanted to be a part of what was being built. (2010)

Such experiences of storytelling and authentic dialogue were important for members to build trust and reciprocity, but also to develop a shared understanding of Community Labor United as a long-term, member-driven alliance. As Lydia Lowe, the executive director of the Chinese Progressive Association, recounted:

There was a whole year or more that was mostly relationship building and the different partners learning about each other. So we went to different organizations, different union halls, and community organizations to meet and then to tell about those different organizations so that we would have more appreciation and understanding of where we were both coming from. And then we tried to do a little bit of mapping who our constituencies and membership were, what are the issues we are working around. Having that basic level of information really laid the groundwork for us to then consider campaigns. And to look at those campaigns not just for the sake of an immediate, short-term campaign but to think about it in terms of how it would help build this alliance. (2009)

As Community Labor United developed an internal culture of joint deliberation, its member organizations not only bridged differences but also cultivated a sense of mutual regard and shared identity.

Power within the Alliance

Beyond facilitating authentic dialogue, Community Labor United ensures that the dialogue is seen as representative and legitimate to all member organizations: it aims to equalize power within the structure of the alliance. Community Labor United's governance is designed for accountability, for opportunities for all members, and for the provision of resources to member organizations with less capacity. The diversity and interdependence of its governing bodies, and their emphasis on consensus-based decision making, help ensure equality and accountability.

Community Labor United typically does not make any major policy decisions without involving member groups and obtaining their sanction.

Additionally, Community Labor United supports leadership and capacity development among its member organizations. The alliance plays the role of a base-building organization, with a twist: its base consists of other base-building organizations. Community Labor United's co-director Darlene Lombos describes how its staff's experience in base building has influenced their approach to developing the alliance.

> [A Community Labor United] organizer's job is to figure out ways to increase leadership and participation at all levels, just the same as in a base-building group. . . . Organizations that are highly involved, that are highly participatory, we try to get them to support other organizations in thinking through how they can get their entire organization participating and involved. So organizing for us also becomes supporting other folks in interacting and developing those relationships and supporting each other and organizing. . . . It is our job as coalition organizers and as base-building groups to always have a very deliberate, intentional plan for increasing that leadership, for finding opportunities for participation and engagement across the board. (2009)

For Community Labor United, the alliance structure requires an emphasis on complementing and facilitating the work of other organizations and avoiding competition with them. The issue of maximizing support and minimizing competition was a central consideration as Clauson developed the structure to be "not staff-heavy, leaner, and also [to use] the organizing to drive resources to the community partners." Accordingly, its fundraising strategy includes regranting funds to members, as well as cowriting foundation grant applications with members. The regranted funds have gone exclusively to community-group members, who are dependent on foundation funding, rather than unions, who receive revenue from member dues. These grant funds allow community-group members to participate more consistently in the activities of the alliance, and this helps to equalize power.

Constantly focusing resources, upholding accountability, and facilitating leadership development among member organizations have helped Community Labor United establish legitimacy and develop member capacity. Founded on the notion that a diverse set of member organizations will disagree on many things, Community Labor United's longer view allows member organizations to find common goals that they can better advance together.

Shared Identity through Campaign Action

Pursuing campaigns based on joint commitment and mutual benefit results in an emphasis on shared interests even as differences are recognized. The assumption is not that benefits from (and commitments to) a particular campaign are necessarily equal, but that enough common interest can justify continued collaboration. Although deliberation can illuminate common interests between parties, conceptual discovery often means little without proof through action. According to Lombos,

> [Community Labor United is] very committed to concrete campaign work as opposed to coming together for "solidarity" and "helping each other out." . . . [Building trust] really is about the day-to-day getting your leaders out in the street, seeing each other in the street together that really makes that bond much more concrete. (2009)

Lombos describes a memorable shift in identity and relationships through action from Community Labor United's "Secure Jobs, Secure Communities" campaign:

> Unions typically go out and do a blitz, where they go out for about a week or two, from 6 a.m. to 6 p.m. or however late. . . . Try to catch as many potential union members as they can. We actually got a bunch of our community groups to do the blitz with them. And the union did pay stipends for folks in the community to go out in the community to make that connection. "You live in my neighborhood. I live here. You should join the union.' That was the idea of it. . . . I went out with a woman from Boston Workers Alliance. . . . We go into one of the buildings downtown. It was during one of the morning shifts. There was this woman she was trying to convince to sign a postcard. She was very union friendly. . . . And then they realized that they knew mutual people, they had shared at some point a neighborhood they lived in, they had shared some experience at some church. . . . I just thought, this is what it is. It is about people seeing themselves not as workers, not as working on community issues but as a community. . . . A

working-class community who is fighting for justice in a ways that we have shared interest, shared goals, shared targets. And having her and also our other community members go out and do the blitz with the union really helped the union. (2009)

Shared experiences and identity gained through joint action are integral to developing the capacity of alliance members to exercise network power. Joint action can serve as a form of authentic dialogue, enabling participants to coconstruct shared identities and meanings. The result is an opportunity to develop new capacity for innovation, including the ability to adapt. Consequently, Community Labor United staff members spend much of their time engaging member organizations in activities. Penn Loh explains:

I would say that [Community Labor United] staff are very, very careful about keeping people involved because they understand that if they end up doing all the work and calling all the shots and getting people to kind of rubber stamp it then you are not really running an alliance. You are running your own show and having some window dressing to go along with it. And those people won't materialize when you really need to exercise your strength. (2009)

To Community Labor United, shared action and leadership development, along with deliberative efforts to identify shared interests and opportunities for mutual gains, serve as forms of authentic dialogue. Such methods develop trust, and that trust fosters reciprocal learning and creativity.

Shared Meaning of "Green Justice"

Community Labor United's latest campaign, "Green Justice," grew from a deliberative process that convened member groups around the issue of creating good green jobs in historically marginalized communities. In 2007, Alternatives for Community and Environment, together with Community Labor United's staff, began to explore the concepts of green jobs and green economy. Penn Loh, then the director of Alternatives for Community and Environment, led a series of discussions that developed "principles of green justice." These principles are effectively a frame that emphasizes economic transformation. Their application aims to generate wealth in communities that typically carry a disproportionate load of environmental burdens. The title of "green justice" (rather than "green jobs") emerged from Community Labor United's emphasis on base building and regional power building. A more narrow formulation of green jobs has often been interpreted to mean sector-specific job training, job-placement programs, and technical assistance for contractors, sometimes targeted to benefit low-income and minority populations. This definition dissatisfied Community Labor United because it would benefit only those directly involved in the programs and would fail to build power for workers or community members more broadly.

The deliberative process that eventually forged a campaign out of the green-justice principles began as a discussion among the staff of a few member organizations and next expanded to include interested community groups. Labor unions followed. This sequencing reflected the desire of Community Labor United's leadership to create a community-driven campaign after having completed two campaigns with union members. Throughout the process, Green Justice participants consulted periodically with the strategy committee to ensure their continued support, while Community Labor United's staff improved the campaign and assessed its value to other members.

The fact that Community Labor United's member organizations broadly recognized the importance of equality of voice between community and labor groups, and had built mutual trust over the course of previous campaigns, allowed them to take a strategic and deliberate approach to developing the Green Justice campaign. This time they sought to create a community-driven, concept-oriented campaign, which differed significantly from the labor-driven, target-oriented campaign led by the security workers and painters. For Community Labor United, the Green Justice campaign was their most ambitious and complex to date, entailing a multiyear engagement in the creation and implementation of statewide energy policy. This was completely new territory in terms of topic, partnerships, duration, and geography.

"Pots of Money" and a Seat on the Council

The Green Justice campaign was Community Labor United's first to articulate a concept rather than identify a target. Instead of focusing on an immediate need, Community Labor United crafted a common frame that was later applied to identify an appropriate campaign. The principles of green justice, along with a detailed conceptual report, preceded any concrete ideas of what an on-the-ground campaign would look like. Eventually, Community Labor United would find itself engaged in another deliberative process, but this time they would be collaborating with nonmovement groups in an official policy-making capacity.

Even two years into its conceptual development, the substance of the Green Justice campaign remained unclear. This changed in early 2009, when Mary Jo Connelly, Community Labor United's research director, developed a "Pots of Money" diagram, revealing the state-regulated utility energy-efficiency programs as the largest and most enduring source of funding for green investments in Massachusetts. The Energy Efficiency Advisory Council was charged with figuring out what the Green Communities Act meant in practice, both for regulation and spending. From Community Labor United's perspective, the council, given its oversight over energy-efficiency programming and control of massive resources, offered a promising opportunity for engaging in green justice.

The council formalized an existing collaborative planning process, the nonutilities parties process, also referred to as the collaborative, which had been in operation in Massachusetts since 1989. The collaborative was an informal forum where stakeholders, largely technocrats, could have input into utility plans before they entered the more formal regulatory process at the Department of Public Utilities. The Massachusetts Department of Energy Resources, in chairing the council, brought in many of the same stakeholders from the collaborative. These continuing members adjusted to their new and officially sanctioned roles in the council, administering dramatic change in utility regulation and the greatest expansion in energy-efficiency spending in the history of the commonwealth. Penn Loh described the significance of these changes:

> This council creates a very interesting dynamic politically. It shakes up the very entrenched interest-group, pluralist approach that there had been in this world, and very insular through the nineties. Not a lot of people were paying a lot of attention, and energy issues hadn't been linked as clearly to so many different issues as it is today. So a lot of the folks who have been doing this work have been in roughly the same

small circle of people for the last twenty-five years. You have a bunch of people who are experts at this kind of stuff in the Department of Energy Resources; they all got their start doing work in the low-income sector or many of them have worked as consultants to utilities or back and forth. It is like this layer of people who have been involved in this work for a long time and now the world has changed around them and many more people have interest in it. (2009)

The council continued the tradition established by the collaborative by operating by majority vote only when consensus could not be reached. Penn Loh described the practical implications of such an approach:

The council was set up and became an organizing platform for the state, for the administration, to really push the utilities to go beyond the envelope, to go beyond their comfort zone. . . . [I]n the end the council is still advisory, but the levels of agreement, the amount of work that went into that process, the amount of political capital spent in that process really assured that whatever we got to real agreement on in the council should give the Department of Public Utilities a real signal of "you know what, don't mess with it. If they came to agreement, you should go with it." (2009)

Community Labor United and the members of Green Justice had never been stakeholders in the advocacy world of the collaborative, and they came late to the formation of the council. As they became increasingly interested in how the regulation of utility energy efficiency could provide important benefits to communities and workers, Community Labor United requested to fill the residential consumer seat on the council, and the Department of Energy Resources approved the request. Penn Loh, who had now transitioned to Tufts University, filled the seat. Mike Prokosch, Community Labor United's internal organizer, described the event's significance:

Penn had the credentials and the chops to be a credible nominee and we campaigned hard to get him on. That was a critical step because then we had direct access to submit proposals. Penn was very careful, as the new kid on the block on the council, to go slow, kind of not push the point, assessed before he moved and figured out how to present things. But he was able to bring idea after idea, proposal after proposal within the council and build relationships with other council members as we were doing from the outside. (2010)

Community Labor United also continued to build their credentials by arranging separate meetings with all the members of the council, including the utilities. The meetings cultivated relationships and served to develop leadership among Community Labor United's member groups. Together, leaders from member groups and Community Labor United staff learned how to ask questions and represent their interests in meetings. As a result, Green Justice became party to a developing shared identity among council members while maintaining their emphasis on an equity-based "green justice" framing of energy efficiency.

The interactions between the council and Green Justice required both bodies to deal with higher levels of diversity and interdependence than they ever had before. Because of its collaborative philosophy, the council had to recognize that Green Justice represented a group with a legitimate stake in the process and could offer valuable assets to the other participants (e.g., access to various communities). Green Justice, for its part, needed to expand its coalition to include partners from around the state, as well as from interest groups like environmentalists and faith communities, to be seen as a legitimate stakeholder in what is traditionally a statewide and technical issue.

"You Always Have to Have an Outsider Strategy"

Community Labor United complemented its collaborative tactics, of participating in collaboration and negotiation through their representative on the council, with strategies of public confrontation. The council shifted from the collaborative's informal, professional, closed-door practices to assume a public-meeting format, complete with public reporting and commenting requirements. As energy-efficiency decision making became something the public could learn about, participate in, and organize around, Community Labor United used the council as a venue not only for negotiation, but for organizing confrontation. The professedly collaborative nature of the council body provided Community Labor United with an opportunity to watchdog its openness and transparency.

This returns us to the event of Green Justice's "extended comment period" action on July 14, 2009, when more than one hundred people testified before the council on the importance of equity in energy-efficiency regulation. Beyond affecting policy decisions and the frame that the council was willing to consider, the action enabled Green Justice to strengthen its internal dynamics. Their principles represented a new idea, and, because of the statewide nature of the campaign, many new member organizations had been recruited and were still adapting to the diverse coalition and the new framing of environmental justice. Through collective action, members of Green Justice were able to make the frame and the goals of the campaign more concrete for themselves. They also made clear their position with regard to the council, as Penn Loh explained:

> What I've learned in my short time there is that Green Justice took kind of a frontal attack on it the same way the many of us in the community-organizing world got used to having to confront decision makers. So we kind of figure out who's the decision maker. Who can we target? Who can give us what we want? And we go after them. . . . And again it was interesting because it was not clear to me from being an insider on the council how much it affected members. From Green Justice's perspective I get the whole routine, you show them you have strength through all these people. (2009)

Jeremy Shenk, senior organizer with Community Labor United, added:

> Even though we were building relationships that were tight, it is like that latent threat that says, "We can do this. We would like you to do it with us. But we have the ability to do this thing that could be very embarrassing, could muck up this process a lot, and we're clearly willing to do that. But we would much prefer to be able to sit down and work on stuff." . . . And then that is how you start talking about policy, but it is all about how far you can move someone. . . . We're having to continue to straddle that line [between insider and outsider], which I think is really hard. But . . . I don't think just an insider strategy works. I think you always have to have an outsider strategy. . . . I think our steering committee will always just make us have that because that is what they do. They are power building, mobilizing kind[s] of groups. (2010)

For Shenk, Community Labor United's dual approach, balancing collaborative and confrontational strategies, went beyond their immediate relationships: it was a matter of maintaining adaptability in a dynamic environment.

"We Need to Start Thinking about Implementation"

Following the extended comment period at the council, Green Justice members met with Ian Bowles, the secretary of energy and environmental affairs, the cabinet-level agency that oversees the Department of Energy Resources. Darlene Lombos of Community Labor United recounted a conversation aimed at getting the council to mandate a "community-driven" approach to implementing energy efficiency:

> He was like, "Look, everybody is supportive of your ideas. Everybody wants to do good, but how do we know it is going to work? We would be really supportive of figuring out some sort of pilot that shows that this works." It dawned on us, we were like, "Oh, this is about implementation. They can do whatever they want in putting the language in but we need to start thinking about implementation." (2009)

At that point, Green Justice shifted from advocating a community-driven model to working with the utilities to design a pilot in order to prove that such a model could work. This transition required that Green Justice view the utilities as partners, not targets, and that meant working together for a shared goal.

The council's final three-year plan for utility-administered energy-efficiency programs was adopted unanimously on October 27, 2009, and included the following provisions:

1. *Financing.* The council established a "Financing and On-Bill Repayment Working Group" to work toward a system where, instead of providing payment upfront, program participants can pay off their energy-investment contribution over time, on their regular utility bill.
2. *Community-driven approach.* The council funded the Community Mobilization Initiatives, a set of community-based building energy-efficiency pilots to be implemented by Green Justice. The pilots were to be evaluated in the first year, toward the goal of replicating them elsewhere in the state.

3. *High-road jobs with standards and career pathways.* The council resolved that utilities should make hiring processes more open and "make reasonable efforts to encourage" contractors to provide "a livable wage, fair benefits, and the opportunity to move along a career path." They also encouraged utility compliance with applicable labor laws.

4. *Equity.* The council convened an equity committee, with Penn Loh among its first members. Loh hopes to establish equity metrics that can be applied to evaluating utility performance. (EEAC 2009a, 2009b)

The Community Mobilization Initiatives were the most tangible win for Green Justice. As defined in the three-year plan, they are

> energy efficiency outreach campaigns where community-based organizations that have long-standing relationships with homeowners, tenants and small businesses in economically marginalized communities and other groups that have a strong record of clean energy education and outreach, develop a "community mobilization outreach model" that implements a large-scale "bundled" neighborhood approach to energy efficiency retrofitting. (EEAC 2009a)

Green Justice conceived the mobilization initiatives as community-run programs to provide outreach, hire and train employees, and implement services. They intended to call on the diverse assets of Green Justice in multiple cities with the idea that every partner could contribute something valuable.

There are two components that distinguish the mobilization initiatives from other energy-efficiency programs. First, the initiatives are implemented by a lead community base-building partner, already established where the pilot will be taking place, and a lead union or workers' cooperative. The building partner coordinates the initial outreach and education on energy efficiency and organizes other community groups to help bundle residential homes, multiunit buildings, and small businesses interested in implementing energy-efficiency measures. The union or cooperative trains hired workers, partnering with a responsible contractor committed to local hiring, providing good wages and benefits, and establishing career pathways for new workers. Accordingly:

- National Grid and NSTAR, the local utility companies, are funding the Community Mobilization Initiatives and paying the higher labor costs required by the pilot programs.
- Community Labor United is hiring staff to coordinate the pilot projects and has raised money for an independent evaluator to identify practices for the utilities to apply statewide.
- The union partners are setting up training programs and allocating staff time to implement the pilot programs. They are bearing the costs of training programs (which are free to workers) and, in at least one case, subsidizing a portion of workers' benefit packages.
- The community partners are contributing staff and member time to negotiate and implement the pilot programs locally.[5]

The mobilization initiatives have four pilot sites: Boston's Chinatown, Lynn, Allston-Brighton, and Springfield, representing the broad geography of the Green Justice Coalition. With these four pilots, Green Justice plans to test and prove their concept in a diverse set of communities, while building relationships with different utilities.

The Chinatown Pilot

Among the mobilization initiatives, the Chinatown pilot has progressed the furthest so far, largely because conversations between Green Justice and NSTAR moved quickly. As the two sides discussed what they wanted, Green Justice saw Chinatown as an opportunity to match their own strengths with their partner's goals. NSTAR indicated an interest in accessing particular market segments, starting with the Asian market. Green Justice had, in the Chinese Progressive Association, a strong community partner with more than thirty years of community-organizing experience in Chinatown, as well as previous experience in energy work.[6] The International Union of Painters and Allied Trades, the most active building-trade union in Community Labor United, also joined the Chinatown pilot to provide preapprentice training for local employees and a pathway to union membership. Moreover, the Union of Painters helped recruit the Aulson Company as the general contractor for the project; this firm had demonstrated responsible labor practices in previous projects and signaled its willingness to abide by the terms of the Chinatown project.

From the Community Labor United perspective, the goals of the Chinatown Mobilization Initiative, which "facilitates the implementation of neighborhood-scale bundled energy-efficiency retrofits in a designated hard-to-reach neighborhood," are manifold. They include the following:

- Promote energy efficiency, energy conservation, and the installation of clean-energy technologies in the designated neighborhood
- Reduce the designated community's energy consumption and energy costs
- Reduce the designated community's greenhouse gas emissions
- Support sustainable development in the community
- Create green-job opportunities for community residents, including new entrants into the workforce, long-term unemployed and underemployed residents, and displaced workers
- Create energy-efficiency job training opportunities for community residents, including on-the-job training and pathways into construction careers
- Pilot innovative community-mobilization outreach mechanisms to engage residents and small businesses in implementing energy-efficiency building improvements and behaviors
- Pilot bundled neighborhood-scale contracting mechanisms to engage a responsible contractor and an adequately trained and compensated workforce to install energy-efficiency building improvements

To accomplish the latter four goals, the Chinese Progressive Association and the Union of Painters, in partnership with the Aulson Company, are developing the Chinatown Green Collar Pathways workforce development program. The training program will create a bilingual workforce of Chinatown residents by preparing two dozen immigrant adults for work in the energy-efficiency industry. Trainees who complete the program will become affiliated with the Union of Painters as weatherization pre-apprentices, be hired at $18.48 plus benefits, and become eligible for the painters' three-year apprenticeship program.

NSTAR foresees a project of narrower and more quantifiable scope as evidenced by their description:

By definition, a pilot is the trial of an alternative program delivery model or measure on a scale that will allow for assessing the merits of the proposed change while minimizing the risk associated with the expenditure of ratepayer funds. Based on these criteria, the scope for a Mobilization Initiative will be limited to:

- 50 homes (each unit is counted separately for buildings with more than one unit)
- 4 multi-family buildings with 20 or fewer units

The utilities likewise define project aims in limited terms:

- Completion of insulation/air sealing in 50 homes (each unit is counted separately for buildings with 2–4 units) and 4 multi-family buildings with 20 or fewer units by September 30, 2010.
- Based on experience gleaned through the outreach efforts, provide the [utilities] with an understanding of the motivations that drove some customers to participate as well as the barriers that prevented others in the same population from participating.

The Chinatown pilot has already fallen behind schedule, largely due to a gap in funding.[7] A central component of the mobilization initiative model is helping moderate-income residents finance the energy-efficiency measures and "preweatherization" building improvements. The required up-front resident contribution (approximately 25 percent of the costs of the installed measures in Massachusetts utility programs) is out of reach for many middle-income people and for those with poor credit. Furthermore, in neighborhoods like Chinatown, the old building stock requires additional improvements to meet building codes before energy-efficiency measures can be installed. The continuing absence of on-bill financing, revolving loans, or other finance mechanisms limits access to building energy-efficiency measures. Although Green Justice had received indications that the city of Boston would help to fill this funding gap, as of May 2010 the funds had not been received.

Regulation as Enabler and Barrier

Another challenge has to do with the different end goals of the various parties in the mobilization initiatives. Green Justice intends for the pilot model to be expanded, while the utilities have made no commitment beyond the initial four pilot sites. The parties have been willing thus far to work together on common short-term goals, but this cooperation will not necessarily persist. The utilities and the council's plan is to evaluate the pilots primarily for cost effectiveness and parity of cost (where they compare favorably in cost to other efficiency programs), as required by law. But Green Justice plans to bring in its own evaluators to capture data on a wider range of issues, including equitable participation in the program, job access, and job quality. They aim to build on their findings to advocate for the expansion of the model. Planning for the pilot evaluation began in early 2010, before a completed agreement on implementing the pilot had even been reached.

The very regulatory constraints that allowed the partnership to begin in the first place are another potential obstacle to continued collaboration. The strong sway of the council made the utilities receptive to new partnerships and experimental programs, but the statutory requirement of least-cost procurement of energy efficiency means that more expensive programs may not get funded precisely because they are more expensive—even if they would provide other benefits to communities and workers. The newly created equity committee (which is part of the council) is working to develop "equity metrics" to measure access to energy-efficiency programs and jobs, but the Department of Public Utilities has ruled that questions of equity are outside its regulatory purview. The introduction of equity considerations into the selection criteria for efficiency programs may prove to be a major test for the council.

Shared Beliefs and Benefits

The cautious partnership between Green Justice and the utilities on the pilots has rested on a shared belief that the relationship is valuable for all parties. For Green Justice, embarking on the pilots was an opportunity to strengthen the coalition, build resources, and demonstrate success. The pilots provided a project-based approach to uniting a diverse and growing coalition through action. By building relationships with the utilities at an early phase in the three-year plans, Green Justice members could access long-term funding opportunities to help drive the development of these community-based efforts. Finally, the pilots proved that communities can improve the built environment at a heavily discounted cost, residents can save money, partnerships can create local jobs, and communities and workers can protect their interests. For the utilities, partnering with Green Justice meant implementing a difficult but potentially valuable program, innovating through existing networks, and satisfying the regulators. It also allowed the utilities to align with a potential opponent.

Balancing Very Different Perspectives

To move beyond the hunch that working together could result in shared benefits and to put a program in place, the partners first had to get to know each other. Participants from the utilities and Green Justice described the beginning of the partnership as an extended learning phase for both sides. Both partners had to learn new vocabulary: utilities became familiar with terms like "coalition," "responsible contractor," and "living wage," while Green Justice learned about utility energy-efficiency implementation. NSTAR outlined all the steps in their energy-efficiency programs for Green Justice so its members could better articulate their interests and goals.

After they learned how to communicate with each other, Community Labor United, NSTAR, utilities, and other partners spent a day mapping out the delivery process for the new program that they were creating. Iteratively, the group put together flow charts on a whiteboard that described how services would actually get to customers. Over the following months, the partners met on a weekly or biweekly basis to figure out the remaining details. In essence, Community Labor United and their community and labor partners were building on the experience and existing models of utility program administrators to implement an entirely new model for delivering energy efficiency. While Community Labor United sees the mobilization initiatives as an opportunity to reframe the value and delivery of energy efficiency in collaboration with the utilities, the process entails balancing very different perspectives. Connelly explains:

> [The pilots] actually are discussed in [the three-year utility plans], but there is no commitment to doing their community outreach in a particular way. So they could do it community mobilization style . . . or they could do some other [version]. . . . The concept of

what [the utilities and the council] think of as community is really odd. Our whole thing is about honoring and building on the role of the community-based organization that is already there, that knows the terrain, that has trust, and can help you wisely negoti-ate and can help you to get people to take on this commitment to doing retrofits. And they have a different ... it's very different, it's a market-based mentality. It's all about individual purchasing deci-sions. (Connelly 2010)

Despite these different starting points, the parties recognize their interdependence, value each other's diversity, and continue to participate in an authentic dialogue. The resultant model will combine technical energy-efficiency expertise with existing community networks and prac-tical knowledge to achieve greater efficiency and provide other benefits for the community. Brought together by Green Justice's social organiz-ing approach and collaborative planning methods, the partners have to-gether realized network power, engendering innovative responses and constructive joint action in the face of collective challenges.

Unpacking Community Labor United's Strategy

Community Labor United developed network power at the intersection of social-movement organizing and collaborative planning in two phases: first among their own member organizations and second through a con-frontal/collaborative process with utilities and other stakeholders on the council. While it would be a mistake to generalize based on a single case, it is important to recognize the key components in their overall strategy.

As a long-term alliance, Community Labor United's organizational mission is to unite diverse groups around issues of common concern and interdependence, that is to say, to build an adaptable structure to support collaborative interactions between progressive social move-ments. Community Labor United has used joint dialogue and joint ac-tion to forge a shared frame among a diverse network of progressive social-movement organizations in the Boston area. The process began when they established an alliance with local base-building organizations, providing initial common reference points. Subsequently, authentic dia-logue, emphasizing similarities and interdependencies, built reciprocity and opportunities for mutual learning and creativity. Joint action toward common goals facilitated the development of shared meanings, identities, and innovations in the face of uncertainty.

Although Community Labor United could not reconcile power differences between the members in their activities outside the alliance, they sought to balance voice and influence within it. In short, they used accountable and democratic procedures to organize the interests and amplify the collective voice of its member groups to achieve authentic representation. Historically marginalized groups and organizing groups affected policy changes, accessed more funding, and found new opportunities around which to organize.

In launching the Green Justice campaign, Community Labor United built a sturdy foundation for dealing effectively with nonmovement partners like energy-efficiency experts and utility companies by undertaking research and recruiting new member organizations to join the alliance. In exploring the green-justice concept, Community Labor United took the powerful new trend and recast it in a way that resonated with its membership, adopting the green-justice frame as their primary approach to messaging and organizing. Community Labor United built an alliance that included environmental, faith-based, and workforce development organizations, and then identified the council as the place to pursue their goals. Within the council, Community Labor United articulated the value of their specific knowledge and skills, successfully arguing that their organizing experience could be put to work to implement energy efficiency. The capacity of Green Justice to activate people on the ground provided an opportunity for Community Labor United to partner with the utilities to test a new type of energy-efficiency program.

As Community Labor United collaboratively engaged with movement outsiders within the council, maintaining its organizing capacity was essential because it allowed Community Labor United not only to gain recognition as a legitimate stakeholder, but also to contribute skills that made new options possible. Even as alliances bridge the practices of organizing and collaborative planning, it is essential that such alliances and their member organizations retain an organizing focus. Organizing allows social-movement groups to fully recognize the value of their own diversity and interdependence. Further, organizing enables social-movement organizations to command entry into, as well as departure from, a policy process. The threat or use of confrontational tactics can prove valuable in enforcing ground rules or simply in ensuring that all parties are meeting their commitments.

Opportunities and Challenges

The role of policy maker and implementer is completely new territory for Community Labor United. If the pilot projects are completed successfully, they can serve as a model for building network power that is transferrable to other cities. Helping to craft and implement policy is a new task for social-movement organizations. In the past, crafting policy and implementing it have largely been handled separately: for example, lobbying and rallies to influence policy and "bucket brigades" for citizen implementation of pollution monitoring. For social-movement organizations intent on combining organizing and collaborative approaches to develop network power, as well as engaging in policy making and implementation, the national energy-efficiency context presents an ideal stage, complete with unprecedented levels of funding, public regulatory and planning requirements, and openness to innovation. However, for many, such involvement first requires a profound shift: from a defensive posture, reacting to the negative consequences of urban development, to a more creative stance that actively pursues an alternative course. The process also includes overcoming oppositional dynamics and building alliances among progressive social movements.

The entry into consensus-based, public decision-making processes by social-movement organizations must be considered as a next step beyond the existing tactics of community-labor partnerships. Community-benefit agreements and project-labor agreements (as in the Clean Energy Works program in Portland, Oregon, a community workforce agreement) that are negotiated with developers on a project-by-project basis have become a common tactic for organizations in the Partnership for Working Families network (Brandin 2010). Community Labor United is taking that tactic one step further, attempting to integrate community benefits and labor standards at the policy level, rather than at the scale of a single development project. The publicly regulated sector of energy-efficiency programs provides a meso-level for organizing, between sector-wide and project-based standards, enabling attached provisions to generate wider impact. Writing job and community standards into energy-efficiency policy would provide a foothold for Community Labor United to engage further and to continue their work, whether through policy or projects. Finally, on a broader level, Community Labor United's organizing and collaborative planning activities in the particular policy subfield of energy efficiency—which brings together community, labor, and environmentalists around a common, prescriptive agenda—represents an important step forward in expanding network power within the ranks of the progressive movement.

Conclusion

It remains to be seen if undertaking the pilots was a good decision, from the perspective of organizational development, for Community Labor United and Green Justice. Even assuming the success of Green Justice in implementing the pilot programs and meeting their goals and the goals of the regulators, the situation raises a whole series of questions. Beyond the risk of "selling out," there is the more persistent challenge of reconciling conflicting frameworks. Will the partial shift into collaboration lead to true collaborative problem solving with opponents over the long term? Or will it lead to half-hearted efforts, lowest-common-denominator outcomes, and reactionary push back from those within the organizations who want to see more confrontational strategies? Ultimately, it seems that the outcome will boil down to Community Labor United's ability to balance organizing and collaborative approaches over the long run. Can Community Labor United stay true to their organizational roots in base building while innovating with other agents through collaborative processes? Time will tell.

Notes

1. A comparable framework is Gaventa's three instruments of power, which includes superior bargaining resources, the ability to construct or eliminate barriers to participation, and the ability to shape shared consciousness through myths, ideology, and control of information (Gaventa 1980).
2. Community groups include Alternatives for Community and Environment, Boston Workers' Alliance, New England United for Justice, Chelsea Collaborative, Chinese Progressive Association, City Life / Vida Urbana, Mass Affordable Housing Alliance, and Project RIGHT. Labor unions include the Boston Teachers' Union, New England Council of Carpenters, Painters and Allied Trades DC35, SEIU Local 1199, SEIU Local 615, UFCW Local 1445, and UNITE HERE. See *massclu.org/leadership-staff* and *massclu.org/green-justice-campaign*.
3. According to the Environmental Protection Agency, environmental justice is the fair treatment and meaningful involvement of all people regardless of race, color, national origin, or income with respect to the development,

implementation, and enforcement of environmental laws, regulations, and policies. U.S. Environmental Protection Agency, "Environmental Justice," *www.epa.gov/environmentaljustice/*.

4. Community groups include Alternatives for Community and Environment, Alliance to Develop Power, New England United for Justice, Boston Workers' Alliance, Chelsea Collaborative, Chinese Progressive Association, Coalition Against Poverty, Coalition for Social Justice, Dudley Street Neighborhood Initiative, Greater Four Corners Action Coalition, MassCOSH, Neighbor to Neighbor, and Project RIGHT. Labor unions include Laborers' New England Regional Organizing Fund, New England Council of Carpenters, Painters and Allied Trades DC35, and Utility Workers Union of America Local 369. Environmental groups included Boston Climate Action Network, Clean Water Action, and Massachusetts Energy Consumers Alliance (Boyd 2010).

5. These details and subsequent ones included in the remainder of this chapter are taken from project planning documents of Green Justice and the utilities.

6. The Chinese Progressive Association had previously collaborated with Alternatives for Community and Environment and the Boston Workers Alliance to create a community-owned energy services company.

7. The original timeline had planned to have program negotiations between the utilities and Green Justice completed in February 2010, the Outreach and Delivery Plan completed in March, initial outreach to be finished by the end of March, the efficiency measures to be installed by the end of September, and the evaluation of the program to be completed by the end of 2010.

References

"2010–2012 Massachusetts Joint Statewide Three-Year Electric Energy Efficiency Plan." 2009. Massachusetts Department of Energy Resources, October 29.

Alinsky, Saul David. 1971. *Rules for Radicals: A Practical Primer for Realistic Radicals.* New York: Random House.

Booher, David E., and Judith E. Innes. 2002. "Network Power in Collaborative Planning." *Journal of Planning Education and Research* 21 (3): 221–36.

Boyd, Soledad. 2010. Personal interview. February 26.

Brandin, B. 2010. "Capitalizing on a Third Wave of Federal Investment: Reenvisioning an Energy Efficiency Retrofit Strategy for Oakland, California." Master's thesis, Massachusetts Institute of Technology.

Clauson, Lisa. 2010. Personal interview. February 15.

Connelly, Mary Jo. 2010. Personal interview. February 12.

Dean, Amy B., and David B. Reynolds. 2009. *A New New Deal: How Regional Activism Will Reshape the American Labor Movement.* Ithaca, NY: ILR Press.

EEAC (Massachusetts Energy Efficiency Advisory Council). 2009a. *2010–2012 Massachusetts Joint Statewide Three-Year Electric Energy Efficiency Plan.* October 29. *www.ma-eeac.org/docs/DPU-filing/ElectricPlanFinalOct09.pdf.*

———. 2009b. *2010–2012 Massachusetts Joint Statewide Three-Year Gas Energy Efficiency Plan.* October 29. *www.ma-eeac.org/docs/DPU-filing/ GasPlanFinalOct09.pdf.*

Gaventa, John. 1980. *Power and Powerlessness: Quiescence and Rebellion in an Appalachian Valley.* Urbana: University of Illinois Press.

Harvey, David. 1989. *The Urban Experience.* Baltimore, MD: Johns Hopkins University Press.

Loh, Penn. 2009. Personal interview. December 8.

Lombos, Darlene. 2009. Personal interview. December 15.

Lowe, Lydia. 2009. Personal interview. December 10.

Piven, Frances Fox, and Richard A. Cloward. 1977. *Poor People's Movements: Why They Succeed, How They Fail.* New York: Pantheon Books.

Prokosch, Mike. 2010. Personal interview. February 2.

Shenk, Jeremy. 2010. Personal interview. February 5.

Sherman, Mike. 2010. Personal interview. February 11.

Tarrow, Sidney G. 1998. *Power in Movement: Social Movements and Contentious Politics.* New York: Cambridge University Press.

Weiss, Marc A. 1987. *The Rise of the Community Builders: The American Real Estate Industry and Urban Land Planning.* Washington, DC: Beard Books.

Reflections

Lorlene Hoyt

An "Ecosystem of Knowledge"

The ecological system of knowledge is complex and
multi-dimensional, often messy and confusing, with
many modes of feedback and many cross connections.
And, at every point of this multiply-connected system
there is learning and enhanced understanding, resulting
in expanded knowledge. —Ernest Lynton (1994, 10)

Transforming Cities and Minds makes the case for a new epistemology
known as reciprocal knowledge: development of knowledge and real
learning on both sides, city and campus, achieved through a diverse, dynamic, and complex network of human relationships.

I have introduced you to the group of six humble and daring students
with whom I collaborated to create this book: Marianna, Gayle, Nick,
Eric, Leila, and Ben. You have been given a front-row seat to the products of their scholarly engagement, as they approached the specific challenges of six of America's old and struggling cities. You now know the
histories, challenges, and aspirations of the cities they explored, and you
have seen examples of how cities can transform themselves by simultaneously engaging the three *E*s: economy, equity, and the environment.

What I have yet to fully detail is the story of our own engagement.
This chapter relies primarily on data I collected over a period of two
years from a variety of sources, including course syllabi and assignments,
meeting notes and transcripts, personal interviews, group discussions,
student blog posts and theses, and my own personal reflections. Here
you will meet and come to understand the interactions among the seven
participants you already know—the six thesis writers and me—as well as
other faculty, students, staff, and community partners. You will witness
our efforts to engage with one another, how we evolved as individuals

and as a group, our relationships with one another, the setbacks, tragedies, and maladies that nearly derailed us, and the victories we celebrated
as we collaboratively produced the book you now hold. Where earlier
chapters are intended to inspire prospective city planning students and
practitioners, this chapter aims to inspire city planning educators. Just
as bold changes in the practice of city planning are needed to transform
America's cities, radical new methods of instruction and mentorship are
the first step in transforming the minds of the profession.

This, then, is the story of the forth *E*, engagement—the essential
link between city planning education and city planning practice. Engagement, a people-centered methodology, is key to transforming minds
and achieving an epistemology of reciprocal knowledge. It challenges
the dominant paradigms in both higher education and local politics,
calling into question the notion of expert knowledge, which drives the
culture of most research universities, as well as top-down approaches to
urban planning that exclude citizens from decision-making processes.
Engagement is risky business for scholars and practitioners alike. It's
not for the faint of heart. And it's exactly what this moment in history
demands.

A Sustained Partnership

Our collaboration began in September 2008 at the dawn of the Great
Recession when Marianna, Gayle, Nick, Eric, and Leila came to campus and made a commitment to working together, with me, and with
the people of Lawrence during their first year at M.I.T. They focused
their time and talents on strengthening the city-campus partnership
and tackling M.I.T.'s tough coursework before the thesis requirement
emerged as a priority.

To create a space for students, staff, and faculty participating in
MIT@Lawrence to build camaraderie, troubleshoot project-related
problems, and reflect on their practice, I created a year-round course
called Theories From, and For, Practice. Mirroring the principles of
community organizing developed by Marianna and other civic leaders in Lawrence, we adopted a horizontal management structure for
the course. Enrolled students and I cocrafted the syllabus. We rotated
agenda-setting, facilitation, note-taking, and time-keeping responsibilities (Hoyt 2010).

To develop a city-campus theory of practice, I worked closely with Marianna and Nick on a documentary about the partnership's ten-year history as told by participants on both sides—city and campus. At first Marianna resisted; she was fiercely loyal to her colleagues in Lawrence, "ambivalent toward MIT@Lawrence," and "skeptical of academia" (Leavy-Sperounis 2010b). Nick also had issues with our work; he wasn't happy with his role as a technical expert for the project (Iuviene 2008d). Motivated by my plans to include the movie in my tenure package and share the film with partnership participants at the end-of-year exposition in downtown Lawrence, I pushed them forward.

In contrast, Gayle immediately invested her mind and heart into Lawrence@MIT. She met with faculty, staff, and students "to review each step of their lesson plan" before the teenagers from Lawrence arrived to participate in monthly workshops at M.I.T. She blogged about the workshops regularly, bringing the events to life for all of us: "Today, a pair of Lawrence students set the record for the length their LEGO car traveled and everyone crowded around and asked them their secret design" (Christiansen 2008b).

Student engagement with the people of Lawrence gathered momentum and intensified during their second semester at M.I.T. as they began using courses as instruments-for-action, blending their work inside the university with their work in the world. For example, Gayle used a required course in statistics, Quantitative Reasoning and Statistical Methods, to investigate the impact of Lawrence@MIT, finding "a statistically significant increase in students believing they will use science and technology in their future careers at the end of the Lawrence@MIT program" (Christiansen 2010a).

Eric, too, hit the ground running in Lawrence. He enjoyed "trying to build relationships" and led a series of meetings throughout Lawrence. The group grew, created "a common campaign agenda," and submitted grant applications together. Some of the group's projects, such as a regular "Green Drinks" social event, continue today—a testament to Eric's early ambition: "Even after I am gone, even if it isn't under the MIT@ Lawrence banner, I want this work to continue and these people to grow their collaboration." Eric told me after he graduated that the Green Jobs Project in Lawrence was the "highlight" of his first year at M.I.T. (Mackres 2008b, 2010b).

Unlike Gayle and Eric, Leila struggled to find traction for her project, dubbed "iHouse." The M.I.T. freshman she expected to collect data on the streets of Lawrence were overloaded with physics and calculus assignments. It was also difficult to finalize a memorandum of understanding between M.I.T. faculty, staff, students, and public officials in Lawrence. She was down, too, in her personal life. After our evening class in the fall, she confided to me that a dear high school friend had committed suicide. I understood her devastation firsthand. As we exited a campus pub called the Muddy Charles and walked slowly along the edge of campus on Memorial Drive, I shared my own experience of losing two family members to suicide. Predictably, she was silent. A few weeks later, Leila took me up on my offer of hospitality. As my daughter introduced Marianna to her Barbies and attempted to braid Leila's very short hair, it occurred to me that this was the first time I had invited students to my home. As for the iHouse project, there were "a few moments" when Leila felt it was "potentially falling apart," but her classmates gave her the support she needed and she later rallied the undergraduates who completed the fieldwork in Lawrence on schedule (Bozorg 2008b).

The group interacted outside the partnership, too. After listening to President Barack Obama's inaugural speech together on the mall in Washington, D.C., in January, Marianna and Leila joined Gayle in New Orleans to kick off the Main Streets Practicum. And all, except Gayle, took Professor Phillip Thompson's Post Stimulus Planning seminar, where Marianna and Eric wrote a paper entitled "Green Jobs in Lawrence" for civic leaders who later incorporated its content into federal stimulus applications (Leavy-Sperounis, Mackres, and Marshall 2009).

End-of-Year Exposition

On a Monday evening in late April 2009, dozens of civic leaders and residents celebrated ten years of partnership with M.I.T. students, faculty, and staff at the Lawrence Heritage State Park facility on Jackson Street. The jazz band's music reverberated throughout the renovated mill as the aroma of rice, beans, and plantains filled the air. Amy Glasmeier, the new department chair, arrived and made her way from one exhibit to the next. She was conspicuously indifferent as students and community partners discussed their projects with her.

Marianna asked the band to take a break, encouraged everyone to take a seat, and enthusiastically unveiled the documentary, *Sustained*

City-Campus Engagement: Reflections on Our Practice (Hoyt et al. 2009). Her attitude about the film project had shifted in January when she began interviewing partnership participants and collaborating with Alexa Mills, a community media specialist at the CoLab. Alexa was an MIT@ Lawrence alumna, having joined the partnership three years earlier when I hired her to work with residents to create a short film, *Predatory Tales.* She had trouble, at first, persuading victims of predatory lending in Lawrence to tell their stories. Her persistence and determination resulted in two stories, one told in English and the other in Spanish, instructing others how to avoid losing their homes to foreclosure (Hoyt et al. 2007).

By the end of their first year at M.I.T., Marianna, Gayle, Nick, Eric, and Leila had developed productive habits of collaboration and a feeling of solidarity while working with the people of Lawrence and with each other. They also launched extracurricular activities, which further united them. Sensing that the department's tradition of transparent decision making was threatened by the new department head, Nick and Eric organized a team of students who interrupted a faculty meeting at the Black Sheep Restaurant in Kendall Square to press for student inclusion. Leila chose to concentrate on creating queer-friendly events at M.I.T.; Marianna joined her. All four participated on the Students of Color Committee.

The end-of-year exposition in Lawrence coincided with Nick's twenty-eighth birthday. He seemed unhappy, so I offered him a ride back to campus. As I drove south on I-93, he explained to me why working on MIT@Lawrence Story Project was "not personally rewarding," but he appreciated the "sense of space and community" being part of the partnership provided (Iuviene 2008b, 2008c). I dropped him off at Drink, a restaurant and bar in south Boston, to celebrate with his friends, among them Benjamin Brandin.

Summer and the Stimulus

During the summer of 2009, everyone but Leila headed off to work side by side in various capacities with civic leaders to secure stimulus funds from the American Recovery and Reinvestment Act. In June, my own real estate development and planning firm, Urban Revitalizers, hired Marianna and Eric to assist the town of Plymouth, Massachusetts, with its Energy Efficiency and Conservation Block Grant application. By this time, both Marianna and Eric had separately asked me to be their thesis advisor. I did not tell them about an idea I had recently begun to contemplate—to cocreate an edited volume with students. But I did share my vision for making the thesis a public good rather than an exclusive commodity, and—after I felt sure that they were receptive to working on their thesis in collaboration with other students—I agreed to advise them.

Meanwhile, with financial support from M.I.T.'s CoLab, Gayle had created an internship for herself at the Camden Empowerment Zone Corporation. We exchanged long e-mails throughout the summer. I sent her journal articles, put her in touch with friends in Philadelphia, and asked questions about the work she was doing; I wasn't her thesis advisor, but I was happy to play the part. As it became obvious that our e-mail exchange was helping her make progress with her thesis research, it occurred to me that other students could also benefit from reflecting on their summer internships in real time. I worked with CoLab staff to create and circulate a set of reflection exercises for that purpose. I was introduced to Ben, so to speak, when I read his mature and nuanced insights about the Lynn Coalition for Green Development in the nearby town of Lynn, Massachusetts. Ben was pragmatic and optimistic about what it would take to assemble a team of civic leaders from all walks of life—educators, business owners, and public officials—for the purpose of applying for federal stimulus funds. He characterized the challenge as "frustrating," noting that "patience is key" (Brandin 2009). I wanted to meet him in person.

Early in a July evening, Ben and I sat and talked on the stairs in front of Building 9 on Massachusetts Avenue. I learned that Ben and Nick had met serendipitously at UCLA's open house for newly admitted graduate students; there Nick convinced Ben to go to M.I.T. Ben, too, had taken Professor Thompson's Post Stimulus Planning seminar in the spring, which led both of them to summer internships with the CoLab. Ben stayed in Boston while Nick returned to New York City to coordinate the Emerald Cities Collaborative, a coalition of national organizations working to "green" cities throughout the United States. I shared with Ben my idea about the graduate thesis as both a product and a process, and I laid out my idea of working with a group of thesis writers. I was curious to know whether he would entertain such a proposition. He was interested.

Leila was far away from where she grew up in Amherst, Massachusetts, working as an intern in her parent's homeland, Iran. At the local development resource center, she researched an early phase of a housing project in the historic district of Ardakan in the Yazd province. The daughter of parents who met by way of "a failed revolution that took the lives of their closest friends," Leila wasn't intimidated by the massive demonstrations that followed the tumultuous presidential elections that summer (Bozorg 2008a, 2010b).

Our "Vegas"

When my students' second and final year at M.I.T. began in September 2009, I knew I would have to hit the ground running to make the edited volume a reality. We were no longer working together in Lawrence, but some of the students were taking Thesis Preparation, a required course for master of city planning students, under my tutelage.

It was a course I had long wanted to teach. I arrived early for the first day of class, raised the blinds, opened the windows, arranged the chairs around the oversized conference table, and welcomed thirteen graduate students, most of whom I knew, to take a seat in the space we would come to know as our "Vegas."

I began class informally, asking each student to tell a funny story about their summer. After an hour of laughter and conversation, I took a provocative position on the thesis requirement: "The thesis experience is broken. Every year, I watch students struggle, often in isolation. I feel they rarely get the support they need and deserve from their advisors. They pour an enormous amount of time and energy into their research, but it rarely sees the light of day. Students, faculty, and society—everyone loses."

The classroom was quiet. Marianna, Gayle, Nick, and Ben, already familiar with my point of view, were unshaken. My aim was to create a respectful space for dialogue as students struggled to define their research interests. I urged the entire class to engage: to show up, to listen, to offer encouragement and constructive feedback to each other, to stick to the deadlines, and to have fun. We reviewed the course syllabus and the small steps that each student would take to create a full-blown thesis proposal by the end of the semester. We agreed to the rules and adopted the mantra: "what happens in thesis prep, stays in thesis prep."

By this time, my strengths and limitations became clear. I felt I could effectively advise and manage a group of five thesis writers, while helping the others formulate thesis topics and find advisors. I did not have a clear strategy for getting the edited-volume project up and running. Without research funds, I couldn't hire students to work on the project with me. Instead, I would have to lure them, gradually, into working together and with me. I sent an e-mail to Marianna, Nick, Gayle, Eric, and Ben asking them to meet with me in the CoLab.

Falling in October

Marianna and Eric were, in large part, on board with my unfolding plan, and I was poised to make my next move by asking Gayle and Ben to join what I was by now referring to as the edited-volume project. Nick, too, was on my mind as a possible participant. But as soon as it seemed we were ready to come together, my experiment began falling apart. The downward spiral began with an e-mail message from Gayle.

> Hi Lorlene,
> I'm sitting at MIT medical waiting to be seen given some persistent flu like symptoms. I will most likely not be in thesis prep today. But believe me, I'd rather be in Vegas than here feeling sick. Please let me know if there is anything I need to do to follow up from class.
> Gayle

At the beginning of October 2009, Gayle was diagnosed with mononucleosis and hepatitis A; she was unlikely to recover quickly. But she came to our first meeting in CoLab, along with everyone else except Leila.

Once they had taken their seats around the small conference table, I grabbed a piece of chalk, approached the blackboard, and drew a tiny makeshift sailboat atop large waves. "This is risky business," I began. For forty-five minutes, I tried to convey the idea of writing a book together, an edited volume, outlining the table of contents for the book based on my interpretation of their individual interests and capabilities. "Each chapter in the book would be a revised version of your thesis," I explained. The response was lukewarm: the students liked the idea of working in a group as they tackled the task of the thesis, but some were not sold on the topics I suggested. Others wondered if I could handle it. I felt entirely deflated.

Two weeks later, I entered CoLab and saw Ben sitting alone, staring at the conference table. He had recently learned his mom was living with cancer. Ben, a self-proclaimed "cynic," needed me to confront his situation directly. I sat down and said, "We'll do whatever it takes to get you through this." I offered to be his thesis advisor. He looked relieved and agreeable. He calmly and methodically laid out his mom's medical options and his plans for supporting her. I listened.

From CoLab, I took the subway home, red line to the green line. I watched the tiny white dinghies bobble on the Charles River as the sun set and the train cars rattled side-to-side over the Longfellow Bridge. As I walked south on Arlington Street, passing the Boston Park Plaza Hotel, I thought about Gayle's "lonely" undergraduate thesis experience. How long would she suffer from these illnesses? I worried Ben might feel overwhelmed by his thesis while coping with the most difficult experience of his life. Without proper support, would he graduate?

When I arrived home, there was a letter from the department chair on my living room coffee table. My tenure review had been postponed. To be considered for tenure the next year, I had to comply with five conditions. The final condition referred to the edited-volume project and starkly concluded this way: "new collaborative initiatives should be deferred." The ultimatum made me realize that I needed the support of like-minded colleagues as much as my students did.

"We Will Be Figuring This Out as We Go."

To encourage students to join me, I took my idea of producing an edited volume from student theses and flipped it on its head. This project, I now realized, had to meet students' needs, not my own. Instead of asking them to write a thesis that would become a chapter in the book that *I* wanted to write, I offered to support their thesis research and writing, and then work to produce a book from *their* research. Three weeks after the edited-volume project meeting, I called another meeting. This time, we discussed the collaborative thesis project.

I invited Alexa Mills and Amy Stitely, the "green hub" program director in the CoLab and a friend of mine. Like Alexa, Amy was an MIT@Lawrence alumna. Born in South Korea and adopted by U.S.

parents, Amy studied architecture at the University of Maryland, near where she grew up, and went on to practice architecture for eight years before coming to M.I.T. to earn a master of city planning degree. As a student, Amy dedicated the bulk of her efforts to practice-based learning, working through CoLab in New Orleans and with me for two years as the teaching assistant for the Lawrence practicum. When Amy and Alexa graduated together in 2008, Alexa joined the CoLab immediately. Building on a long-standing interest in "sustainable building practices," Amy spent a year working for Urban Revitalizers on a Massachusetts state public-housing assessment before joining CoLab in June 2009 (Stitely 2006, 2007).

Now, at the collaborative thesis project meeting, Amy, Alexa, and I started by clarifying our individual interests and roles. Amy wanted to learn about new efforts to "green" America's cities, offering to help students create short, easy-to-read, how-to guides from their research once their theses were complete. Like me, Alexa wanted students to use plain language, to make ideas accessible to a public audience; she wanted to help students disseminate their research by way of short films and blog posts. After Marianna, Gayle, Nick, Eric, and Ben described their research plans, we decided to meet in the CoLab regularly—for an hour every two weeks. At the end of this meeting, I concluded, "It isn't all figured out; we will be figuring this out as we go." A few people nodded their heads in agreement. I felt a sense of possibility.

The "Syllabus"

On separate occasions, Nick, Eric, and I heard about Leila's work with the people of Kansas City and their districting strategy for attracting stimulus dollars. After a brief discussion, the group unanimously invited her to join. Leila's thesis advisor, Professor Anne Spirn, however, was reluctant initially; she was concerned that there were too many people involved and that the group's writing schedule would not align with the one she typically asked her advisees to follow. Leila was torn. She wrote,

> Anne and I met today about my thesis, and her thoughts on joining the collaborative thesis group were straight-forward: she felt that if I would like to be part of the group, that I should switch advisors. As you know, I was excited about potentially being part of the group, and

contributing to your work and that of the CoLab, but I've also really been looking forward to working with Anne as my advisor.

I offered to join Leila's thesis committee as a reader, and she came to our meeting in early December. At this time, there was nothing officially binding us together, save the fact that I was a member of each student's thesis committee. Gayle had asked me to be her thesis advisor and Nick asked me to join his committee, headed by Professor Phil Thompson. An obvious way to formalize our schedule and articulate our commitment to working together would be to create a course for the students to take during the spring semester, but, based on the warnings I had already received about this kind of work, the new department chair would surely deny such a proposal. How could I be certain each student was committed to the project? How would we coordinate our busy schedules for the next six months?

The holiday break is six weeks long at M.I.T. and students would need to make significant progress with their research while we were apart. I called a four-hour meeting in CoLab in mid-December, asking each student to identify the city where they planned to engage, the issue they expected to investigate, and research methods they would apply. To gauge whether we could commit to a common timetable, I asked each student to rate, using a scale from one to ten, the importance of graduating in June. Marianna picked eight. Ben picked eleven. The others picked numbers in between. I was relieved to see there was little variation. We were in agreement on the project deadline, a crucial aspect of collaboration.

At her kitchen table in Somerville, Massachusetts, on a Sunday afternoon in January, Amy and I fleshed out a detailed schedule for the project. Later, I created a document that looked like a syllabus to function as a binding agreement for our group. It pinpointed when we would meet and outlined a series of writing and other assignments. It also included a placeholder for a conference-like event called "Thesis Defense Week," scheduled for April; instead of holding their thesis defense behind closed doors, each student agreed to hold a public defense accessible to students, staff, and faculty in our department.

Unlike a traditional course syllabus, there was no reading list. Instead of imposing subject material on students, I allowed space for improvisation. As we had done when we were engaged in the city of Lawrence, we would rotate meeting responsibilities. Once students formally agreed to the assignments and deadlines for their thesis as well as a short film or blog post, a how-to guide, and a book chapter, I distributed the "syllabus" to their committee members. We were all relieved when Professor Spirn responded,

> I met with Leila today to review her field work in Kansas City and to discuss how that experience has refined her research questions. Given the increased focus and importance of the stimulus funding to her principal case, I think it would be invaluable for her to meet this semester with you and the thesis students working with you and advised her to join the group.

"We Can Help Each Other Dig Deep"

The collaborative thesis project was underway, but now the heavy lifting would begin. In late January 2010, before students returned from the holiday break, Nick sent me an e-mail. He would be unable to participate in our next meeting and expressed concern about how we had been using our time together. He wrote,

> My hope is that in this space we can help each other dig deep into the issues we are exploring and get beyond surface level "solutions" and through that process develop some common language and concepts that may weave throughout our theses. I'm also a little concerned that our group sessions are going to become mostly reporting and accountability sessions.

I replied, "I share these aspirations. They may require more time and effort for all of us."

I read Nick's e-mail to the group when we met in CoLab on February 8, 2010. Ben responded first, "I don't expect any of our solutions to be 'surface level.'" Leila redirected the conversation, asking, "What is the solution and *how* do we get there?" Gayle backed her up, "we need to start this conversation." Eric pulled everyone's sentiments together, "It's a difficult thing to talk about, but we must, even if it's at a surface level right now." Then he proposed, "Can we focus, each week, on one person's research and issues?"

This was exactly the kind of leadership I expected from this group. I suggested we organize a daylong retreat to do some deep digging. Amy was reluctant. She explained, "All of our energy might be spent on the first few people." I agreed. With an interest in including other faculty in our group conversations, I added, "In the spirit of collaboration, we don't want advisors and readers on the outskirts until the defense." Marianna reinforced my proposal, "We could organize several sessions around different topics. Professor Spirn could join us and talk about sustainability. Professor Thompson could come and talk about labor unions and job creation."

I suddenly felt we were drifting, with the problem Nick had posed remaining unanswered. I stood up, approached the chalkboard, and drew CoLab's "sweet spot," a conceptual diagram used to guide engagement with community partners. The "sweet spot" was the area at the intersection of three big ideas: economy, equity, and environment. These were the three issues we agreed on—all of them were important to all of us. Ben called the sweet spot "elusive." Marianna agreed, but added, "I would like to discuss all the pieces of the sweet spot, even if I don't delve into them. I want to be aware of them." Gayle explained, "Everyone defines the sweet spot differently."

Alexa entered the room and jumped into the conversation: "The closest example we have is what the Beloved Community Center of Greensboro, North Carolina, tries to do. They are training people in the neighborhood to retrofit their own houses. They want to pool the savings to address other community needs." A dynamic discussion ensued. Amy elaborated on CoLab's understanding of economy, what they refer to as shared wealth generation, "it's the inverse of a global economy based on the exploitation of resources and people." This resonated with Gayle, who had been discovering business owners in Camden "committed to giving back." Marianna wove together notions of engagement and economy: "Engagement is based in local knowledge. Shared wealth involves locally owned businesses that hire locally. These are small enough that if any go under it doesn't destroy the community's wealth. A diversified economy is sustainable." Eric added, "Engagement emphasizes a longer view, based on strategic planning and thinking." In the end, Ben saw a relationship between the sweet spot and his research in Oakland, explaining that "the city has a huge amount of money right now and they are not sharing it. Retrofitting can be used to achieve energy efficiency and as an economic driver. But, there's a disconnect between what the city and the community wants to do. Right now, the city is making decisions for the community. The community groups are at odds with the city. I want to show that real engagement is missing." As the meeting drew to a close, Ben, Alexa, and others agreed with Gayle's earlier point that the sweet spot has a different meaning in different cities.

We had, as Nick suggested, done some digging and started to develop common concepts for the theses. Later, in an e-mail, I conveyed to Nick what we had accomplished. Nick replied, "It looks like I missed a great meeting. It figures." And, thanks to Nick, we didn't spend our precious time together resolving the logistics associated with a retreat. Digging deep into each other's research is exactly what we needed to do before the individual arguments were fully formed. Focusing on a handful of key concepts prompted students to make sense of the data they had collected. My eye was on the book, which needed to be a coherent whole, but I opted to let them put the pieces together. Imposing my ideas on them at this stage in their research might derail a student or the entire group.

Miniretreats

We held two, three-hour-long "miniretreats" in the CoLab in early March. By spending an hour on each student's research, we aspired to "hear more about each investigation, ask deeper questions, offer more thoughtful insights, and explore meaningful connections across cases." Each student was struggling to make sense of his or her data; all needed encouragement and useful feedback; each was vulnerable.

When we later reflected on the various phases of the collaborative thesis project, our assessment of the miniretreats was mixed. Gayle thought they were "a great learning experience" and "came at a time when constructive feedback was essential." Ben "enjoyed hearing what everyone was working on," and Eric characterized the discussions as our "best example of digging and finding common themes." In contrast, Nick thought people "could have been more critical." Leila's time was cut short, and I felt that Marianna had been challenged on issues that weren't relevant to her investigation (Christiansen 2010b; Brandin 2010a; Mackres 2010b; Iuviene 2010b).

Searching for Common Themes

Our story, so far, has been told from my perspective. To give the reader a sense of the way we interacted with one another as we shaped the ideas in this book, I offer below a partial record of the conversation we had in CoLab after the miniretreats, on a Monday afternoon during spring break, five days before Ben's wedding. Eric initiated the exchange in the first excerpt by responding to a question Amy posed: "What are the common themes across your research?"

Eric: One thing that really stood out to me is that we're all looking at, for a lack of a better term, alternative decision-making regimes. Not all of us, but that was something that came out a lot, something that really stood out from Mariana, Nick. . . .

Lorlene: Regimes?

Eric: Regimes. So, you know, not necessarily the formal governance structure, but how cities actually . . .

Leila: Mine's like that too.

Eric: And Leila's as well. The other one that I heard that doesn't really apply to me as much is the role of institutions in communities as anchors or forces for change. Those are two I remember.

Marianna: I'm envisioning a matrix where we have themes that we think crosscut and then a check for the people who it applies to.

Amy: We could do that.

(Amy begins drawing a matrix on the chalkboard)

Lorlene: Ask and you will receive.

Marianna: Another one that came up was also the question of spatial districting or targeting for these initiatives. That came up with mine, Leila's, and Eric's. Nick? Ben?

Gayle: Postindustrial cities, older cities.

Amy: Is everyone in a postindustrial city?

Eric: What does that mean?

Marianna: It means that they had at one time an economic industrial base.

Ben: I'm an affirmative on that one.

Amy: Nick?

Nick: Well, Cleveland yes. The Bronx, kind of.

Leila: Kansas City is. I mean I wouldn't say it was one industry.

Marianna: And we could maybe classify it as places that have struggled since most manufacturing left the U.S. If there has been any negative impact on that local economy because of the loss of manufacturing, then that might be something we would all have in common. But the effect could be larger or smaller depending on which city we're talking about.

Having agreed that their research uncovered the vital role of rooted institutions as forces for change in postindustrial cities, we began to explore the idea that urban planning involves simultaneously tackling issues of economy, equity, and environment.

> Nick: So the part that I'm trying to get to in mine is related to this. Two things: one is that we always look externally to jumpstart investment and there is also a way—sometimes more powerful and overlooked—to look internally. To organize what seems like limited resources, more intelligently, internally. And the other thing is we constantly make an argument from a social justice perspective that development has got to be more equitable: wages, jobs, access. . . . But, there is almost always a missing piece of the argument: how is it going to work? So, we assume that the development piece will just happen. It needs to be tweaked. You know, to make it work with equity. We don't talk about that.
>
> Marianna: You can't layer equity onto something and expect it to work . . .
>
> Nick: How they connect makes a much stronger argument.
>
> Leila: What changes in that? What's so different from the older version?
>
> Eric: I think . . . there is a connection to investing in communities and creating markets . . . in the sense of juxtaposing extreme capitalism with a more locally based market economy. The idea is that if you are investing in communities and, for example, you bring people's heating bills down, they're going to have more money to spend. Lower-income people are more likely to spend their money locally and invest in their community anyway. So, that's another local economic stimulus measure. And that's one argument for the prosperity of the United States in general. For a long time we have been a middle-class society that has created tons of consumers and that has kept

tons of people in jobs. And that's, at least partially, why we are having issues with our economy right now.

Nick: Well, now we consume and don't produce.

Leila: Well, yeah. My first reaction to what you said is that, it's still more about consumption from a part of the population that maybe wasn't as actively . . .

Amy: Greening isn't consumption. I mean in the terms of buying a good. You know, I mean retrofitting isn't the same as consuming a good.

Leila: No, I know, but when you were saying . . .

Ben: Whoa whoa whoa, wait! That's not necessarily true because a lot of the jobs that they continue to claim will come out of the retrofit market is the development of materials for retrofitting. So there's a huge production and consumption model to be built in order for this to be successful.

Amy: OK!

Marianna: But it's a different kind of consumption we're talking about. We're consuming the products, but it's not disposable stuff. I mean, we're not consuming.

Amy: They're infrastructure products.

Marianna: Right. Maybe I'm misunderstanding where we're going, but I feel like that's the kind of consumption we're talking about.

Eric: Well, it's conservation, in a way, instead of new development, if you want to think about it on the building scale. Instead of greenfields housing that nobody can afford and nobody can live in, you're helping to make investments in communities that are closer to jobs and transit.

Leila: Yeah. What's interesting is that it's conservation but it almost seems like, at least in some of my interviews, there's this influx first of additional consumption to conserve, right? Like new furnaces, new refrigerators, new appliances. We've got to weatherize your home. We're going to give you this meter. Everybody's going to be given stuff to then stop consuming resources.

Amy: I like the word investment, while we're consuming. I get it.

Leila: What was the word?

Amy: I like the word investment, while we're consuming. Because it's supposed to pay back, right? That's the whole idea.

Eric: But if you think about it, too, there's a lot of studies that show people of lower or middle income are more likely to invest locally and to invest in things that they need to survive rather than boats and things like that. So, in that sense it's consumption but it's . . .

Leila: Out of necessity.

Marianna: Less frivolous.

Eric: Yeah, out of necessity.

Thesis Defense Week

At the very end of our conversation, Marianna and Amy made the observation that each student thesis was, in effect, proposing a new strategy for transforming cities that were suffering from disinvestment even *before* the advent of the Great Recession. Their discovery prompted Eric, who could see we needed a title for our upcoming event, to take issue with our "syllabus."

Eric: I'm not crazy about the title.

Amy: What title?

Eric: Thesis Defense Week.

Lorlene: That's a wonderful reaction. So you've got alternative suggestions?

Eric: How about something with *creating* rather than, something slightly less militant, something exciting. There you go.

Lorlene: So, creating, got it.

Eric: Creating knowledge, creating communities. Defending our theses while . . .

Leila: While recognizing Earth Day.

Marianna: Celebrating the paradox of . . .

Leila: Wait. I hate Earth Day.

Marianna: It's my birthday!

Leila: Every day should be Earth Day. Maybe that's our . . .

Eric: Making Every Day Earth Day—Theses for the Future.

Amy: These are all really bad.

Lorlene: We don't have to play off of thesis defense or play off of Earth Day. Just create a really great title.

Marianna: New Strategies for an Old Crisis.

Amy made posters and brochures advertising the week long event entitled "New Strategies for an Old Crisis." The thinking behind "thesis defense week" was to make each student's defense a public conversation with a large and diverse audience instead of a discussion with two or three committee members behind closed doors. It was also an attempt to keep the group on the same schedule; everyone was expected to have a full and "defendable" draft of their thesis by the third week in April. We aimed to share our collaborative approach to research and the research itself with the university community through a series of individual student presentations, which were flanked on one end by a roundtable discussion to introduce the idea of the collaborative thesis project and on the other by an end-of-week celebration at the Cambridge Brewing Company in Kendall Square.

In the end, all of the student presentations were well attended, with an audience of faculty, staff, students, friends, and family asking tough, thoughtful questions and offering helpful insights and suggestions. In an effort to share the student work with people outside the university, Alexa paired the second-year thesis writers with first-year students who attended the talks and wrote and posted summaries on CoLab Radio (Brickman 2010; Emig 2010; Feeney 2010; Goodspeed 2010; Ritoper 2010; Xypolia 2010).

As was the case with the "miniretreats," our evaluation of "thesis defense week" yielded mixed results. I felt the quality of each talk was very high because each student had been honing an argument within the group for several months. Ben and Marianna agreed that the presentation pushed them to organize a clear argument. Leila enjoyed seeing everyone's ideas "resonate with other people," especially first-year students (Bozorg et al. 2010). Gayle was pleased to see "more similarities" across their work by the end of the week but thought "it would have been nice" if everyone defended their thesis during the week, as originally planned (Christiansen 2010b). Ironically, Ben and Gayle, the two students who had hit rock bottom six months earlier, were the only two in the group of six who defended their thesis as planned. The others, for various reasons, were not ready to defend, although everyone presented their work in progress. Eric was very disappointed that he missed the deadline and felt he "let the group down" (Mackres 2010b). Others felt similarly, but I was relieved that they succeeded in sticking together and, ultimately, graduating together. By design, "thesis defense week" took place several weeks before their final thesis document was officially due, and everyone in the group avoided the all-too-common pitfall of missing the thesis deadline by only a few hours or days.

Reflecting on Our Engagement

Benefits of Engaged Scholarship

We held our final meeting in CoLab on Monday, May 17, 2010. To my astonishment, my students (excepting Ben and Gayle) looked haggard, clearly in a state of exhaustion I had hoped to help them avoid. Amy and I crafted a set of questions to structure their reflection on our engagement with cities and with each other.

The transcripts reveal powerful patterns as well as a variety of individual feelings and opinions. The most salient theme points to the collaborative thesis project as a different and good way of learning from one another. Leila remarked, "I really did benefit from drawing on the research that everyone else was doing." Ben explained, "One day Eric brought up the issue of partnerships, which I had totally overlooked. There are these times where you have information but you're not taking notice of it until one of your peers points it out to you." Nick credited the project with pushing him to think differently, "Having a number of counterpoints and perspectives and a constant dialogue with people struggling with similar issues really pushed and challenged the breadth and perspective of the research I was doing. That was really important. It challenged me to think differently" (Bozorg et al. 2010).

Students found the regular meetings, dialogue, and feedback beneficial as it provided the support and validation they needed to feel secure and confident about their research. Gayle explained, "I found in the group the type of education I was expecting to get when I came here. Digging into stuff, the hands on, and this kind of horizontal structure. . . . It's not just a professor that's just telling you the right answer, but you had people in this group who were all working together with you on something and thinking that your points were really valid and at the same time pushing you, but in a very different way." Marianna echoed Gayle's experience, adding, "I came in with pretty strong opinions about what I wanted to say in January and February, but wouldn't have necessarily moved ahead with them as confidently without hearing certain things resonating with people." Leila agreed and highlighted how our regular meetings mitigated, in large part, the feeling of isolation students commonly experience, "I had three days last week of feeling very isolated, trying to write a lot of edits. It freaked me out. I thought, 'I can't imagine doing this all freaking semester.' That is, trying to pump this out on my own and not getting constant feedback" (Bozorg et al. 2010).

When prompted to answer the question: "What held us together? Why didn't it fall apart?" Marianna suggested that we had established "habits of collaboration" and "trust that evolved on its own" as we worked together over the course of their first year in Lawrence. Nick highlighted the importance of respect, "Respect is a huge, huge piece of it. Respect was often lacking in my other group projects among members." Ben added, "You don't always have to like everyone that you work with. But if you can respect them and you appreciate what they bring to the table, then the product will always be better. And I think this is one of those cases. Everyone stuck it out. Everyone showed the guts" (Bozorg et al. 2010).

Leila and Eric offered two different yet related theories for the project's success. For Leila, personality traits were key. She explained, "Everyone was humble, yet each person was capable of being an alpha and taking charge." She described the group as "selfless," each of us "willing to listen" and "willing to talk." It was a "positive experience," she continued, because "we were all engaged, but no one was putting their ideas ahead of anyone else's or their needs ahead of anyone else's." Eric agreed with Leila, adding, "I think it has a lot to do with pedagogy and how we decided to approach learning. We value learning from each other within a research group in addition to learning from people in the outside world" (Bozorg et al. 2010).

Challenges of Engaged Scholarship

The process was far from perfect; there were areas where we fell short. For example, Leila and Nick expressed regret that they did not take full advantage of their thesis advisors. I had not invited faculty to our "miniretreats," few faculty engaged in the project in a meaningful way, and some students did not seek guidance from committee members because we spent so much time together as a group. And, admittedly, I was stretched too thin and was unable to give each student timely feedback near the end of the thesis-writing process.

With respect to the longer view, we only scratched the surface in practicing an epistemology of reciprocal knowledge. While students engaged with community partners in their respective cities, recognized their expertise, and shared their ideas and products with them, we could have done more. For example, students led the research design; because of the way the project unfolded slowly throughout the fall semester, we did not have time to include community partners in this part of the process. In large part, students developed the questions as well as the methods of data collection and analysis in consultation with me, CoLab staff, and their thesis committee members; they established a timeline for their research that aligned with the academic calendar. Though each student interacted with several civic leaders and residents by way of personal on-site interviews, only two students engaged people outside the university as coinvestigators during the early stages of their research.

Gayle and Marianna came closer than others in the group to realizing an epistemology of reciprocal knowledge. Each had deep and ongoing personal and professional ties with the people living and working in the cities where they were working. Gayle spent countless hours in Camden, visiting and talking with business owners who provided consistent feedback along the way; she recalibrated her questions and findings accordingly. Marianna made the rounds, too, meeting with numerous civic leaders and residents in Lawrence and Lowell during the summer and into the fall, in effect cocrafting her topic of inquiry. Both Marianna and Gayle were able to lure community partners into their research in real time because they had worked for several years in these cities and remained in partnership with people outside the university while they were students inside the university. Both Gayle and Marianna traveled along a continuum between the ever-present themes of practice and knowledge. Each, in her own unique way, overcame the false dichotomy through sustained engagement (Hoyt 2010).

In a way, all of the thesis writers engaged with civic leaders and residents in the latter stages of the research process. For example, several students shared draft copies of their theses with partners outside the university who suggested improvements and edited portions of their text. And all of the students creatively disseminated their findings to civic leaders and residents by reworking their theses into such formats as short films, blog posts, community presentations, how-to guides, op-eds, radio shows, conferences, and online magazine articles. Looking back on our experiment, it is increasingly clear that reciprocal knowledge, the development of knowledge and real learning inside and outside the university in a diverse and complex network of human relationships, is an idea that is as vital as it is difficult to realize. And engaged scholars like me and my former students, now practitioners, need environments like Co-Lab in order to collaborate with each other and with the outside world. CoLab performs a unique and important function at M.I.T., connecting and supporting innovative partnerships among faculty, staff, and students with community partners, including alumni, in cities throughout the country. Its leadership, resources, and expertise made possible the collaborative thesis project and its products. Centers like CoLab have long been crucial to the civic engagement movement. The next necessary step, however, is to rethink standard notions of scholarship and reinvent faculty roles and reward systems.

"Scholarship in Action"

> The concept of an eco-system of knowledge is not just a convenient metaphor. It has profound implications for faculty roles because the system of knowledge is the *territory of scholarship.*
>
> Wherever knowledge emerges, scholarship can exist. Any intellectual activity in every part of the system that results in true learning, in added understanding, in an increase in knowledge—as distinct from a mere accretion of facts and figures—is scholarship in action. —Ernest Lynton (1994, 11)

Tenured faculty living in university and college cultures dominated by technical rationality hold the exclusive power to incrementally enlarge the customary paradigm of knowledge generation. They can call into question and take steps to modernize faculty reward systems such as tenure to assign value to new forms of scholarship. I believed that a majority of my tenured colleagues would view my tenure case as an opportunity to reignite a productive conversation, among faculty both inside and outside our department, about the promises and consequences of introducing an epistemology of reciprocal knowledge into a renowned research university like M.I.T. Without question, my scholarly dossier initiated a debate among tenured faculty in our department, but the conversation took place behind closed doors where, in October 2011, the majority voted to deny (what I perceived to be) my right to an external review of my scholarship. I was stunned to learn that esteemed colleagues in my field at peer institutions would not have the opportunity to assess my scholarship and weigh in on the promotion decision at M.I.T. For me, the tenure review process was cut short, and I did not get tenure.

I understood, yet chose to resist, the institutional culture and prevailing epistemology. Despite the numerous warnings I received, in writing and in person, I explored the idea of reciprocal knowledge with my students and other colleagues. I felt, and continue to believe, that the "battle of snails" is worth fighting (Schön 1995, 32). My experience with the tenure review process is not unique; I am in good company. The reality is that while department chairs and senior faculty encourage early-career faculty to engage with communities, tenure and promotion policies are not aligned to reward such work. Moreover, faculty evaluation is a decentralized, value-laden, and highly political process, continuing to reinforce rather than challenge the status quo (O'Meara 2011).

In contrast, a movement in higher education is underway both at home and abroad. There are many disciplines and institutions of higher education that have revised their faculty assessment and promotion guidelines to include scholarly engagement and to reward faculty who undertake such activities. At present, 115 universities and colleges across the United States enjoy the honor and prestige of a voluntary ranking known as the Carnegie Community Engagement Classification. The issue of faculty assessment and rewards is emerging as a fertile area for development as evidenced by imminent changes to the Carnegie application, which will include questions about institutional policies for promotion and tenure that reward the scholarship of community engagement. Additionally, systems of higher education in such places as Australia, Canada, Portugal, and the United Kingdom are expanding their missions and enlarging their understanding of what constitutes scholarly work for faculty (Rice 2005).

What I learned from this experience is embedded in the story of our engagement and may be useful to those seeking to replicate the collaborative thesis project inside their own universities or colleges. Below are guiding principles of engagement for developing an epistemology of reciprocal knowledge; they can be adopted to transform institutions of higher education and other rooted institutions into agents of democracy in an increasingly diverse and rapidly changing world.

1. Everybody possesses expert knowledge. Attention to the wholeness
    and uniqueness of individuals and institutions facilitates the flow of
    people and ideas inside and among rooted institutions.
2. Relevant knowledge is generated by creating and sustaining mean-
    ingful human relationships. It takes time for people to get to know
    each other, develop trust, commit to issues of common cause, and
    effect change.
3. New knowledge is developed in complex, dynamic, and diverse
    networks of collaboration. It is crucial to rethink both space and
    time—where we meet and deliberate, how frequently and continu-
    ously we engage.

Transforming Cities and Minds

With support from Alexa, Marianna published a short film, *Green Jobs
on the Ground in Lawrence, Massachusetts*, on MIT's TechTV and distributed her thesis to community partners (Leavy-Sperounis 2010b).
Today, she is special assistant to the assistant secretary for community
planning and development at the United States Department of Housing and Urban Development in Washington, D.C., where "every day"
she finds herself working on policies that "treat community partners as
partners, not clients, of the federal government and that help to build
comprehensive local capacity for community and economic development, based on a thorough understanding of the local market."

Gayle published an op-ed with Ray Lamboy of Camden in the *Philadelphia Inquirer* and appeared with him on NBC10's *@Issue* program.
Ray spoke about the op-ed in a segment for WHYY's *RadioTimes,* and
Gayle published a short piece in *Next American City*. She is working
at Project H.O.M.E. in North Central Philadelphia, teaching a class
on entrepreneurship and placing high school and college students in
internships with small-business owners.

Nick, with help from Amy, produced a how-to guide entitled *Sustainable Economic Democracy: Worker Cooperatives for the Twenty-First
Century,* which was posted on CoLab Radio. As a consequence, he was
invited to present his ideas at a cooperative conference in Richmond,
California. Nick is a program manager at the M.I.T. Community Innovators' Lab, where he is the New York project lead for the Emerald Cities Collaborative and is supporting the creation of a cooperative network

in the Bronx. In August 2011, he visited Mondragon with a delegation of civic leaders, academics, and entrepreneurs.

Eric is the manager of the Communities Program at the American Council for an Energy Efficient Economy in Washington, D.C., developing research and policy for energy-efficient communities. His thesis research helped him to "understand energy planning processes and the methods through [which] diverse stakeholders can work together to develop innovative solutions using both collaboration and confrontation." He is providing technical assistance to local governments and community as they develop energy-efficiency plans, programs, and projects.

Leila presented her research at the Towards a Just Metropolis conference in Berkeley, California, shortly after graduation. Her thesis helped her to "develop and define" her "own sense of what it means to have quality public participation," which she applies to her work as a presidential management fellow in the United States Department of Housing and Urban Development. She finds that "the things HUD is trying to advance are very much connected to the ideals of the collaborative thesis group's research."

Ben presented his scholarship to the Urban Strategies Council in Oakland, California, the lead party organizing Emerald Cities in the East Bay. He is living in San Francisco with his wife, Kate Levitt, who assisted in transforming his thesis into a chapter in this book. His thesis gave him "a much clearer understanding of how public money flows to local municipalities and community nonprofit organizations," which informs his work as an assistant project manager at Eden Housing where he is designing green development and retrofit strategies.

I wrote the introduction and concluding chapter of this book and edited the other chapters during my final year at M.I.T., while I was on the job market. Today, I am a visiting scholar at the University of Massachusetts in Boston where I coteach classes in the College of Higher Education. I am also the director of programs and research for the Talloires Network, a global coalition of 266 engaged universities in sixty-seven countries with a combined student enrollment of more than six million. The network's secretariat functions are based in the Department of Urban and Environmental Policy and Planning at Tufts University where I am coteaching a new graduate course that explores the nexus between rooted institutions and community revitalization.

Conclusion

People inside rooted institutions, perhaps beginning with our universities and colleges, need to work collaboratively to generate new knowledge to solve old problems. By studying and taking action together, my students felt less isolated and thus had the resources to learn from each other and the support to develop novel ideas. People in cities, all caught in an economic morass even before the Great Recession, now need more than just an influx of money—they need constructive ways to engage with the resources already available in their communities. By developing new relationships, building trust, and formulating a collective vision of the future, people can come together across long-held divisions of race, class, and politics to create a healthier and more productive civic sphere. Of course, the problems confronting the postindustrial cities are different, in kind and in quantity, from those that bedevil the higher education and thesis system. But there is a current of connection, an underlying issue of being hidebound, overly committed to outmoded and limiting ways of thinking, that must, in both cases, be constructively confronted.

References

Bozorg, L. 2008a. Personal statement. Massachusetts Institute of Technology.
———. 2008b. MIT@Lawrence. September 24.
———. 2010a. Resume. March 29.
———. 2010b. Personal interview. August 3.
Bozorg, L., B. Brandin, G. Christiansen, L. Hoyt, N. Iuviene, M. Leavy-Sperounis, E. Mackres, and A. Stitely. 2010. Group meeting. May 17.
Brandin, B. 2008. Personal statement. Massachusetts Institute of Technology.
———. 2009. "CoLab Leveraging the Stimulus Reflection Exercises." Summer.
———. 2010a. Phone interview. August 3.
———. 2010b. Resume. August 6.
Brickman, A. 2010. "Boston, MA: Movement Building and Changing Energy Policy." *CoLab Radio*. Massachusetts Institute of Technology, April 24.
Christiansen, G. 2008a. Personal statement. Massachusetts Institute of Technology.
———. 2008b. MIT@Lawrence. September 21.
———. 2010a. Resume. March 1.
———. 2010b. Phone interview. July 9.
Emig, A. 2010. "Oakland, CA: Designing an Energy Efficiency Retrofit Strategy." *CoLab Radio*. Massachusetts Institute of Technology, April 23.
Feeney, K. 2010. "The Bronx, NY: A Strategy for Economic Democracy and

Cooperative Development." *CoLab Radio.* Massachusetts Institute of Technology, April 28.

Goodspeed, R. 2010. "Lawrence and Lowell, MA: A Networked Approach to Green Jobs." CoLab Radio. Massachusetts Institute of Technology, April 28.

Hoyt, L. 2010. "A City-Campus Engagement Theory From, and For, Practice." *Michigan Journal of Community Service Learning* 17 (1): 75–88.

Hoyt, L., C. Balderas-Guzman, J. Bonilla, A. Bopp Stark, L. Caraballo, C. Espinoza-Toro, A. Mills, D. Rich, L. Rodda, M. Rotzel, and R. Ochshorn. 2007. *Predatory tales.* DVD. Cambridge, MA: MIT@Lawrence, U.S. Department of Housing and Urban Development.

Hoyt, L., A. Dougherty, M. Leavy-Sperounis, D. Martin, A. Mills, and E. Sisk. 2009. *Sustained City-Campus Engagement: Reflections on Our Practice.* DVD. Cambridge, MA: MIT@Lawrence, U.S. Department of Housing and Urban Development.

Iuviene, N. 2008a. Personal statement. Massachusetts Institute of Technology.
———. 2008b. MIT@Lawrence. September 30.
———. 2008c. MIT@Lawrence. October 22.
———. 2008d. MIT@Lawrence. November 18.
———. 2010a. Resume. June 13.
———. 2010b. Phone interview. July 14.

Leavy-Sperounis, M. 2008a. Personal statement. Massachusetts Institute of Technology.
———. 2008b. MIT@Lawrence. September 21.
———. 2008c. MIT@Lawrence. September 28.
———. 2010a. "Resume." March, 26.
———. 2010b. "Green Jobs on the Ground: Lawrence, Massachusetts." *Tech TV.* Massachusetts Institute of Technology, May 27.
———. 2010c. Personal interview. July 27.

Leavy-Sperounis, M., E. Mackres, and S. Marshall. 2009. "Green Jobs in Lawrence." Unpublished paper, Massachusetts Institute of Technology.

Lynton, E. 1994. "Knowledge and Scholarship." *Metropolitan Universities* 5 (1): 9–17.

Mackres, E. 2008a. Personal statement. Massachusetts Institute of Technology.
———. 2008b. MIT@Lawrence. September 28.
———. 2010a. Resume. March 1.
———. 2010b. Phone interview. August 3.

O'Meara, K. A. 2011. "Faculty Civic Engagement: New Training, Assumptions, and Markets Needed for the Engaged American Scholar." In *"To Serve a Larger Purpose": Engagement for Democracy and the Transformation of Higher Education,* edited by J. Saltmarsh and M. Hartley, 177–98. Philadelphia: Temple University Press.

Rice, R. E. 2005. "The Future of Scholarly Work of Faculty." In *Faculty Priorities*

Reconsidered: Rewarding Multiple Forms of Scholarship, edited by K. A. O'Meara and R. E. Rice, 303–13. San Francisco: Jossey-Bass.

Ritoper, S. 2010. "Camden, New Jersey: Small Businesses as a New Economic and Community Development Strategy." *CoLab Radio.* Massachusetts Institute of Technology, April 26.

Schön, D. A. 1995. "Knowing-in-Action: The New Scholarship Requires a New Epistemology." *Change* 27 (6): 26–34.

Stitely, A. 2006. Personal statement. Massachusetts Institute of Technology.

———. 2007. Resume. July 13.

Xypolia, A. 2010. "Kansas City, MO: Spatializing Social Justice and the Green Impact Zone." *CoLab Radio.* Massachusetts Institute of Technology, April 26.

Contributors

Leila Bozorg: Leila's professional experience includes work with the National Trust for Historic Preservation, Pathfinder International, the World Affairs Council of Northern California, and Saath—an Indian nongovernmental organization working on quality-of-life issues in informal settlements. She has worked in San Francisco, California; Cambridge, Massachusetts; Washington, D.C.; Ahmedabad, Gujarat (India); and in the Yazd province, Iran. While at M.I.T., Leila served as a research assistant with MIT@Lawrence. Leila earned a bachelor of arts in government from Wesleyan University, as well as a master in city planning and certificate in urban design from M.I.T. She is currently a presidential management fellow in the U.S. Department of Housing and Urban Development.

Benjamin Brandin: Ben has worked as the outreach coordinator for Amnesty International's San Francisco office, where he served as the Western Region representative on the organization's Gender Audit task force. Ben also worked as the organizational development consultant for the Lynn Coalition for Green Development in Lynn, Massachusetts, where he sought federal funding to put disadvantaged minority residents in new green jobs. Ben has a bachelor of arts in American studies from the University of California, Berkeley, and a master in city planning from M.I.T. He is currently an assistant project manager at Eden Housing, designing green development and retrofit strategies.

Gayle Christiansen: Gayle previously taught seventh- and eighth-grade science in Camden, New Jersey, under the auspices of Teach for America, and contributed to the development of an economic development strategy for the city of Camden while working at the Camden Empowerment Zone Corporation. She led and significantly expanded Lawrence@MIT, bringing dozens of eighth-grade students from Lawrence, Massachusetts, to M.I.T. monthly to take part in science and technology workshops. Gayle has a bachelor of arts in sociology from Kenyon College and a master in city planning from M.I.T. She is currently working at Project H.O.M.E. in Philadelphia, Pennsylvania, placing high school and college students in internships with small-business owners.

Lorlene Hoyt: Lorlene is currently the director of programs and research for the Talloires Network at Tufts University, a global coalition of 266 universities in 67 different countries. She is also a visiting scholar in the New England Resource Center for Higher Education at the University of Massachusetts, Boston. Lorlene founded and led MIT@Lawrence, a sustained city-campus partnership between M.I.T. and the city of Lawrence, Massachusetts as an assistant/associate professor in the Department of Urban Studies and Planning at M.I.T. (2002–2011). MIT@Lawrence was recognized when she received the Ernest A. Lynton Award for the Scholarship of Engagement (2007) and the Martin Luther King Jr. Leadership Award (2008), and the partnership received the President's Higher Education Community Service Honor Roll (2007) and the Massachusetts Campus Compact Presidents' Community Partnership Award (2011). She has a Ph.D. in city and regional planning from the University of Pennsylvania, a master of landscape architecture from the State University of New York, and a B.S. in landscape architecture from the Pennsylvania State University.

Nick Iuviene: Nick worked for the Northwest Bronx Coalition where he was lead staff for a large-scale, grassroots economic development project, negotiating strategic alliances with labor unions, city agencies, and real estate developers. During the same period he worked with youth leaders to develop an art-and-technology center in the Bronx. He also cofounded Black Leaf Studios, a web development firm focused on serving nonprofit organizations, artists, and small businesses. While enrolled at M.I.T., Nick worked with on the MIT@Lawrence Story Project, producing an interactive web-based timeline depicting the ten-year history of the partnership. Nick holds a bachelor of science in urban studies and planning from the State University of New York, Empire State College and a master in city planning from M.I.T. He is currently a program manager at the M.I.T. Community Innovators' Lab where he works on the Bronx Cooperative Development Initiative and is the New York project lead for the Emerald Cities Collaborative.

Marianna Leavy-Sperounis: Marianna worked as a community organizer with Lawrence CommunityWorks from 2003 to 2007, where she helped craft the organization's network organizing approach. In 2008, she joined the Obama campaign to train field organizers in Denver, Colorado. Marianna has also worked as an urban-policy intern with the Massachusetts Smart Growth Alliance and as a community engagement consultant to the Emerald Cities Collaborative. At M.I.T., Marianna cotaught a practice-based planning practicum with Lorlene Hoyt and managed numerous aspects of the MIT@ Lawrence partnership. Marianna holds a master's degree in city planning from M.I.T. and a bachelor's degree in politics from Oberlin College. She currently serves as special assistant to the Assistant Secretary for Community Planning and Development at the U.S. Department of Housing and Urban Development in Washington, D.C.

Kate Levitt: Kate has done extensive fieldwork in New York, California, and Mexico, and has presented and published her research at conferences throughout the United States and Mexico. Kate has also worked with the Social Science Research Council and the United Nations on various programs concerning international relations and human rights in the developing world, with a particular focus on Latin America. In addition, she teaches classes on media, culture, and politics at the University of California, San Diego and Berkeley campuses. Kate is currently a doctoral degree candidate in communication at the University of California, San Diego. She holds a master in communication from University of California, San Diego, and a bachelor of arts in political theory from Barnard College, Columbia University.

Eric Mackres: Eric has worked with the StatePIRGs on environmental and consumer advocacy in Michigan and on statewide affordable housing policy in California. At M.I.T. he acted as an organizer for green-job development with the MIT@Lawrence partnership and as a researcher with the Community Innovators' Lab and Professor Harvey Michaels on developing energy-efficiency strategies for local communities. Additionally, Eric has completed research related to environment and community development in the European Union, South Africa, and India. Eric has a master in city planning and certificate of environmental planning from M.I.T. and a bachelor of arts in political science from Albion College. He currently works as the manager of the Communities Program at the American Council for an Energy Efficient Economy, developing research and policy for energy-efficient communities and providing technical assistance to communities beginning or expanding energy-efficiency efforts.

Lily Song: Lily's professional experience includes community organizing around issues of substance-abuse prevention and electoral representation, as well as conducting policy analysis around community workforce agreements. Lily holds a bachelor of arts in ethnic studies from the University of California, Berkeley, and a master in urban planning from the University of California, Los Angeles. Lily is currently a doctoral student in urban studies and planning at M.I.T., where she is a Martin Family Fellow for Sustainability.

Index

www.ingramcontent.com/pod-product-compliance
Lightning Source LLC
Chambersburg PA
CBHW030646270326
41929CB00007B/223